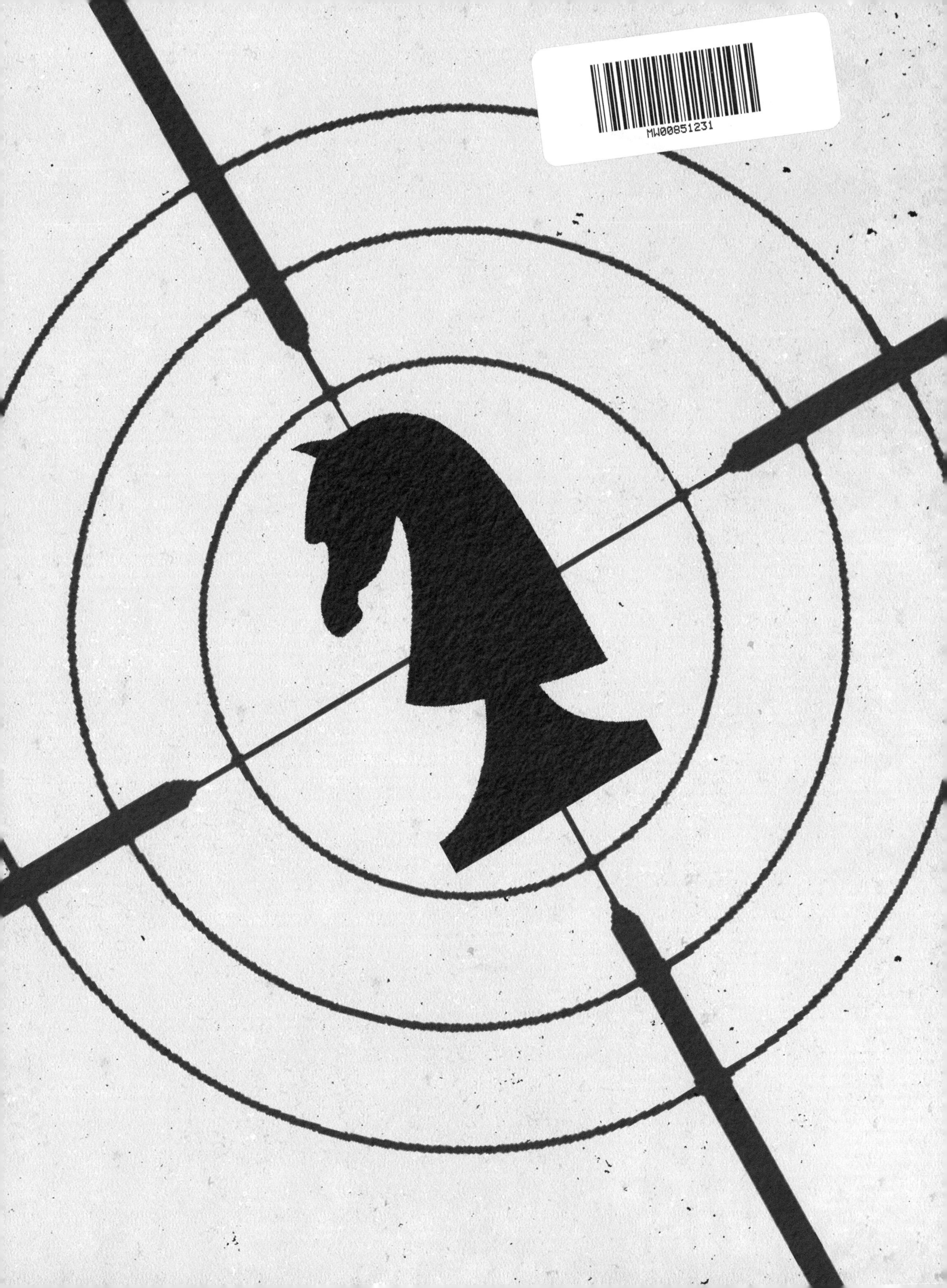

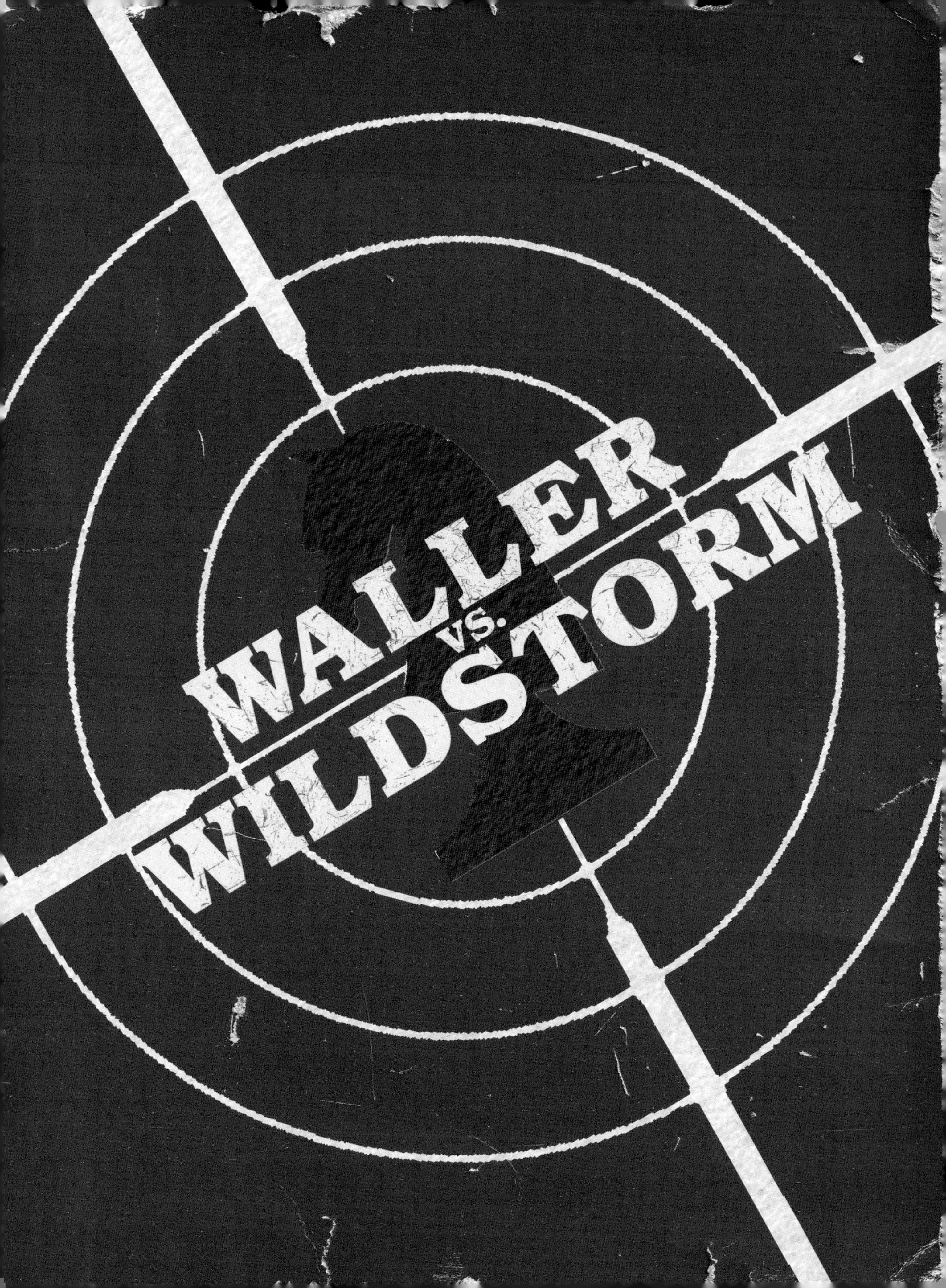
WALLER
VS.
WILDSTORM

**SPENCER ACKERMAN
EVAN NARCISSE**
writers

JESÚS MERINO
penciller

**VICENTE CIFUENTES
JESÚS MERINO**
inkers

MICHAEL ATIYEH
colorist

DAVE SHARPE
letterer

JORGE FORNES
series & collection cover artist

WALLER VS. WILDSTORM

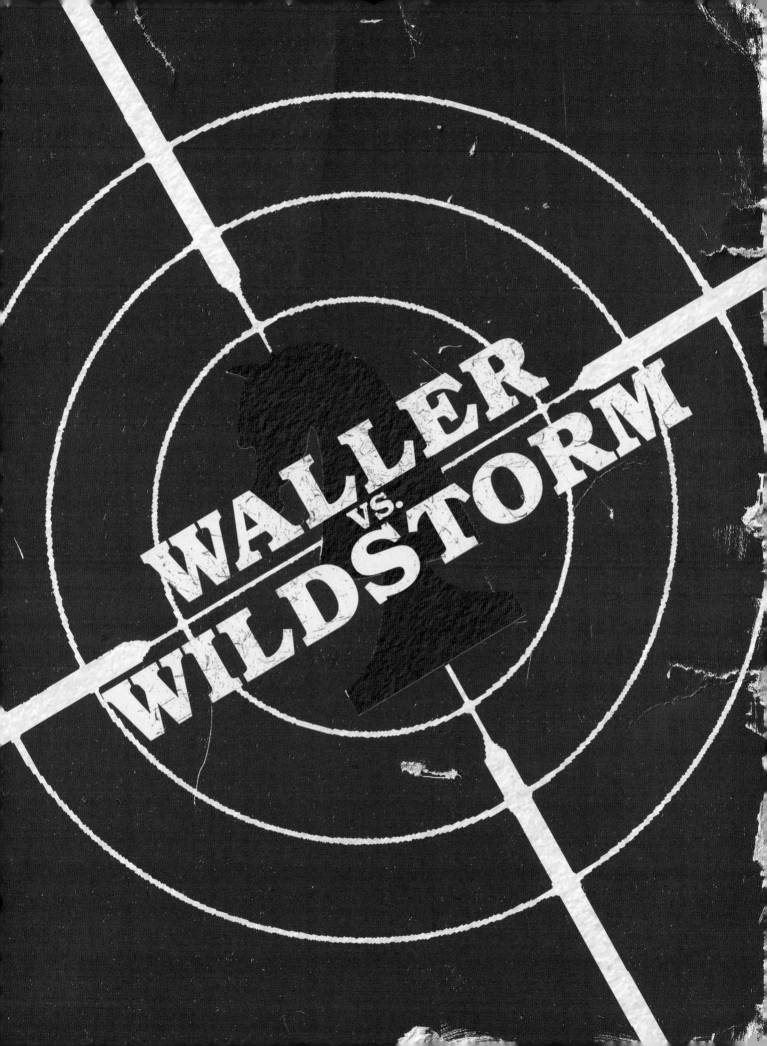

CHRIS CONROY
Editor – Original Series & Collected Edition

MARQUIS DRAPER
Associate Editor – Original Series

STEVE COOK
Design Director – Books

DAMIAN RYLAND
Publication Design

SUZANNAH ROWNTREE
Publication Production

MARIE JAVINS
VP – Editor-in-Chief

JIM LEE
President, Publisher & Chief Creative Officer

ANNE DePIES
Senior VP & General Manager

LARRY BERRY
VP – Brand Design & Creative Services

DON FALLETTI
VP – Manufacturing & Production

LAWRENCE GANEM
VP – Editorial Programming & Talent Strategy

ALISON GILL
Senior VP – Manufacturing & Operations

NICK J. NAPOLITANO
VP – Publishing & Business Operations

NANCY SPEARS
VP – Sales & Marketing

WALLER VS. WILDSTORM

DC Comics, 4000 Warner Blvd., Bldg. 700, 2nd Floor, Burbank, CA 91522
Printed by Transcontinental Interglobe, Beauceville, QC, Canada.
12/15/23. First Printing. ISBN: 978-1-77951-751-7

Library of Congress Cataloging-in-Publication Data is available.

PEFC Certified
This product is from sustainably managed forests and controlled sources
PEFC/01-31-106 www.pefc.org

SPENCER ACKERMAN · EVAN NARCISSE · JESÚS MERINO · MICHAEL ATIYEH

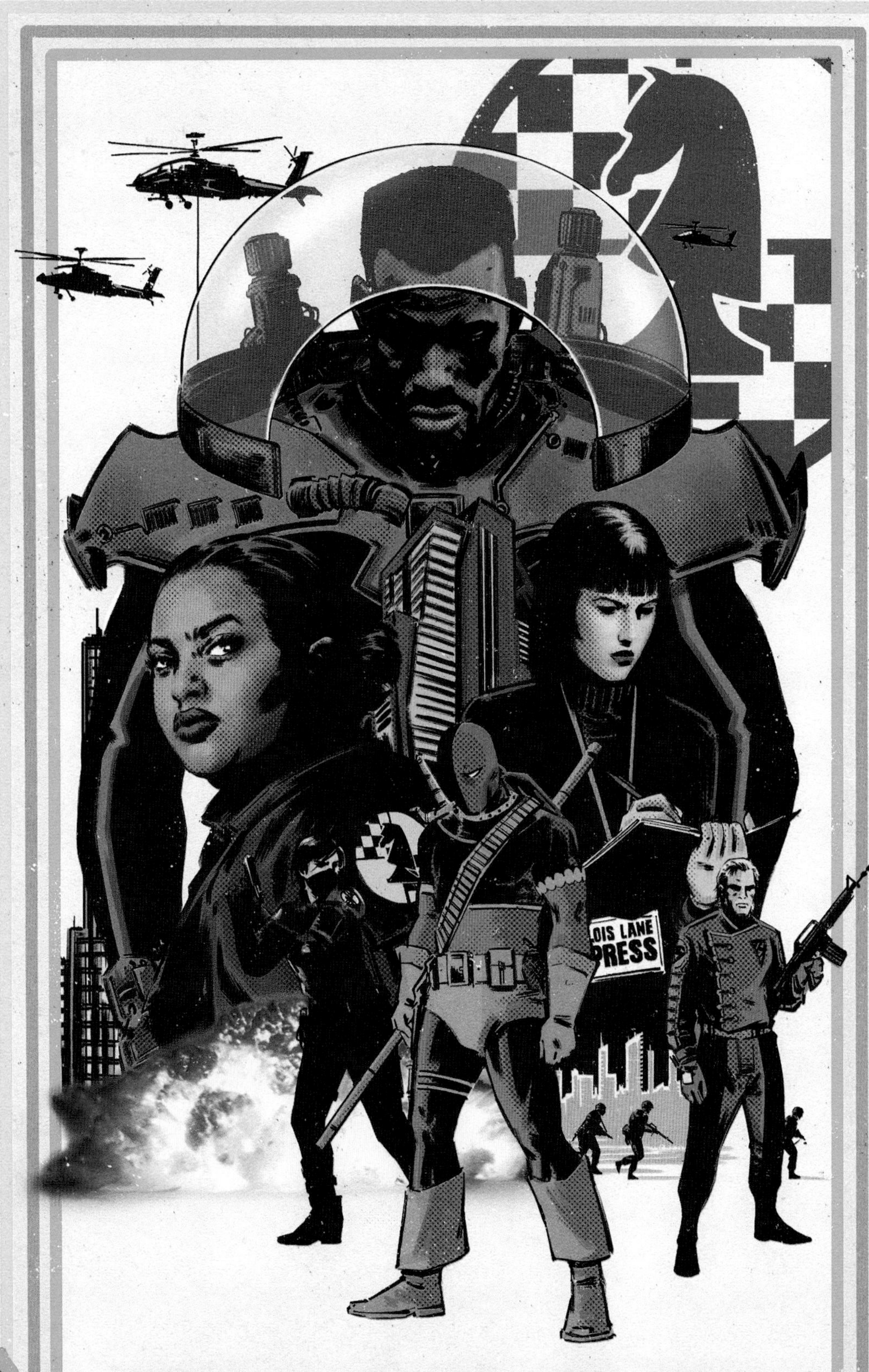
LOIS LANE
PRESS
FORNÉS

SPECIAL OFFER
$5.99
Ages 17+

$5.99

WALLER VS. WILDSTORM

"MS. LANE, HAVE YOU EVER HEARD OF A WOMAN NAMED **AMANDA WALLER?**

"SHE'S THE REASON MY FRIEND IS **DEAD.**"

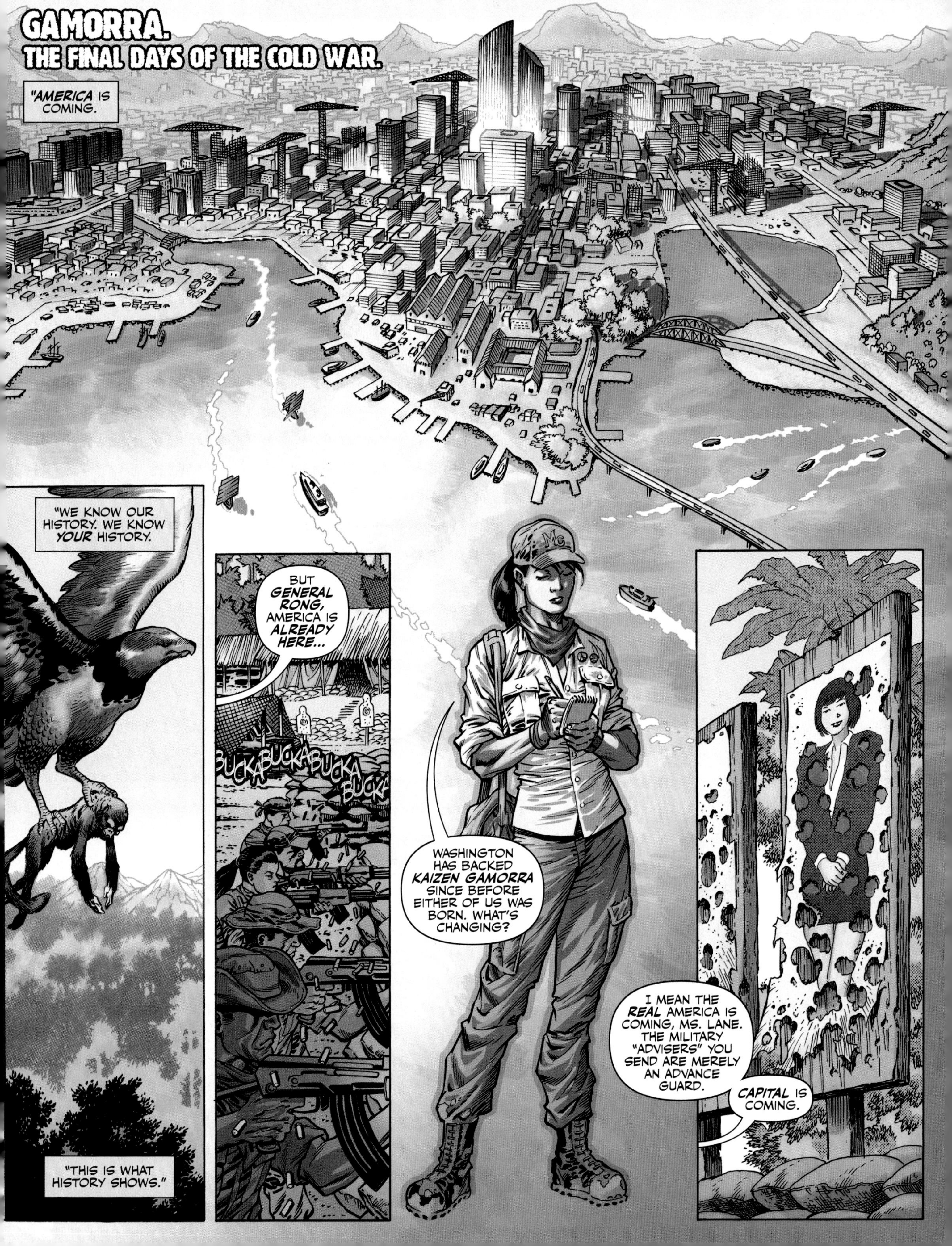
GAMORRA.
THE FINAL DAYS OF THE COLD WAR.
"AMERICA IS COMING.
"WE KNOW OUR HISTORY. WE KNOW YOUR HISTORY.
"THIS IS WHAT HISTORY SHOWS."
BUT GENERAL RONG, AMERICA IS ALREADY HERE...
BUCKABUCKABUCKA BUCKA
WASHINGTON HAS BACKED KAIZEN GAMORRA SINCE BEFORE EITHER OF US WAS BORN. WHAT'S CHANGING?
I MEAN THE REAL AMERICA IS COMING, MS. LANE. THE MILITARY "ADVISERS" YOU SEND ARE MERELY AN ADVANCE GUARD.
CAPITAL IS COMING.

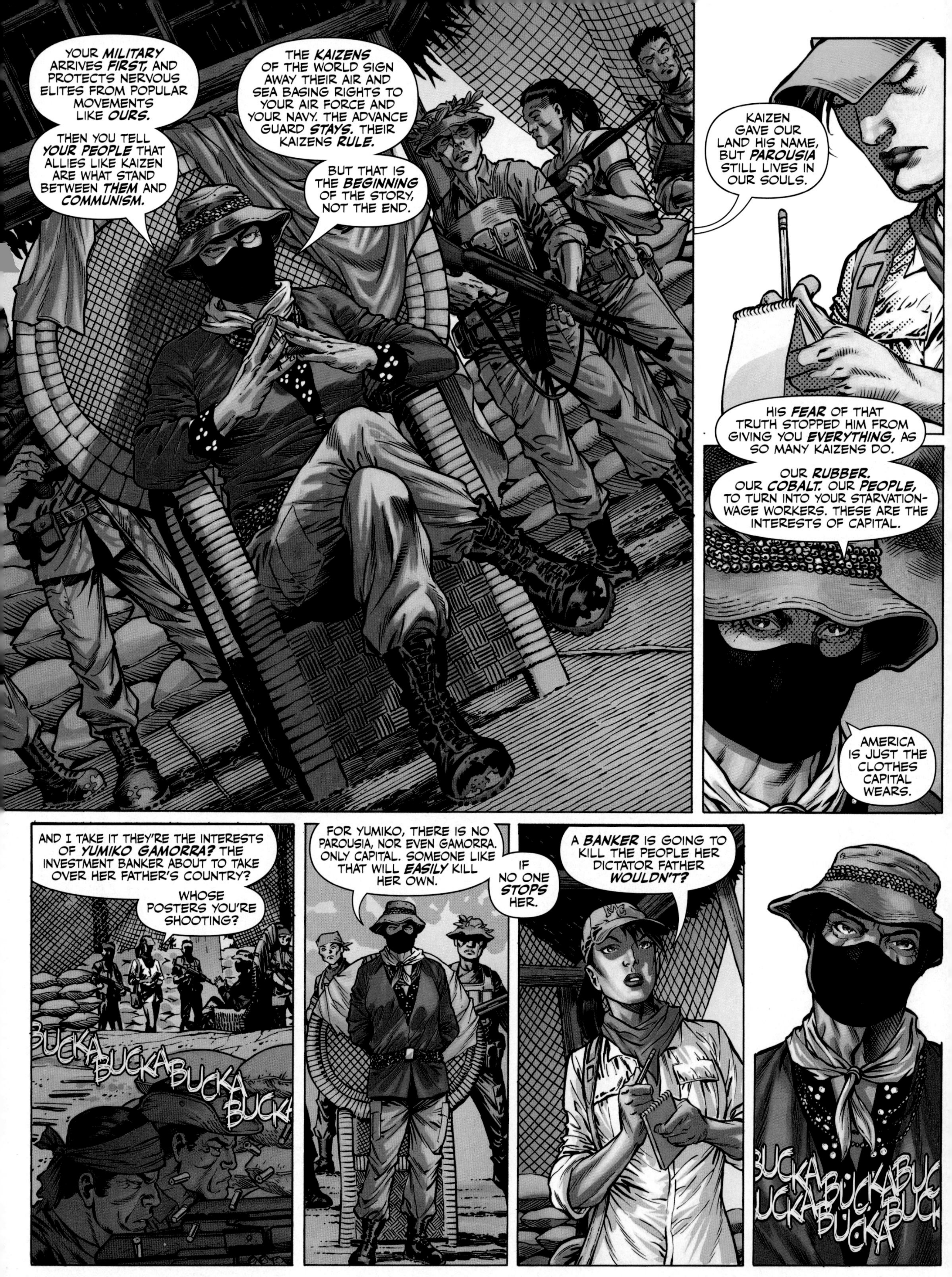
YOUR MILITARY ARRIVES FIRST, AND PROTECTS NERVOUS ELITES FROM POPULAR MOVEMENTS LIKE OURS.
THEN YOU TELL YOUR PEOPLE THAT ALLIES LIKE KAIZEN ARE WHAT STAND BETWEEN THEM AND COMMUNISM.
THE KAIZENS OF THE WORLD SIGN AWAY THEIR AIR AND SEA BASING RIGHTS TO YOUR AIR FORCE AND YOUR NAVY. THE ADVANCE GUARD STAYS. THEIR KAIZENS RULE.
BUT THAT IS THE BEGINNING OF THE STORY, NOT THE END.
KAIZEN GAVE OUR LAND HIS NAME, BUT PAROUSIA STILL LIVES IN OUR SOULS.
HIS FEAR OF THAT TRUTH STOPPED HIM FROM GIVING YOU EVERYTHING, AS SO MANY KAIZENS DO.
OUR RUBBER. OUR COBALT. OUR PEOPLE, TO TURN INTO YOUR STARVATION-WAGE WORKERS. THESE ARE THE INTERESTS OF CAPITAL.
AMERICA IS JUST THE CLOTHES CAPITAL WEARS.
AND I TAKE IT THEY'RE THE INTERESTS OF YUMIKO GAMORRA? THE INVESTMENT BANKER ABOUT TO TAKE OVER HER FATHER'S COUNTRY?
WHOSE POSTERS YOU'RE SHOOTING?
BUCKA BUCKA BUCKA BUCKA
FOR YUMIKO, THERE IS NO PAROUSIA, NOR EVEN GAMORRA. ONLY CAPITAL. SOMEONE LIKE THAT WILL EASILY KILL HER OWN.
IF NO ONE STOPS HER.
A BANKER IS GOING TO KILL THE PEOPLE HER DICTATOR FATHER WOULDN'T?
BUCKA BUCKA BUC BUCKA BUCKA BUCKA BUCK

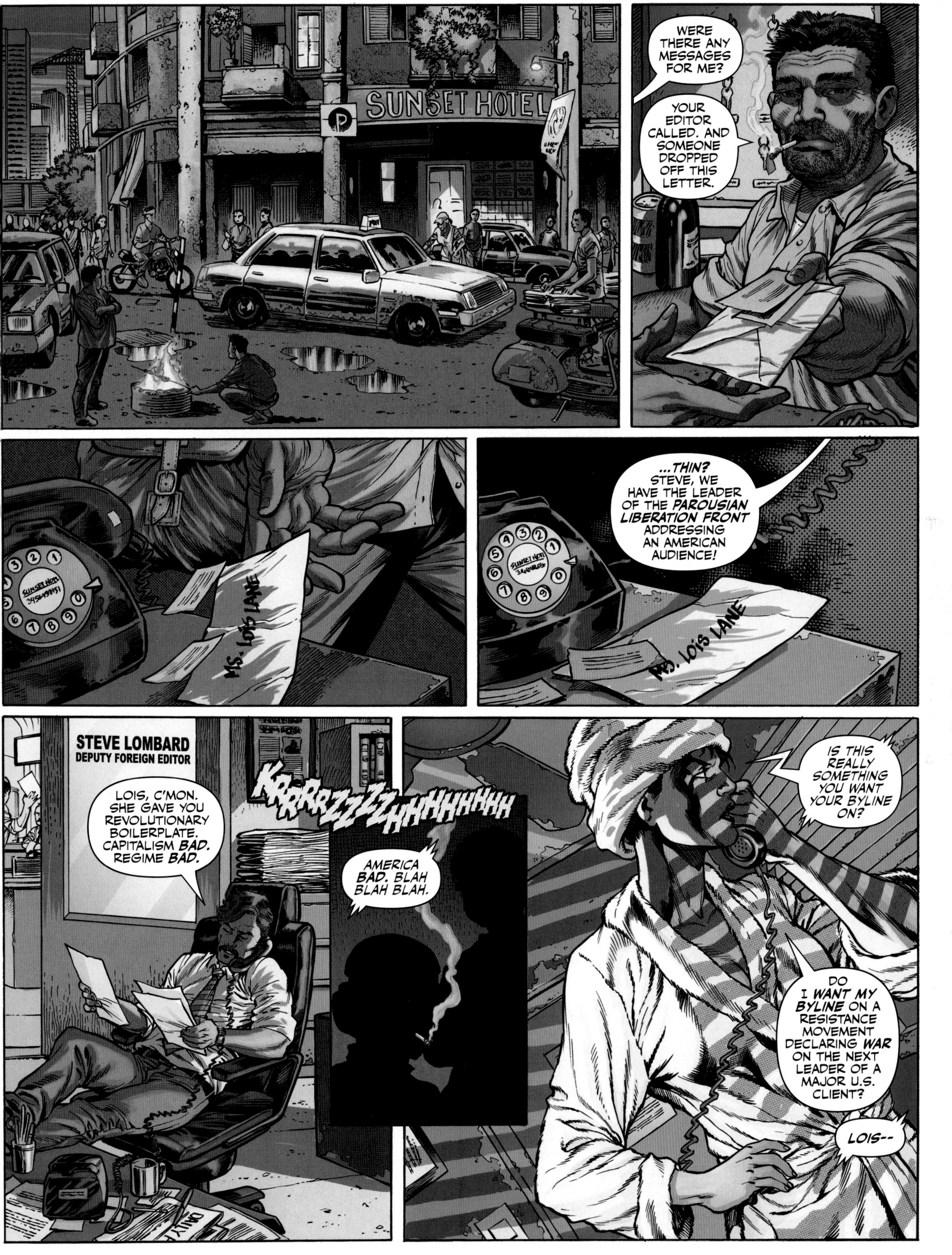
SUNSET HOTEL
WERE THERE ANY MESSAGES FOR ME?
YOUR EDITOR CALLED. AND SOMEONE DROPPED OFF THIS LETTER.
MS. LOIS LANE
...THIN? STEVE, WE HAVE THE LEADER OF THE PAROUSIAN LIBERATION FRONT ADDRESSING AN AMERICAN AUDIENCE!
MS. LOIS LANE
STEVE LOMBARD
DEPUTY FOREIGN EDITOR
LOIS, C'MON. SHE GAVE YOU REVOLUTIONARY BOILERPLATE. CAPITALISM BAD. REGIME BAD.
KRRRRZZZZZHHHHHHHHH
AMERICA BAD. BLAH BLAH BLAH.
IS THIS REALLY SOMETHING YOU WANT YOUR BYLINE ON?
DO I WANT MY BYLINE ON A RESISTANCE MOVEMENT DECLARING WAR ON THE NEXT LEADER OF A MAJOR U.S. CLIENT?
LOIS--

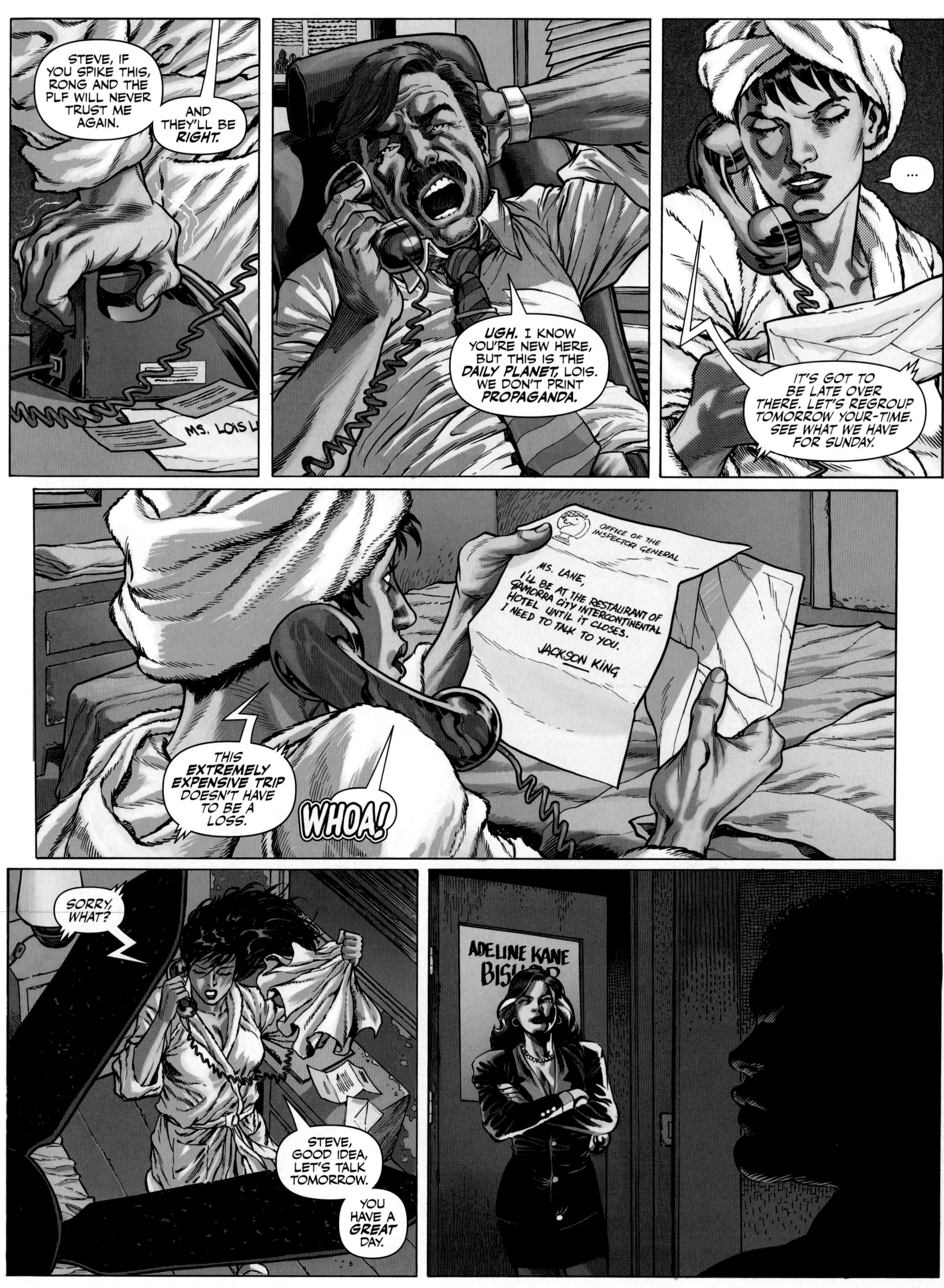
STEVE, IF YOU SPIKE THIS, RONG AND THE PLF WILL NEVER TRUST ME AGAIN.
AND THEY'LL BE RIGHT.
MS. LOIS L
UGH. I KNOW YOU'RE NEW HERE, BUT THIS IS THE DAILY PLANET, LOIS. WE DON'T PRINT PROPAGANDA.
...
IT'S GOT TO BE LATE OVER THERE. LET'S REGROUP TOMORROW YOUR-TIME. SEE WHAT WE HAVE FOR SUNDAY.
OFFICE OF THE INSPECTOR GENERAL
MS. LANE,
I'LL BE AT THE RESTAURANT OF GAMORRA CITY INTERCONTINENTAL HOTEL UNTIL IT CLOSES. I NEED TO TALK TO YOU.
JACKSON KING
THIS EXTREMELY EXPENSIVE TRIP DOESN'T HAVE TO BE A LOSS.
WHOA!
SORRY, WHAT?
STEVE, GOOD IDEA, LET'S TALK TOMORROW.
YOU HAVE A GREAT DAY.
ADELINE KANE

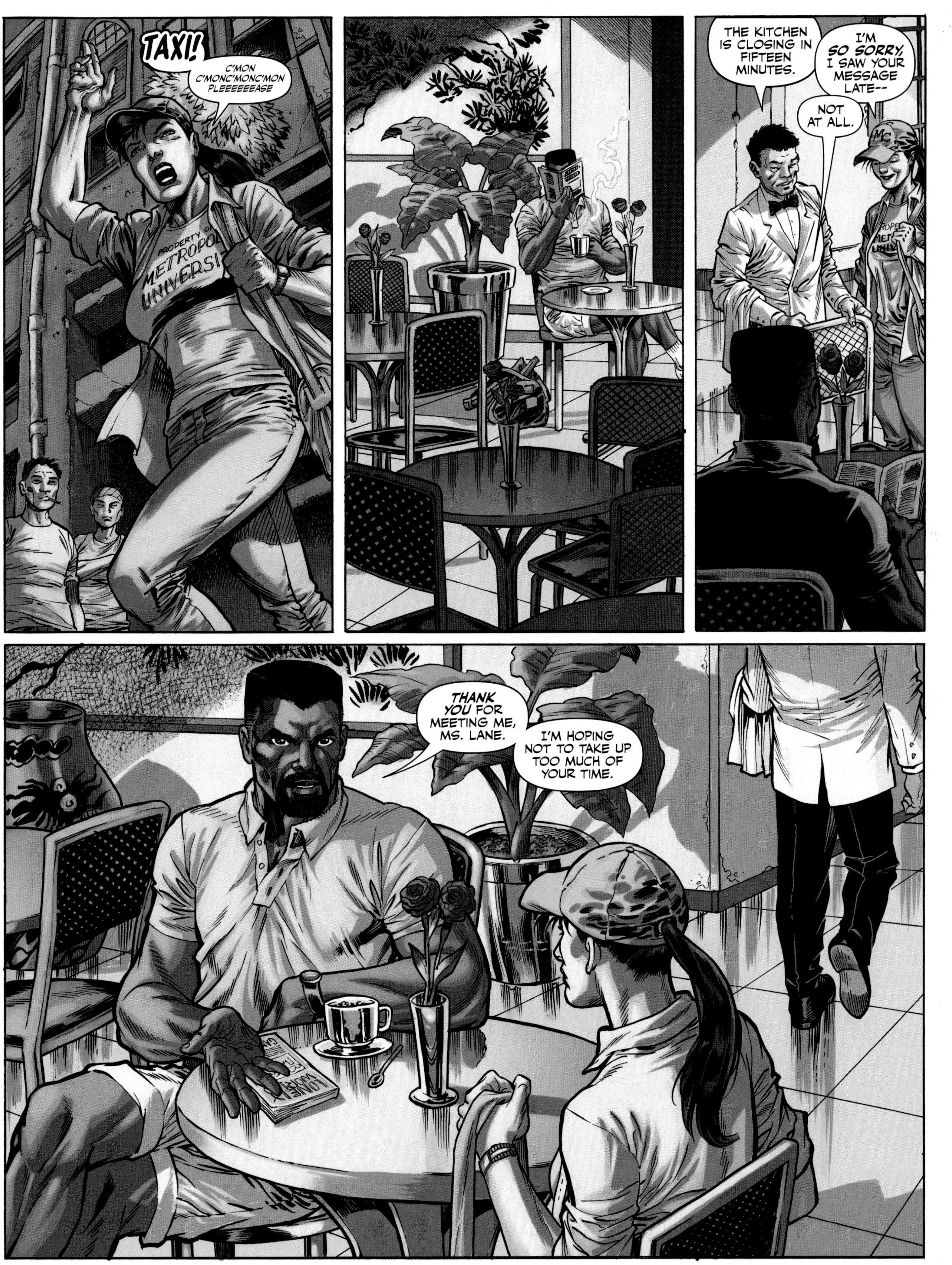
TAXI!
C'MON C'MONC'MONC'MON PLEEEEEEASE
THE KITCHEN IS CLOSING IN FIFTEEN MINUTES.
I'M SO SORRY, I SAW YOUR MESSAGE LATE--
NOT AT ALL.
THANK YOU FOR MEETING ME, MS. LANE.
I'M HOPING NOT TO TAKE UP TOO MUCH OF YOUR TIME.

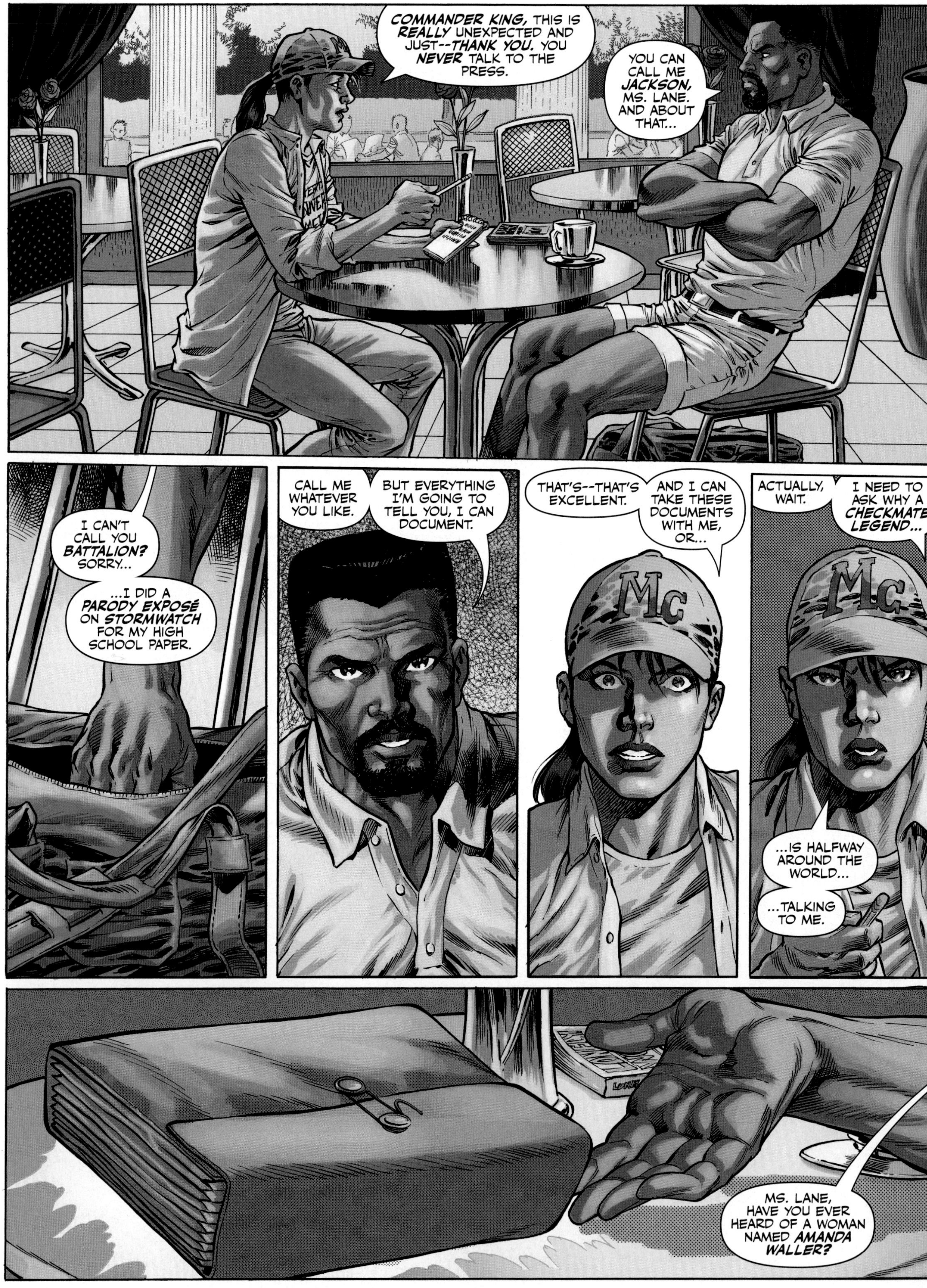
COMMANDER KING, THIS IS REALLY UNEXPECTED AND JUST--THANK YOU. YOU NEVER TALK TO THE PRESS.
YOU CAN CALL ME JACKSON, MS. LANE. AND ABOUT THAT...
I CAN'T CALL YOU BATTALION? SORRY...
...I DID A PARODY EXPOSÉ ON STORMWATCH FOR MY HIGH SCHOOL PAPER.
CALL ME WHATEVER YOU LIKE.
BUT EVERYTHING I'M GOING TO TELL YOU, I CAN DOCUMENT.
THAT'S--THAT'S EXCELLENT.
AND I CAN TAKE THESE DOCUMENTS WITH ME, OR...
ACTUALLY, WAIT.
I NEED TO ASK WHY A CHECKMATE LEGEND...
...IS HALFWAY AROUND THE WORLD...
...TALKING TO ME.
MS. LANE, HAVE YOU EVER HEARD OF A WOMAN NAMED AMANDA WALLER?

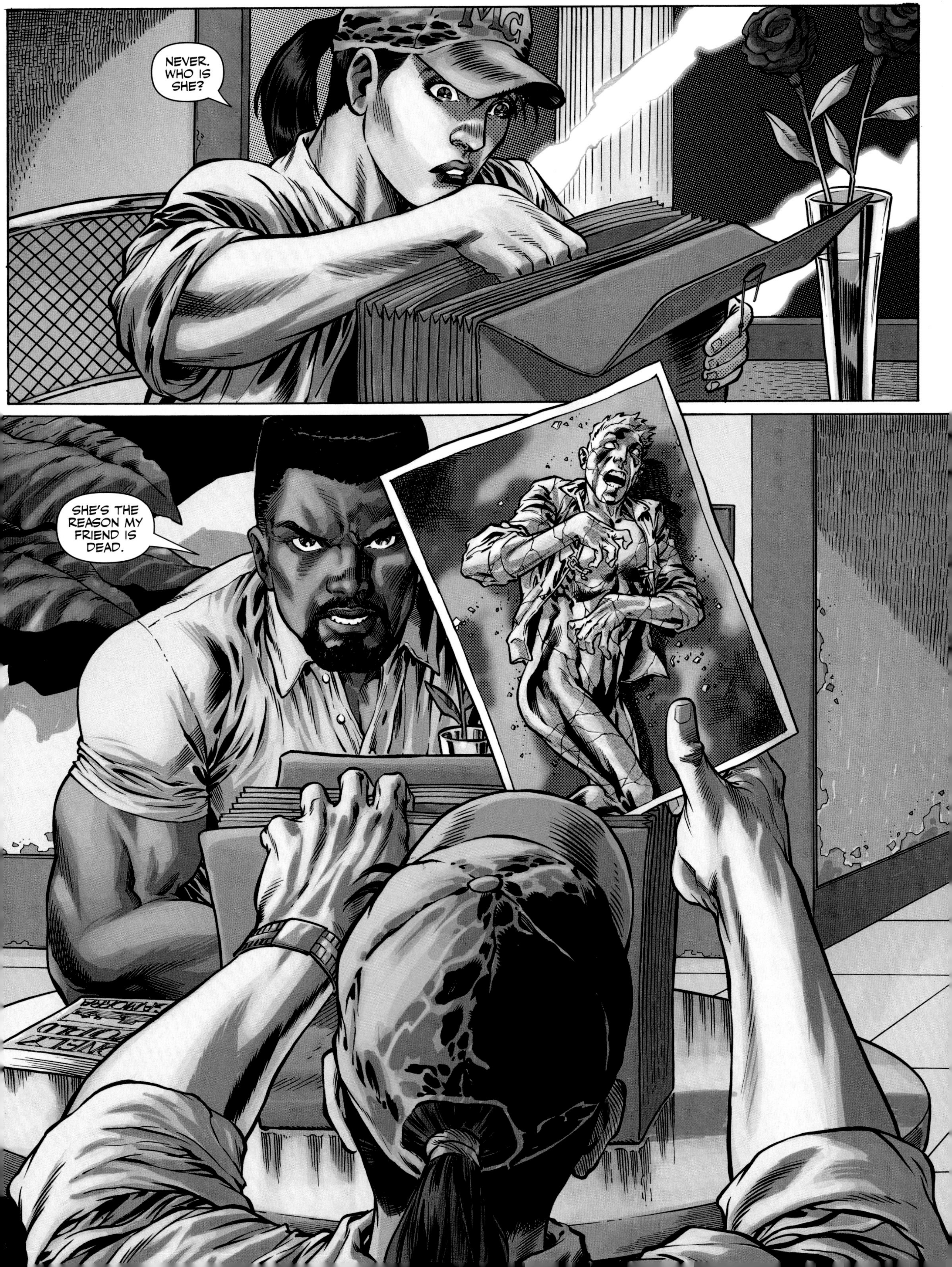
NEVER. WHO IS SHE?
SHE'S THE REASON MY FRIEND IS DEAD.

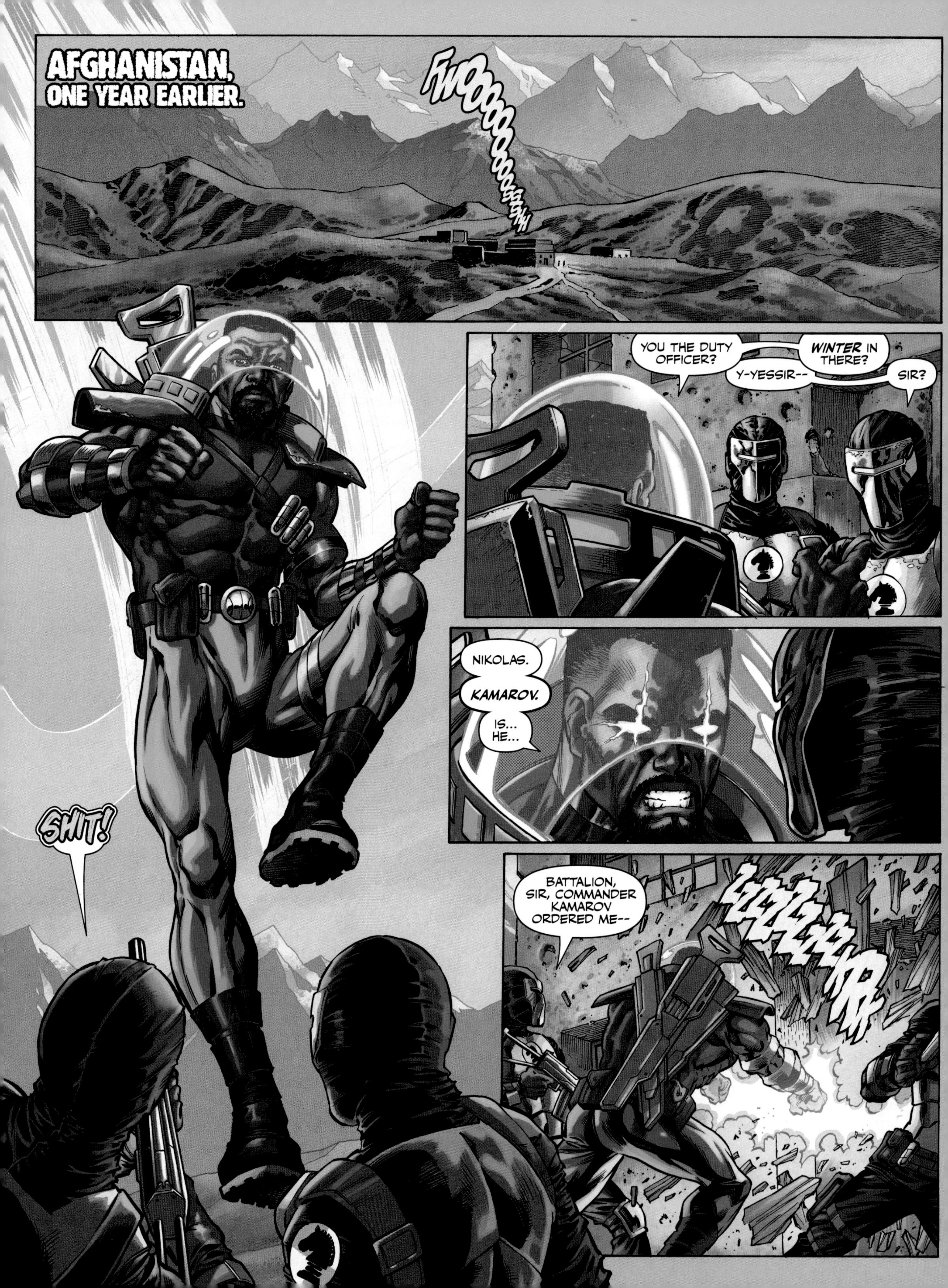
AFGHANISTAN, ONE YEAR EARLIER.
FWOOOOOOOOOSSSHH
YOU THE DUTY OFFICER?
Y-YESSIR--
WINTER IN THERE?
SIR?
NIKOLAS.
KAMAROV.
IS... HE...
SHIT!
BATTALION, SIR, COMMANDER KAMAROV ORDERED ME--

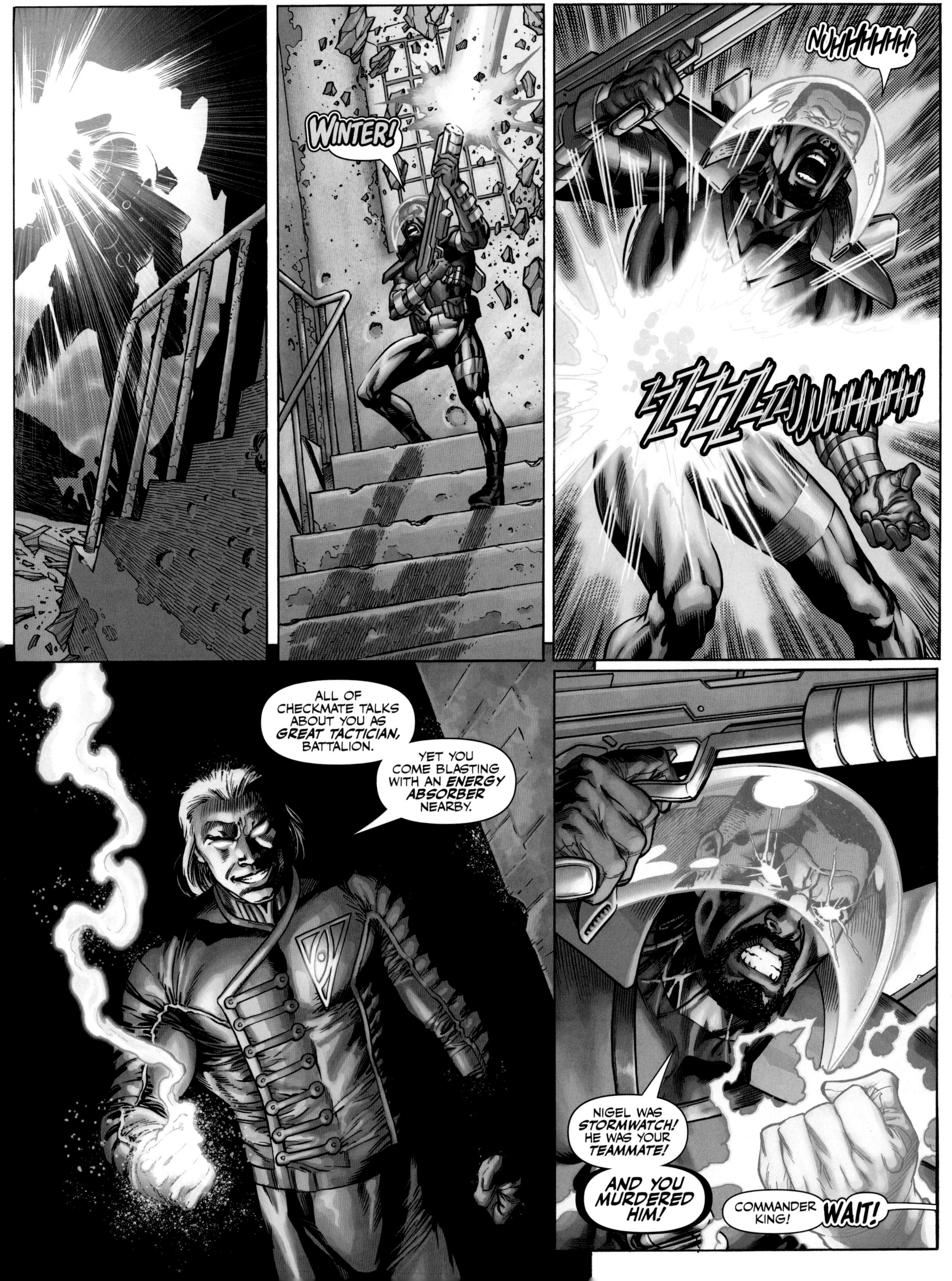

WINTER!
NUHHHHHH!
ZZZZZAWHHHHH
ALL OF CHECKMATE TALKS ABOUT YOU AS GREAT TACTICIAN, BATTALION.
YET YOU COME BLASTING WITH AN ENERGY ABSORBER NEARBY.
NIGEL WAS STORMWATCH! HE WAS YOUR TEAMMATE!
AND YOU MURDERED HIM!
COMMANDER KING!
WAIT!

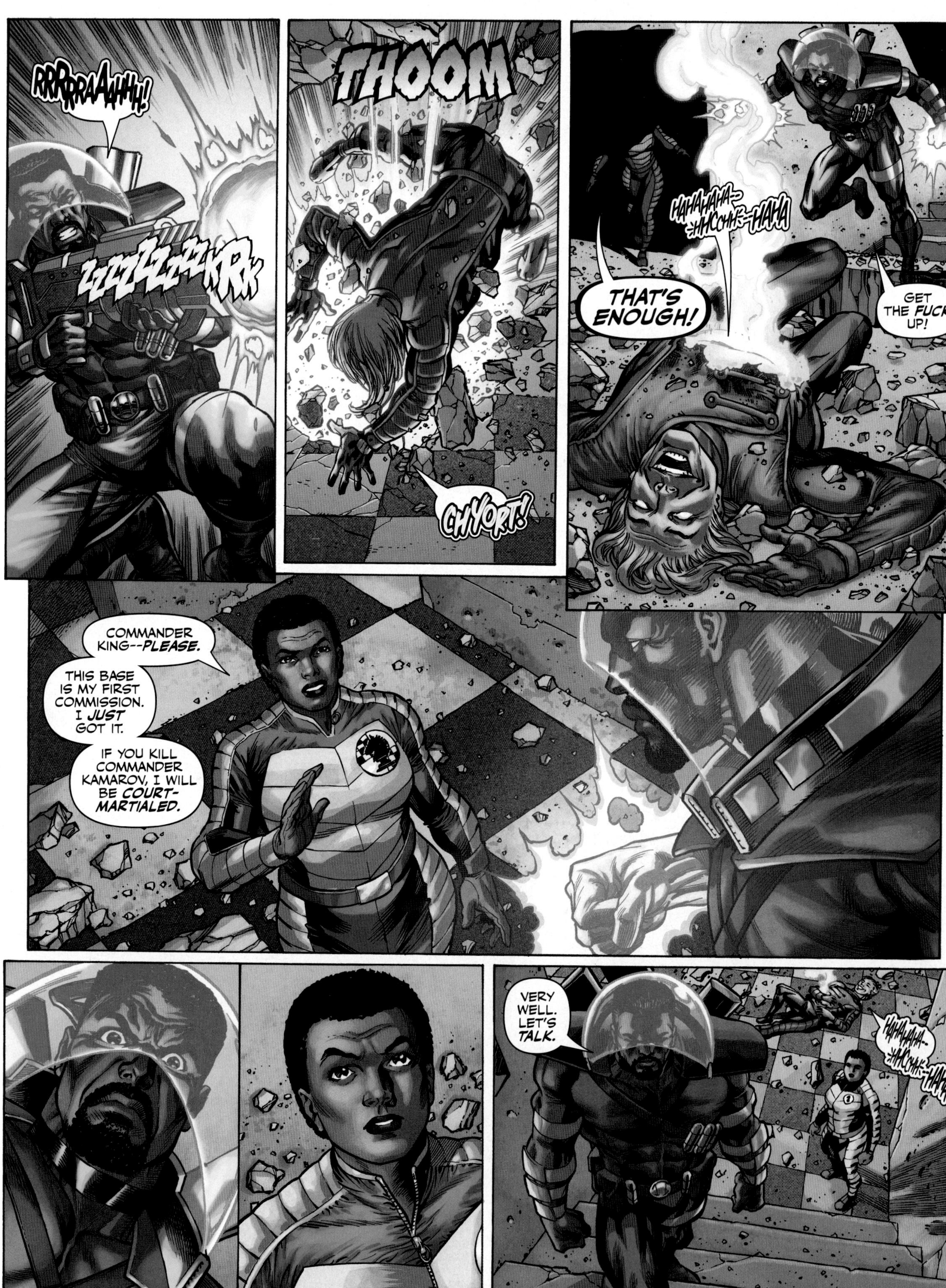
RRRRRAAAHHH!
ZZZZZZZZZZZKRRK
THOOM
CHYORT!
HAHAHAHA--HHCHHK--HAHA
THAT'S ENOUGH!
GET THE *FUCK* UP!
COMMANDER KING--*PLEASE.*
THIS BASE IS MY FIRST COMMISSION. I *JUST* GOT IT.
IF YOU KILL COMMANDER KAMAROV, I WILL BE *COURT-MARTIALED.*
VERY WELL. LET'S *TALK.*
HAHAHAHA--HHCHHK--HAHA

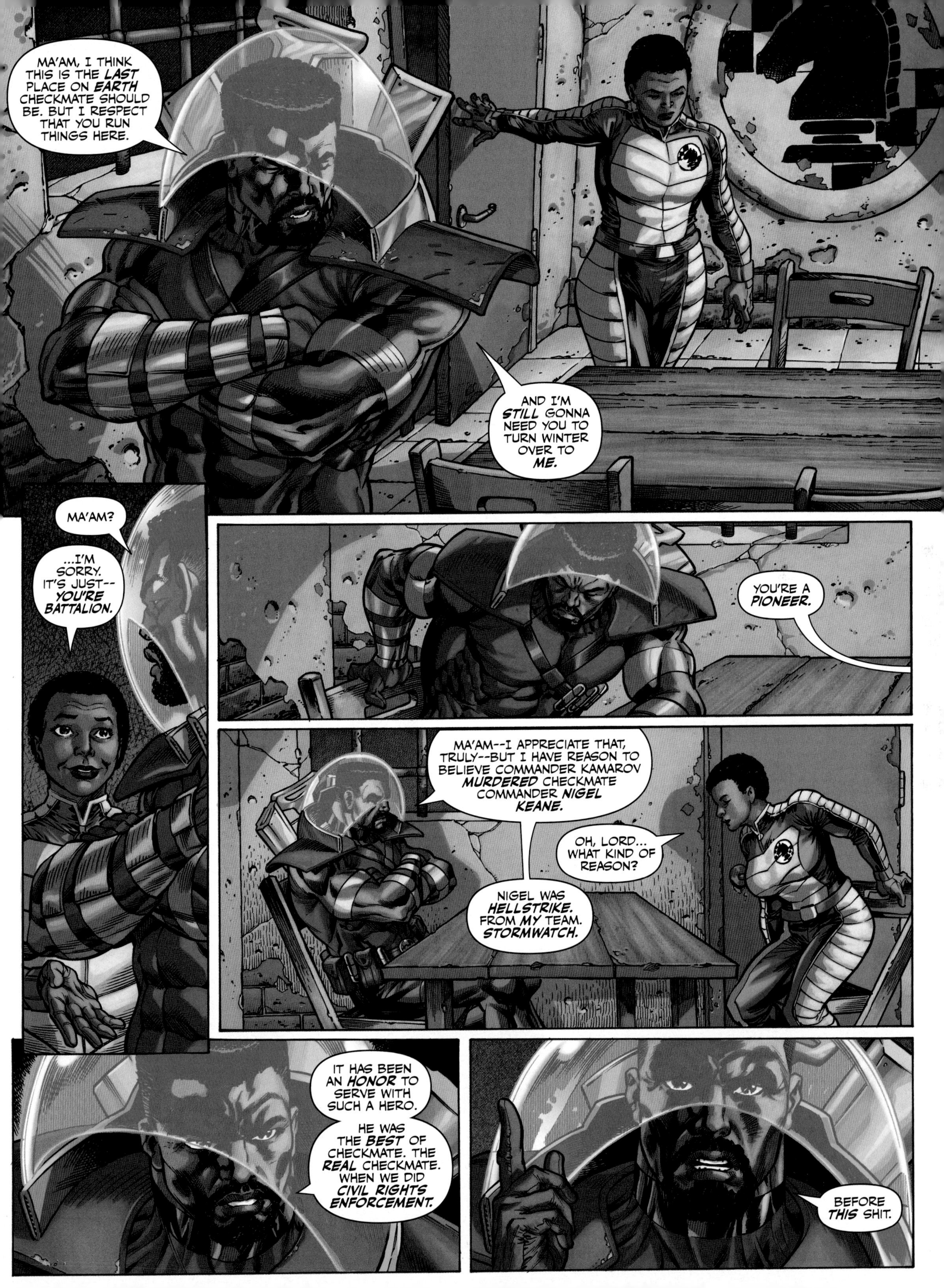
MA'AM, I THINK THIS IS THE LAST PLACE ON EARTH CHECKMATE SHOULD BE. BUT I RESPECT THAT YOU RUN THINGS HERE.
AND I'M STILL GONNA NEED YOU TO TURN WINTER OVER TO ME.
MA'AM?
...I'M SORRY. IT'S JUST-- YOU'RE BATTALION.
YOU'RE A PIONEER.
MA'AM--I APPRECIATE THAT, TRULY--BUT I HAVE REASON TO BELIEVE COMMANDER KAMAROV MURDERED CHECKMATE COMMANDER NIGEL KEANE.
OH, LORD... WHAT KIND OF REASON?
NIGEL WAS HELLSTRIKE. FROM MY TEAM. STORMWATCH.
IT HAS BEEN AN HONOR TO SERVE WITH SUCH A HERO.
HE WAS THE BEST OF CHECKMATE. THE REAL CHECKMATE. WHEN WE DID CIVIL RIGHTS ENFORCEMENT.
BEFORE THIS SHIT.

"THIS SHIT"?

MA'AM, I APOLOGIZE IF I COME ACROSS AS DISMISSIVE. YOU JUST GOT HERE AND I RESPECT THAT.

BUT LOOK AROUND. YOU RUN A BLACK SITE.

THAT'S WHAT PEOPLE IN OUR LINE OF WORK CALL A *TORTURE CHAMBER.*

LIKE I SAID, I SERVED WITH HELLSTRIKE. WE WENT *THROUGH THINGS* TOGETHER.

HE *TRUSTED* ME.

NIGEL *NEVER* BELIEVED CHECKMATE HAD *ANY* BUSINESS OUTSIDE OUR BORDERS, BUT HE WENT WHERE THEY SENT HIM. HERE.

A *SUPPLY OUTPOST.* BUT REALLY, WHERE WE TAKE PEOPLE WHO MIGHT HAVE *POWERS.*

"WHY DID THEY SEND HELLSTRIKE THERE?

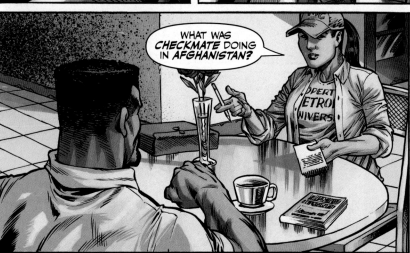

WHAT WAS *CHECKMATE* DOING IN *AFGHANISTAN?*

ALL I KNOW FOR SURE IS THEY MANNED A SUPPLY OUTPOST.

FOR THE FIGHTERS AGAINST THE SOVIETS.

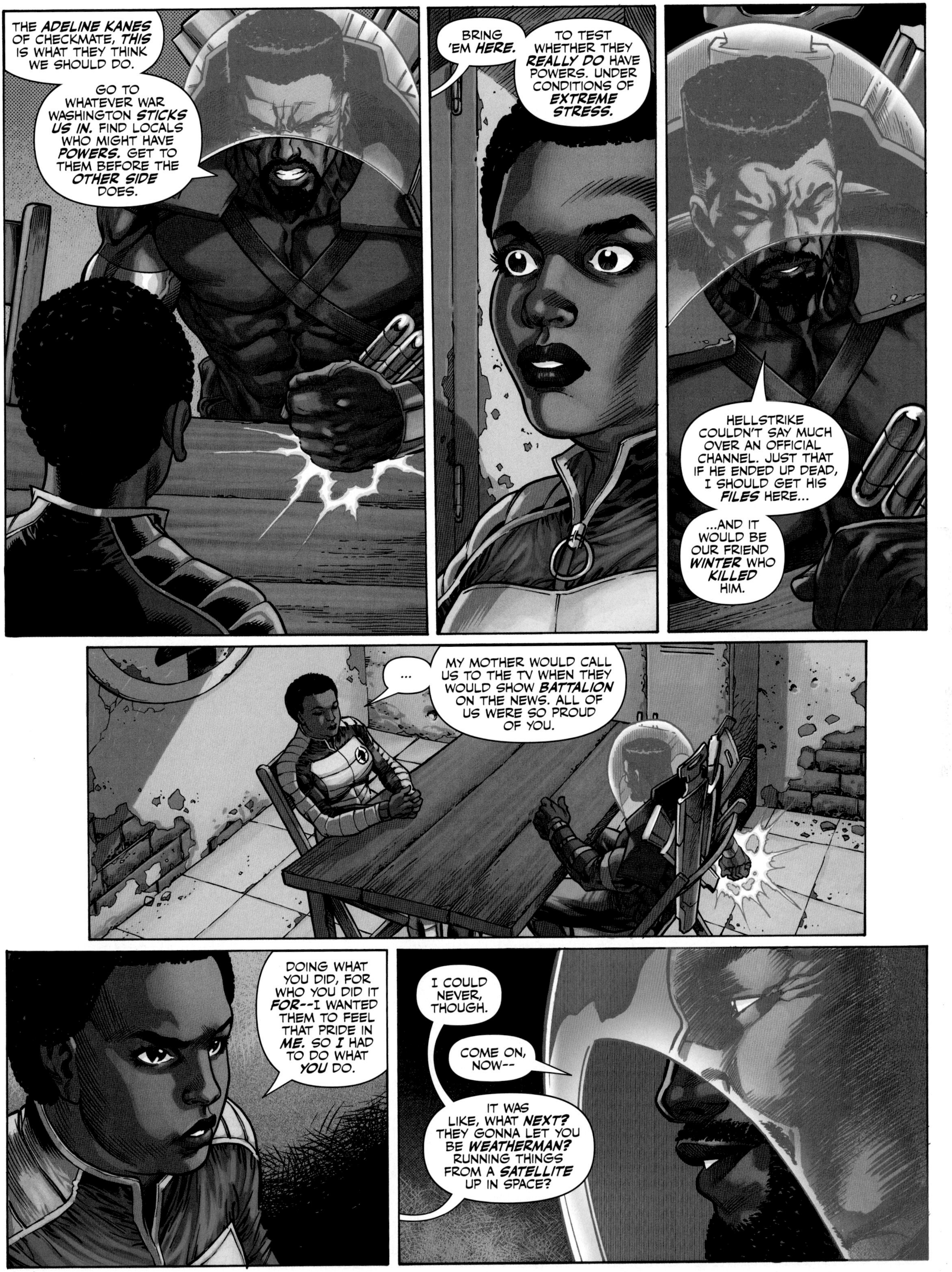
THE ADELINE KANES OF CHECKMATE, THIS IS WHAT THEY THINK WE SHOULD DO.
GO TO WHATEVER WAR WASHINGTON STICKS US IN. FIND LOCALS WHO MIGHT HAVE POWERS. GET TO THEM BEFORE THE OTHER SIDE DOES.
BRING 'EM HERE.
TO TEST WHETHER THEY REALLY DO HAVE POWERS. UNDER CONDITIONS OF EXTREME STRESS.
HELLSTRIKE COULDN'T SAY MUCH OVER AN OFFICIAL CHANNEL. JUST THAT IF HE ENDED UP DEAD, I SHOULD GET HIS FILES HERE...
...AND IT WOULD BE OUR FRIEND WINTER WHO KILLED HIM.
...
MY MOTHER WOULD CALL US TO THE TV WHEN THEY WOULD SHOW BATTALION ON THE NEWS. ALL OF US WERE SO PROUD OF YOU.
DOING WHAT YOU DID, FOR WHO YOU DID IT FOR--I WANTED THEM TO FEEL THAT PRIDE IN ME. SO I HAD TO DO WHAT YOU DO.
I COULD NEVER, THOUGH.
COME ON, NOW--
IT WAS LIKE, WHAT NEXT? THEY GONNA LET YOU BE WEATHERMAN? RUNNING THINGS FROM A SATELLITE UP IN SPACE?

I'M GRATEFUL TO HAVE HAD THAT IMPACT.

WEATHERMAN, THOUGH--I'LL TELL YOU...MA'AM, I APOLOGIZE, I DON'T THINK I HEARD YOUR NAME?

CHIEF OF BASE *AMANDA WALLER.* IT'S AN *HONOR*, SIR.

WELL, CHIEF WALLER--*AMANDA*--WHEN I SAW THEM LAUNCH *SKYWATCH*, I KNEW I HAD TO GET UP THERE.

YOU *TOO*?

ME TOO. RECKONED *CHECKMATE*--THIS *SUIT*--MIGHT BE THE WAY.

IF THEY'RE GONNA HAVE A *GIANT SPACE STATION* UP ABOVE US, ONE OF *US* HAS TO BE ON IT.

EXACTLY, SIR.

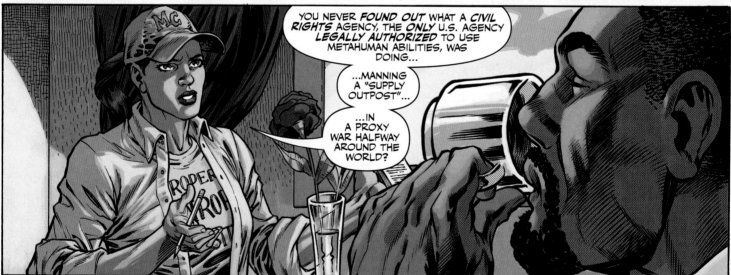

YOU NEVER *FOUND OUT* WHAT A *CIVIL RIGHTS* AGENCY, THE *ONLY* U.S. AGENCY *LEGALLY AUTHORIZED* TO USE METAHUMAN ABILITIES, WAS DOING...

...MANNING A "SUPPLY OUTPOST"...

...IN A *PROXY* WAR HALFWAY AROUND THE WORLD?

MS. LANE. I SAID I CAN *DOCUMENT* WHAT I TELL YOU.

YOU, ME, AND EVERYONE ELSE HAS AN *OPINION* ABOUT WHAT CHECKMATE DOES IN WHATEVER PLACE. I CAME HERE TO *DOCUMENT* SOMETHING.

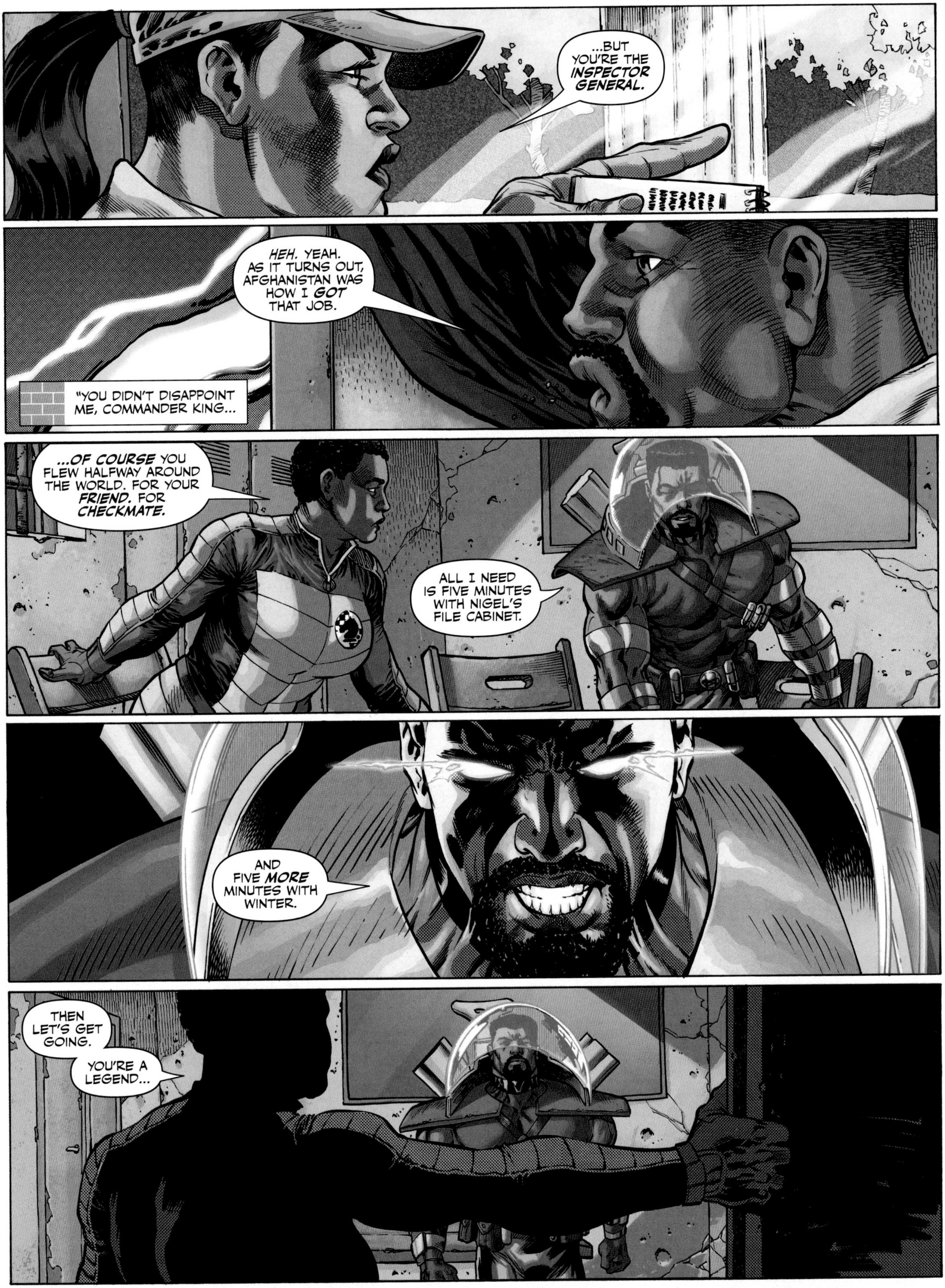
...BUT YOU'RE THE INSPECTOR GENERAL.
HEH. YEAH. AS IT TURNS OUT, AFGHANISTAN WAS HOW I GOT THAT JOB.
"YOU DIDN'T DISAPPOINT ME, COMMANDER KING...
...OF COURSE YOU FLEW HALFWAY AROUND THE WORLD. FOR YOUR FRIEND. FOR CHECKMATE.
ALL I NEED IS FIVE MINUTES WITH NIGEL'S FILE CABINET.
AND FIVE MORE MINUTES WITH WINTER.
THEN LET'S GET GOING.
YOU'RE A LEGEND...

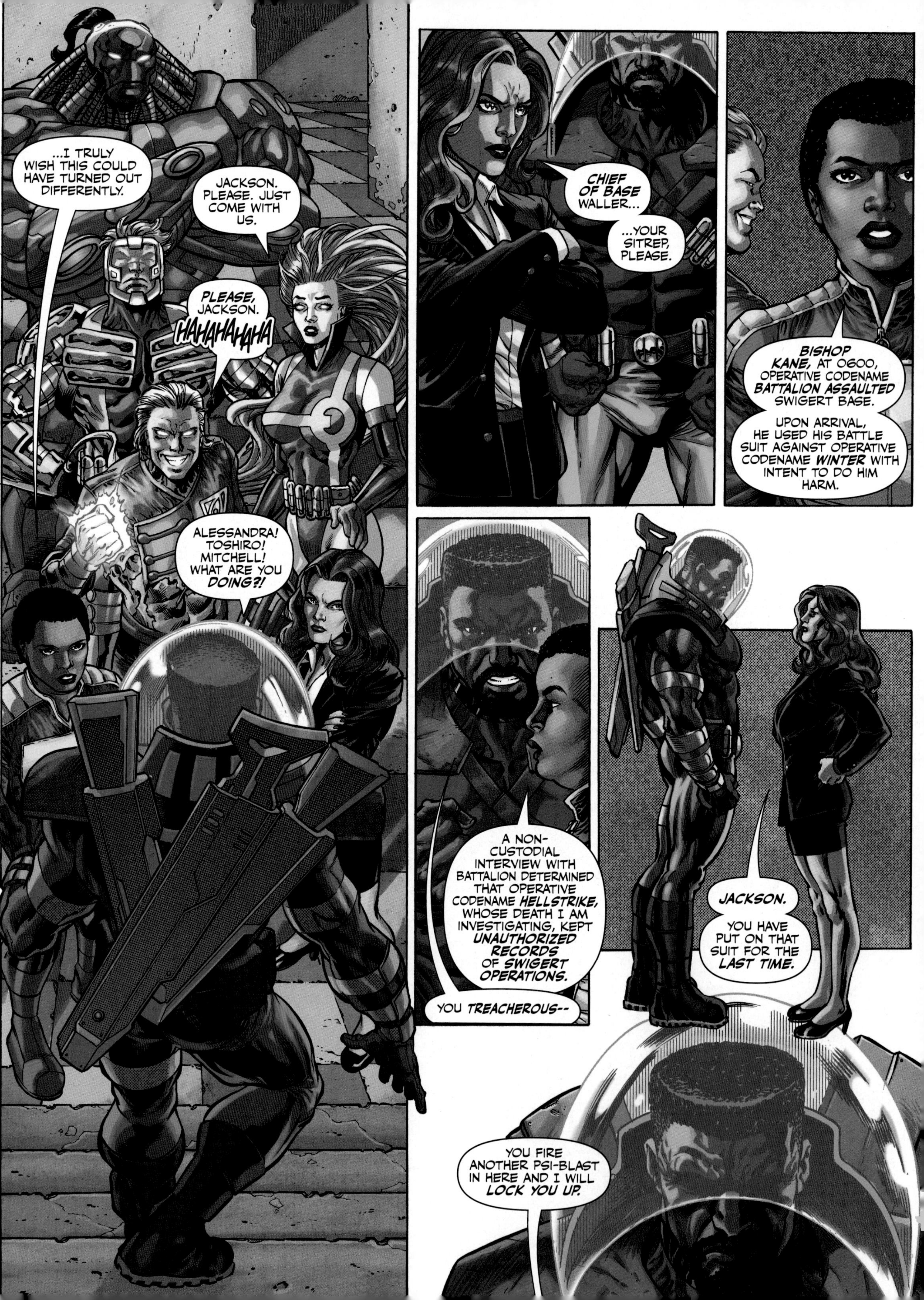
...I TRULY WISH THIS COULD HAVE TURNED OUT DIFFERENTLY.
JACKSON. PLEASE. JUST COME WITH US.
PLEASE, JACKSON.
HAHAHAHAHA
ALESSANDRA! TOSHIRO! MITCHELL! WHAT ARE YOU DOING?!
CHIEF OF BASE WALLER...
...YOUR SITREP, PLEASE.
BISHOP KANE, AT 0600, OPERATIVE CODENAME BATTALION ASSAULTED SWIGERT BASE.
UPON ARRIVAL, HE USED HIS BATTLE SUIT AGAINST OPERATIVE CODENAME WINTER WITH INTENT TO DO HIM HARM.
A NON-CUSTODIAL INTERVIEW WITH BATTALION DETERMINED THAT OPERATIVE CODENAME HELLSTRIKE, WHOSE DEATH I AM INVESTIGATING, KEPT UNAUTHORIZED RECORDS OF SWIGERT OPERATIONS.
YOU TREACHEROUS--
JACKSON.
YOU HAVE PUT ON THAT SUIT FOR THE LAST TIME.
YOU FIRE ANOTHER PSI-BLAST IN HERE AND I WILL LOCK YOU UP.

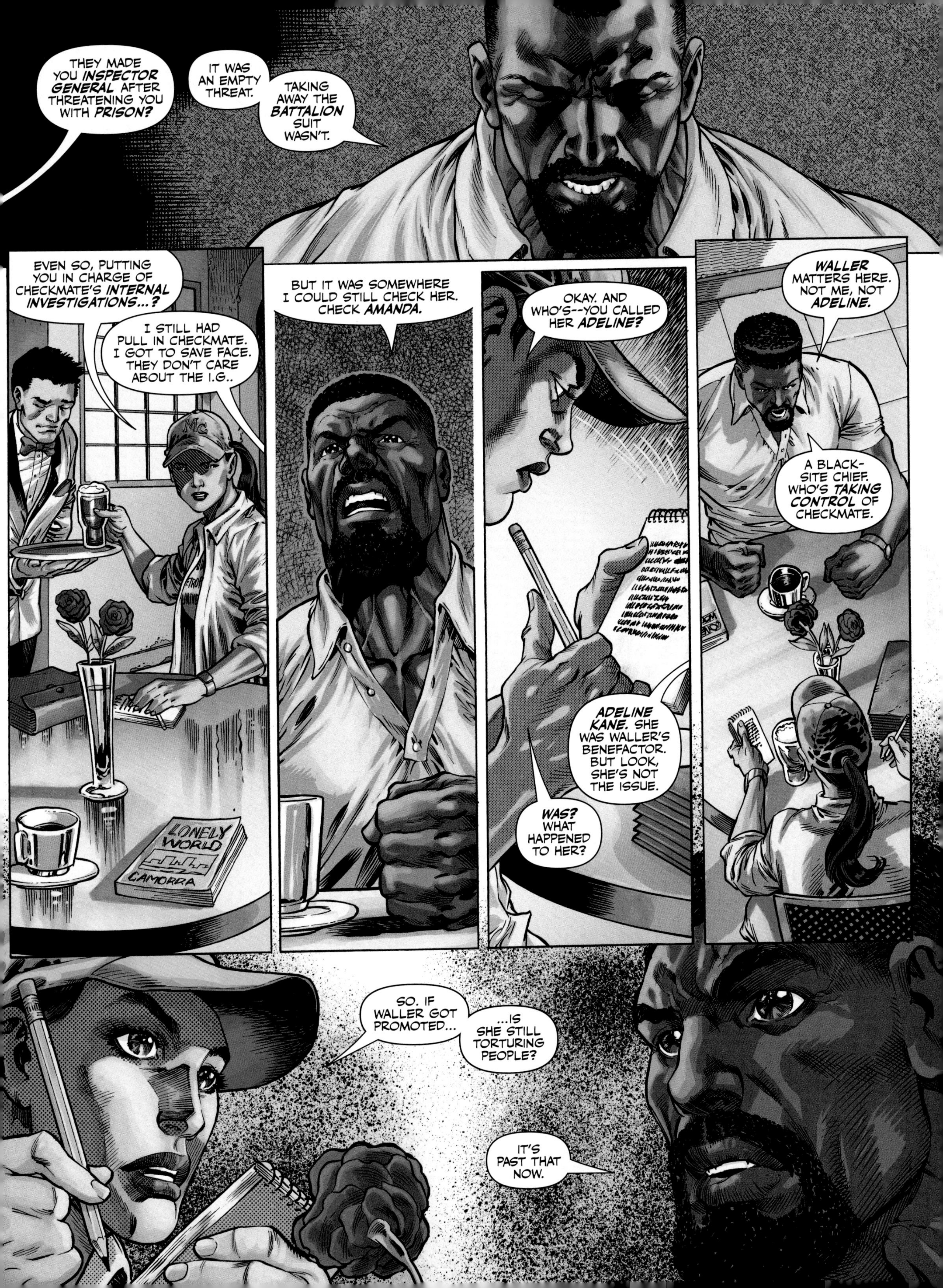
THEY MADE YOU INSPECTOR GENERAL AFTER THREATENING YOU WITH PRISON?
IT WAS AN EMPTY THREAT.
TAKING AWAY THE BATTALION SUIT WASN'T.
EVEN SO, PUTTING YOU IN CHARGE OF CHECKMATE'S INTERNAL INVESTIGATIONS...?
I STILL HAD PULL IN CHECKMATE. I GOT TO SAVE FACE. THEY DON'T CARE ABOUT THE I.G..
LONELY WORLD
CAMORRA
BUT IT WAS SOMEWHERE I COULD STILL CHECK HER. CHECK AMANDA.
OKAY. AND WHO'S--YOU CALLED HER ADELINE?
ADELINE KANE. SHE WAS WALLER'S BENEFACTOR. BUT LOOK, SHE'S NOT THE ISSUE.
WAS? WHAT HAPPENED TO HER?
WALLER MATTERS HERE. NOT ME, NOT ADELINE.
A BLACK-SITE CHIEF. WHO'S TAKING CONTROL OF CHECKMATE.
SO. IF WALLER GOT PROMOTED...
...IS SHE STILL TORTURING PEOPLE?
IT'S PAST THAT NOW.

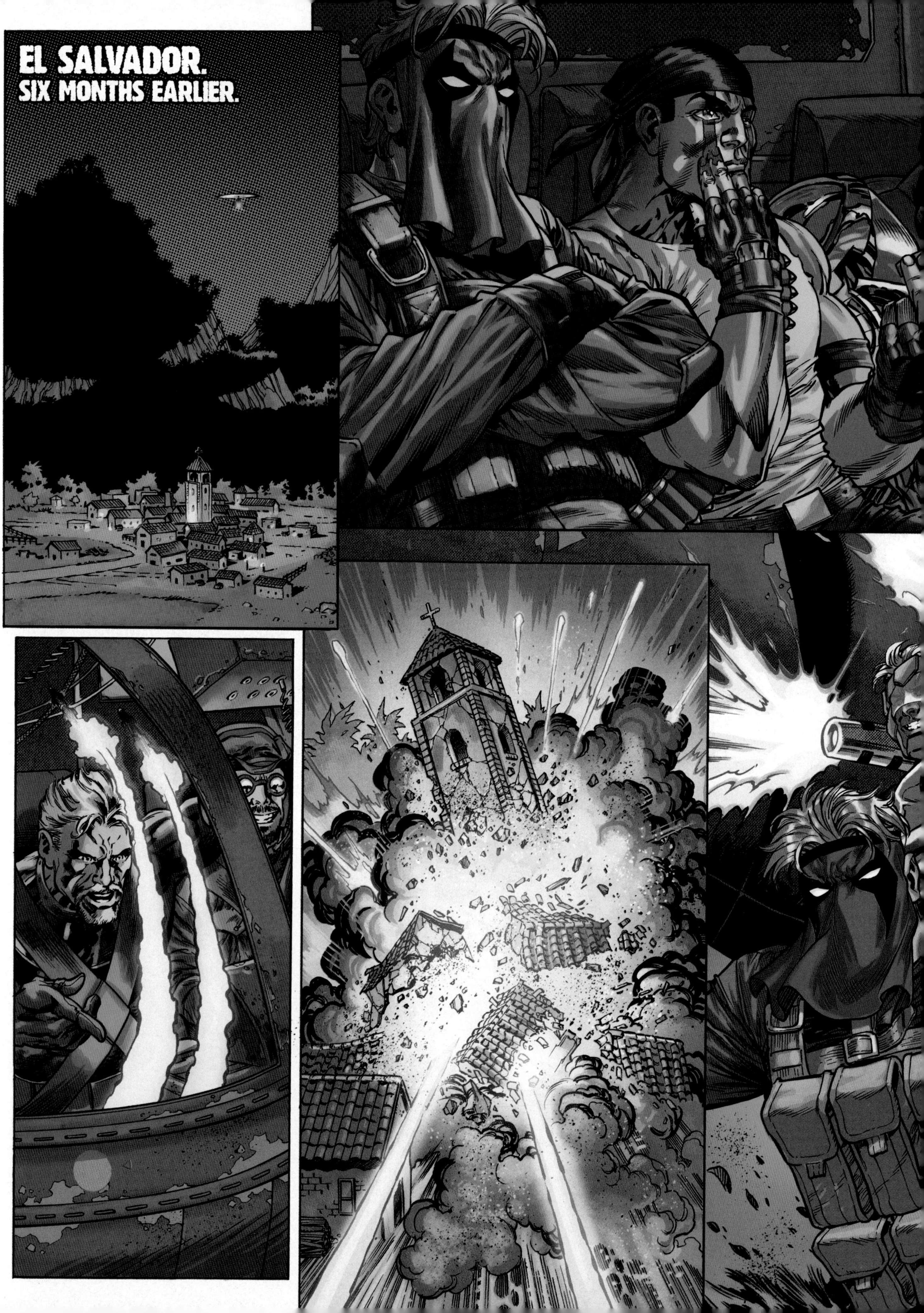
EL SALVADOR.
SIX MONTHS EARLIER.

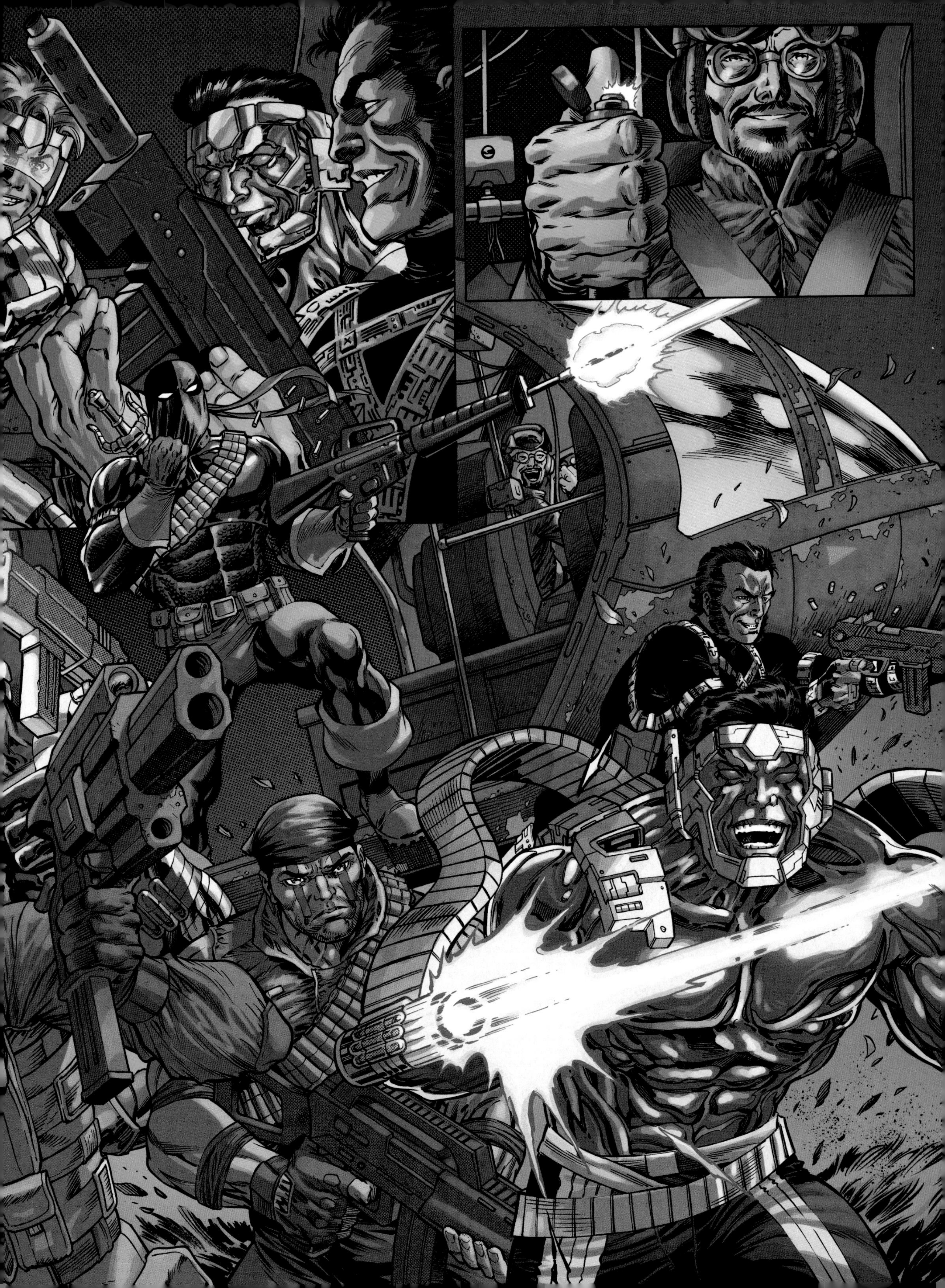

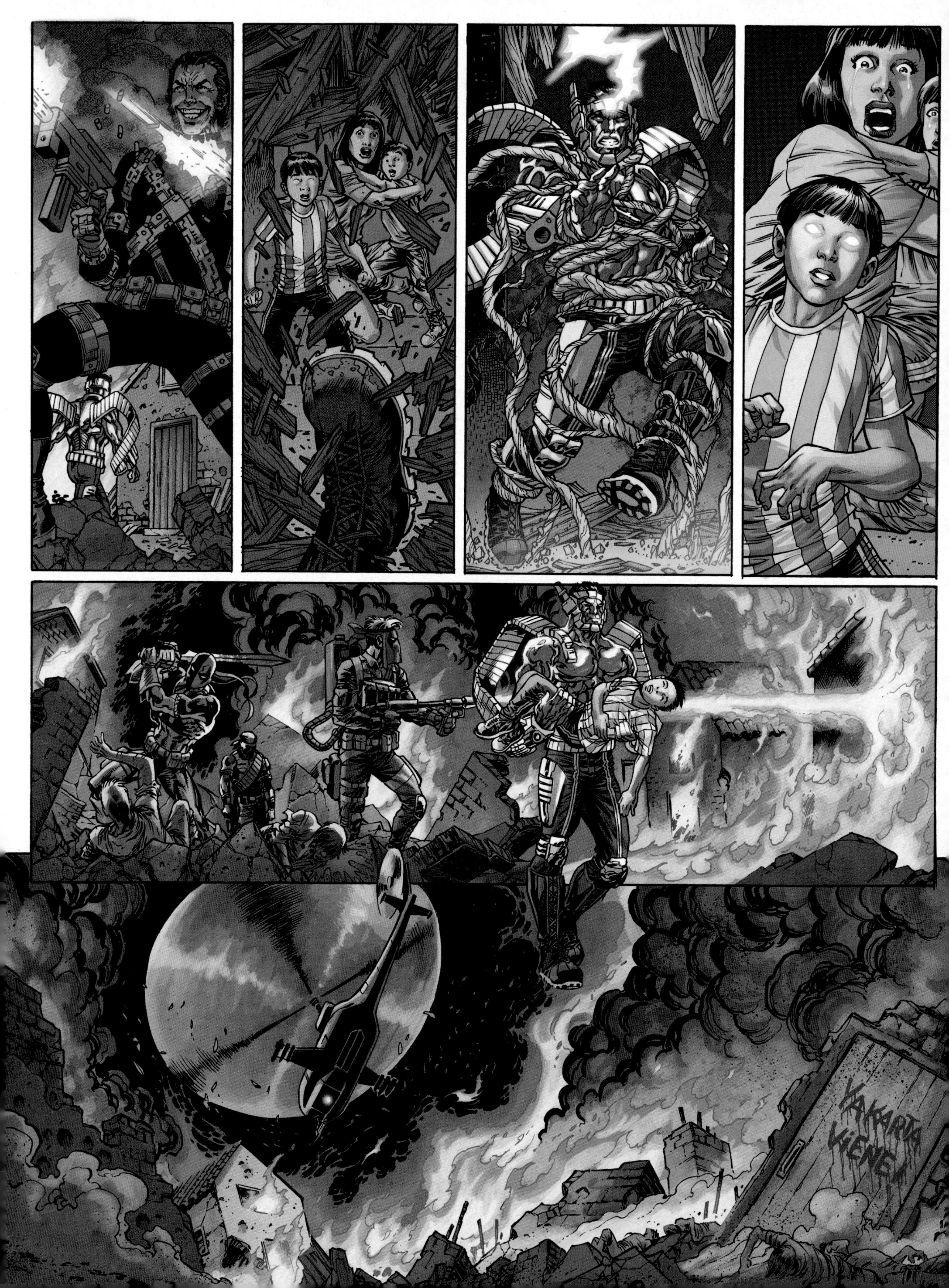
YAKARTA
VIENE

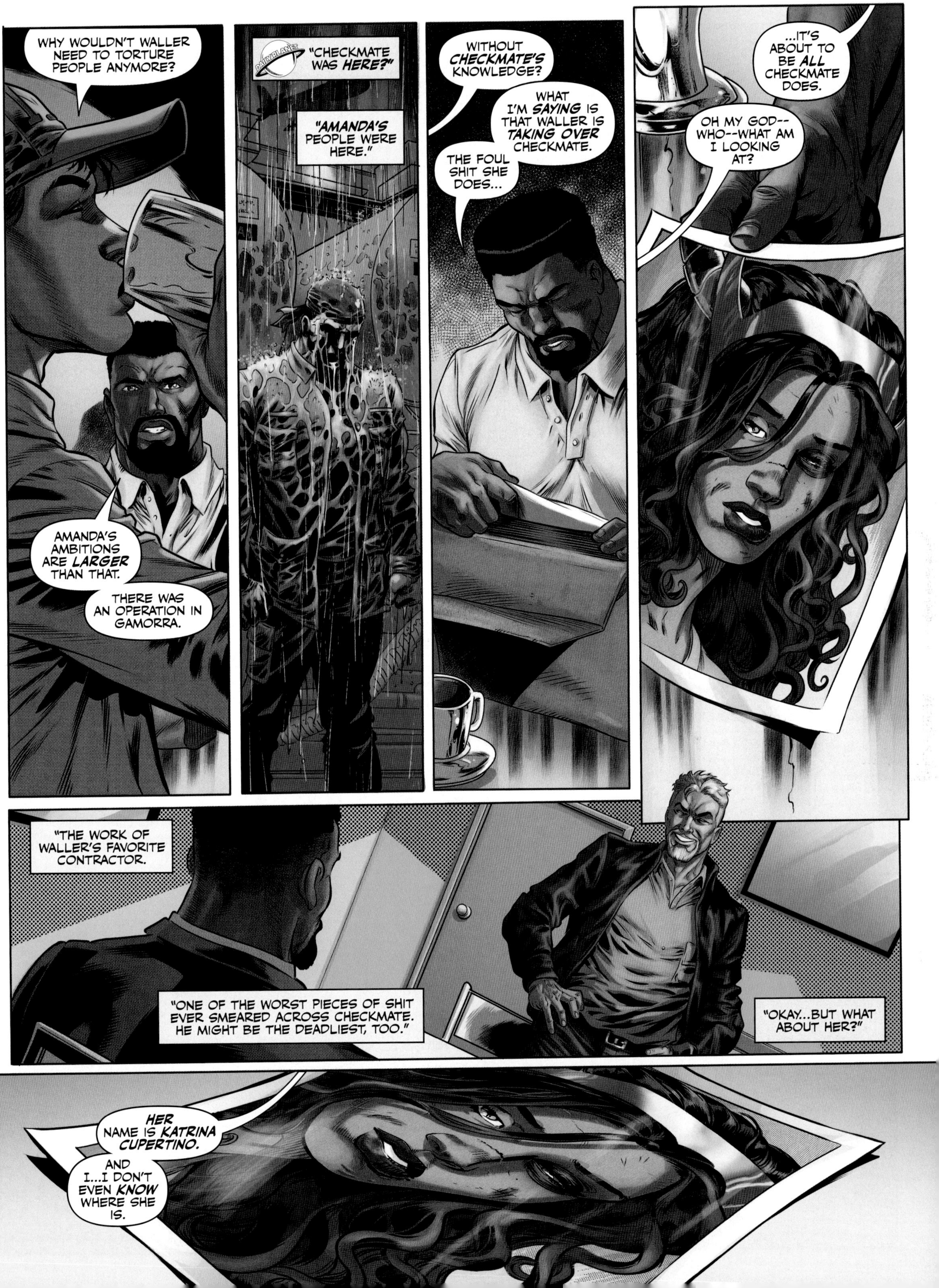
WHY WOULDN'T WALLER NEED TO TORTURE PEOPLE ANYMORE?
AMANDA'S AMBITIONS ARE LARGER THAN THAT.
THERE WAS AN OPERATION IN GAMORRA.
DAILY PLANET
"CHECKMATE WAS HERE?"
"AMANDA'S PEOPLE WERE HERE."
WITHOUT CHECKMATE'S KNOWLEDGE?
WHAT I'M SAYING IS THAT WALLER IS TAKING OVER CHECKMATE.
THE FOUL SHIT SHE DOES...
...IT'S ABOUT TO BE ALL CHECKMATE DOES.
OH MY GOD-- WHO--WHAT AM I LOOKING AT?
"THE WORK OF WALLER'S FAVORITE CONTRACTOR.
"ONE OF THE WORST PIECES OF SHIT EVER SMEARED ACROSS CHECKMATE. HE MIGHT BE THE DEADLIEST, TOO."
"OKAY...BUT WHAT ABOUT HER?"
HER NAME IS KATRINA CUPERTINO.
AND I...I DON'T EVEN KNOW WHERE SHE IS.

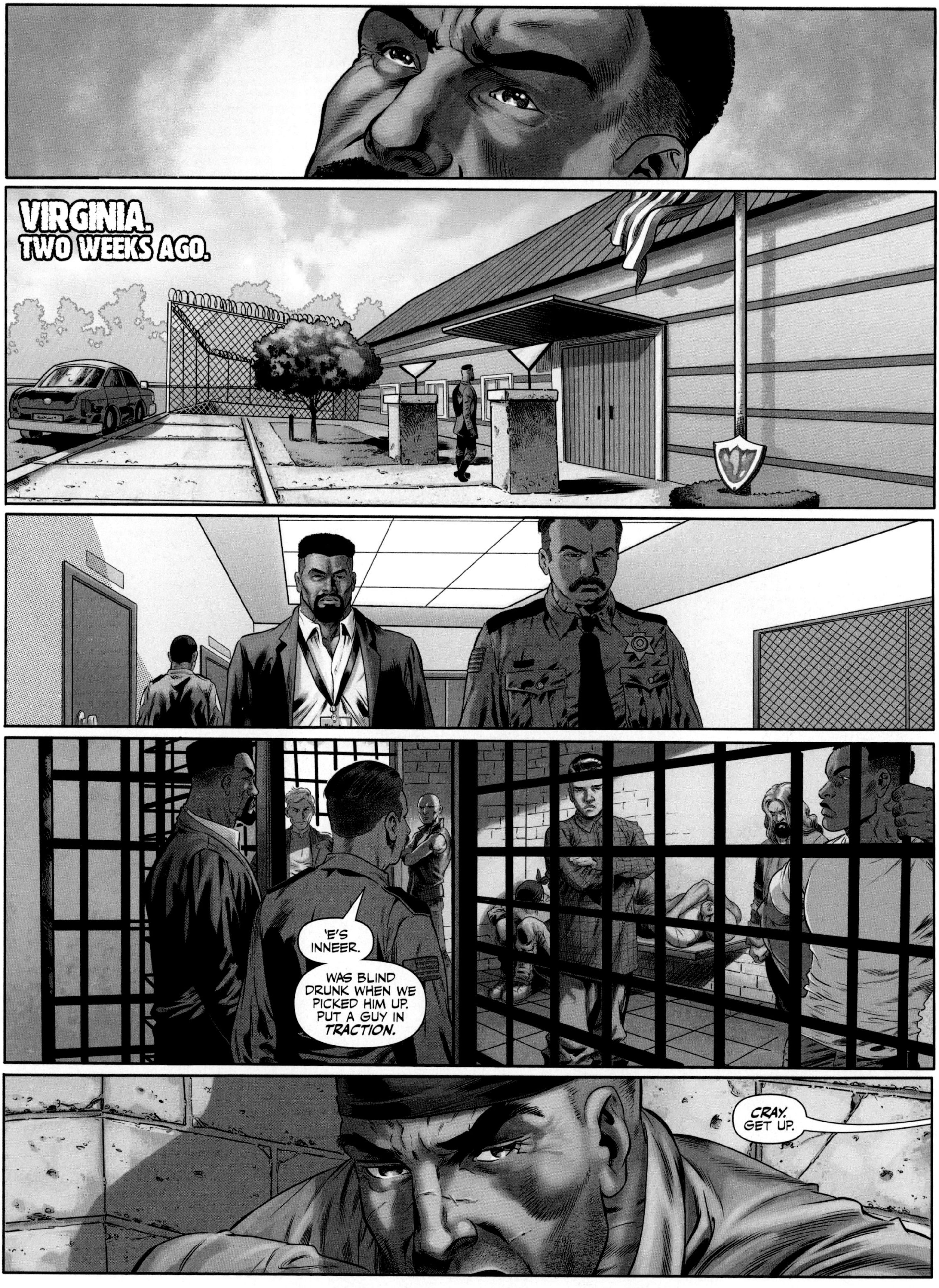
VIRGINIA.
TWO WEEKS AGO.
'E'S INNEER.
WAS BLIND DRUNK WHEN WE PICKED HIM UP. PUT A GUY IN *TRACTION.*
CRAY. GET UP.

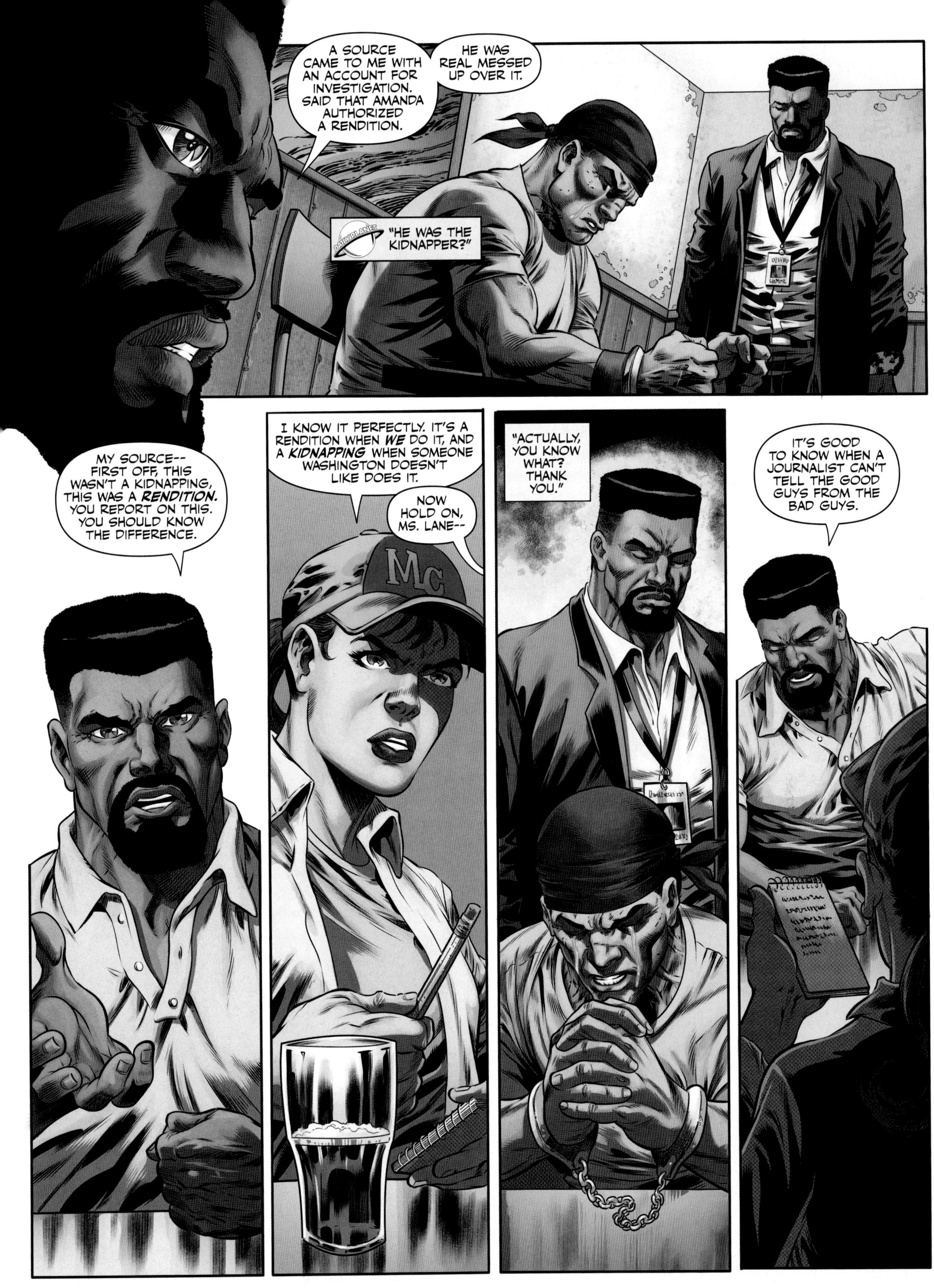
A SOURCE CAME TO ME WITH AN ACCOUNT FOR INVESTIGATION. SAID THAT AMANDA AUTHORIZED A RENDITION.
HE WAS REAL MESSED UP OVER IT.
"HE WAS THE KIDNAPPER?"
MY SOURCE-- FIRST OFF, THIS WASN'T A KIDNAPPING, THIS WAS A RENDITION. YOU REPORT ON THIS. YOU SHOULD KNOW THE DIFFERENCE.
I KNOW IT PERFECTLY. IT'S A RENDITION WHEN WE DO IT, AND A KIDNAPPING WHEN SOMEONE WASHINGTON DOESN'T LIKE DOES IT.
NOW HOLD ON, MS. LANE--
"ACTUALLY, YOU KNOW WHAT? THANK YOU."
IT'S GOOD TO KNOW WHEN A JOURNALIST CAN'T TELL THE GOOD GUYS FROM THE BAD GUYS.

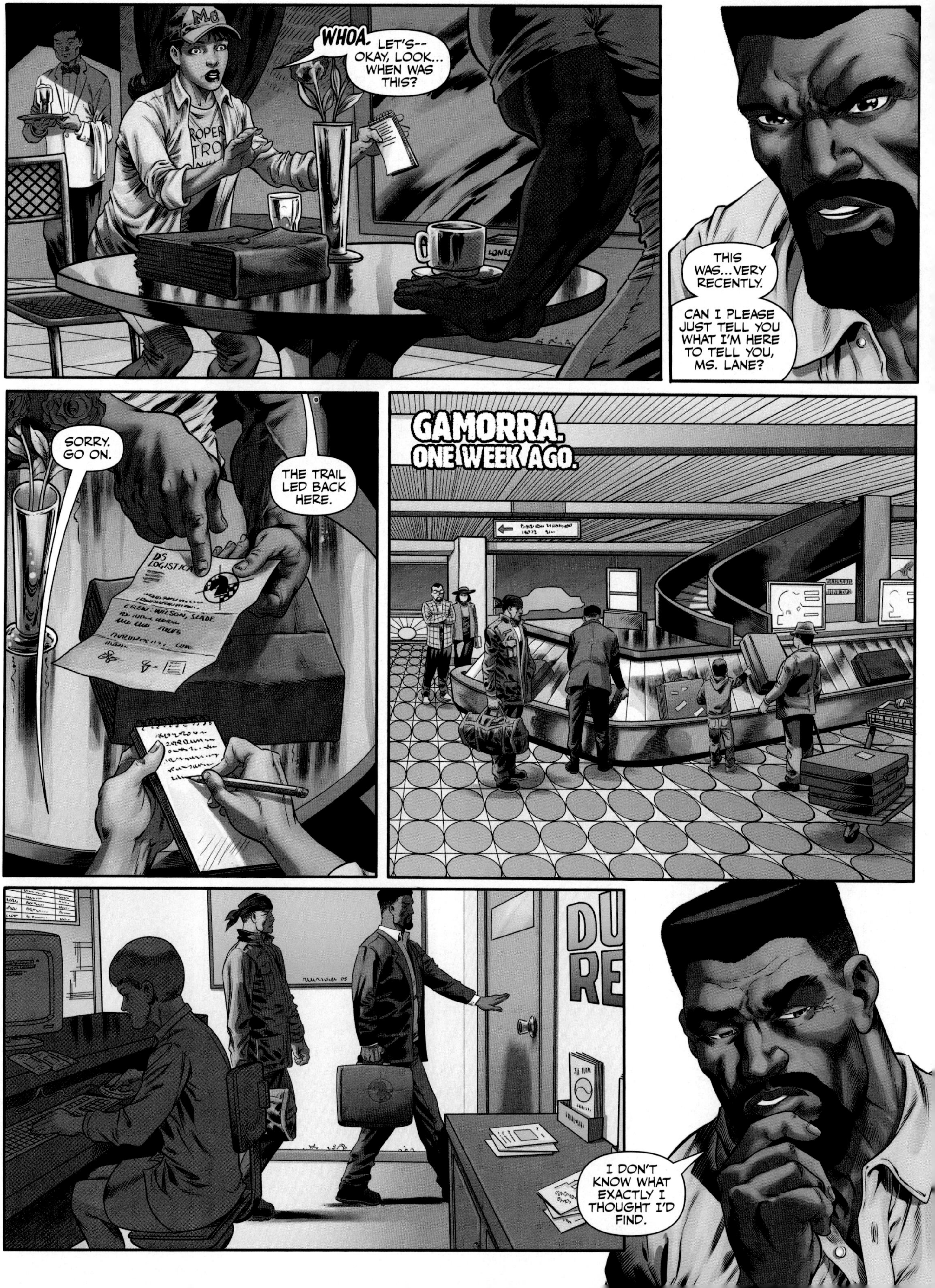

WHOA.
LET'S-- OKAY, LOOK... WHEN WAS THIS?
THIS WAS...VERY RECENTLY.
CAN I PLEASE JUST TELL YOU WHAT I'M HERE TO TELL YOU, MS. LANE?
SORRY. GO ON.
THE TRAIL LED BACK HERE.
DS LOGISTICS
CREW: WILSON, SLADE
GAMORRA. ONE WEEK AGO.
I DON'T KNOW WHAT EXACTLY I THOUGHT I'D FIND.

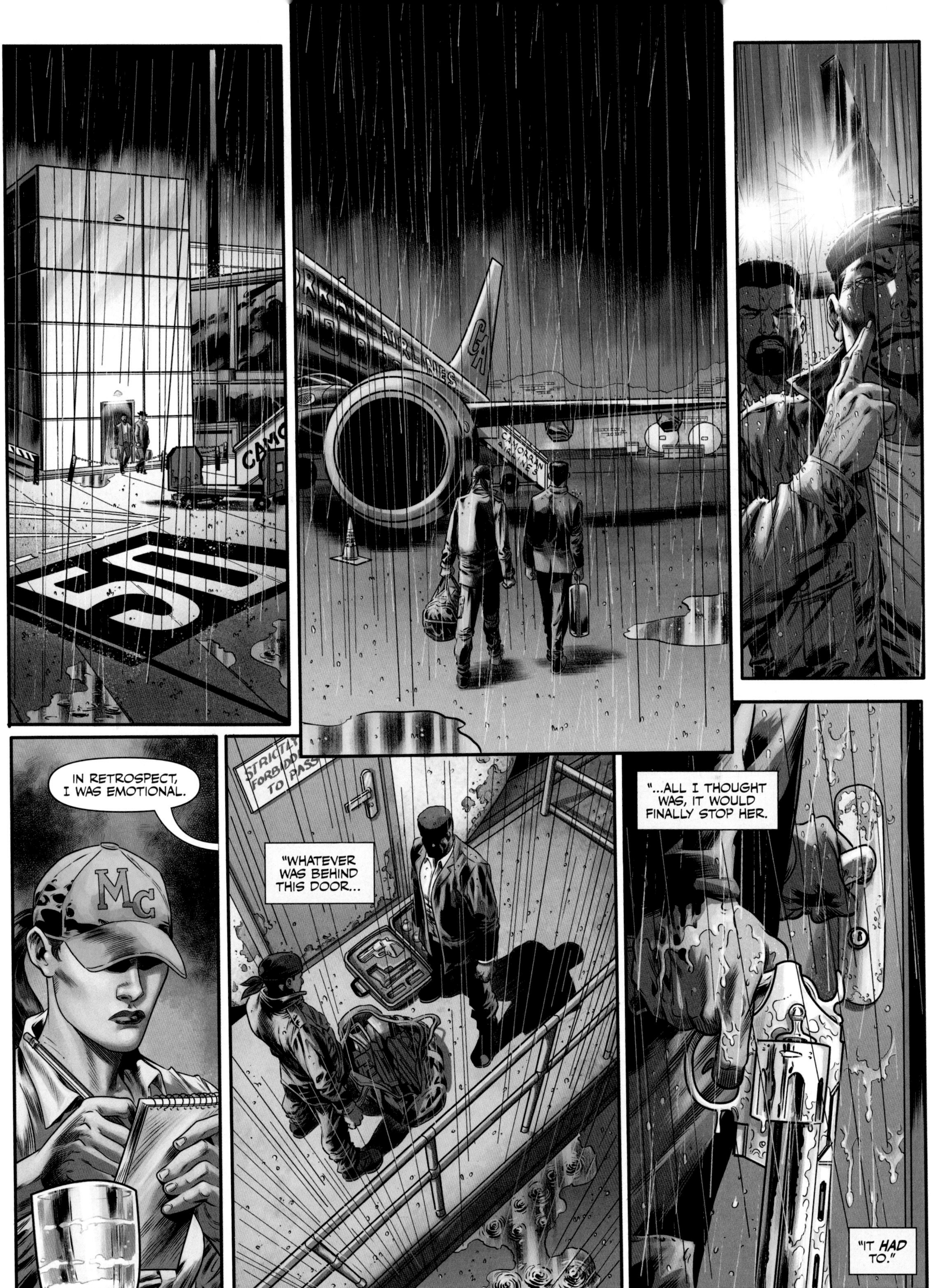
IN RETROSPECT, I WAS EMOTIONAL.
"WHATEVER WAS BEHIND THIS DOOR...
"...ALL I THOUGHT WAS, IT WOULD FINALLY STOP HER.
"IT *HAD* TO."

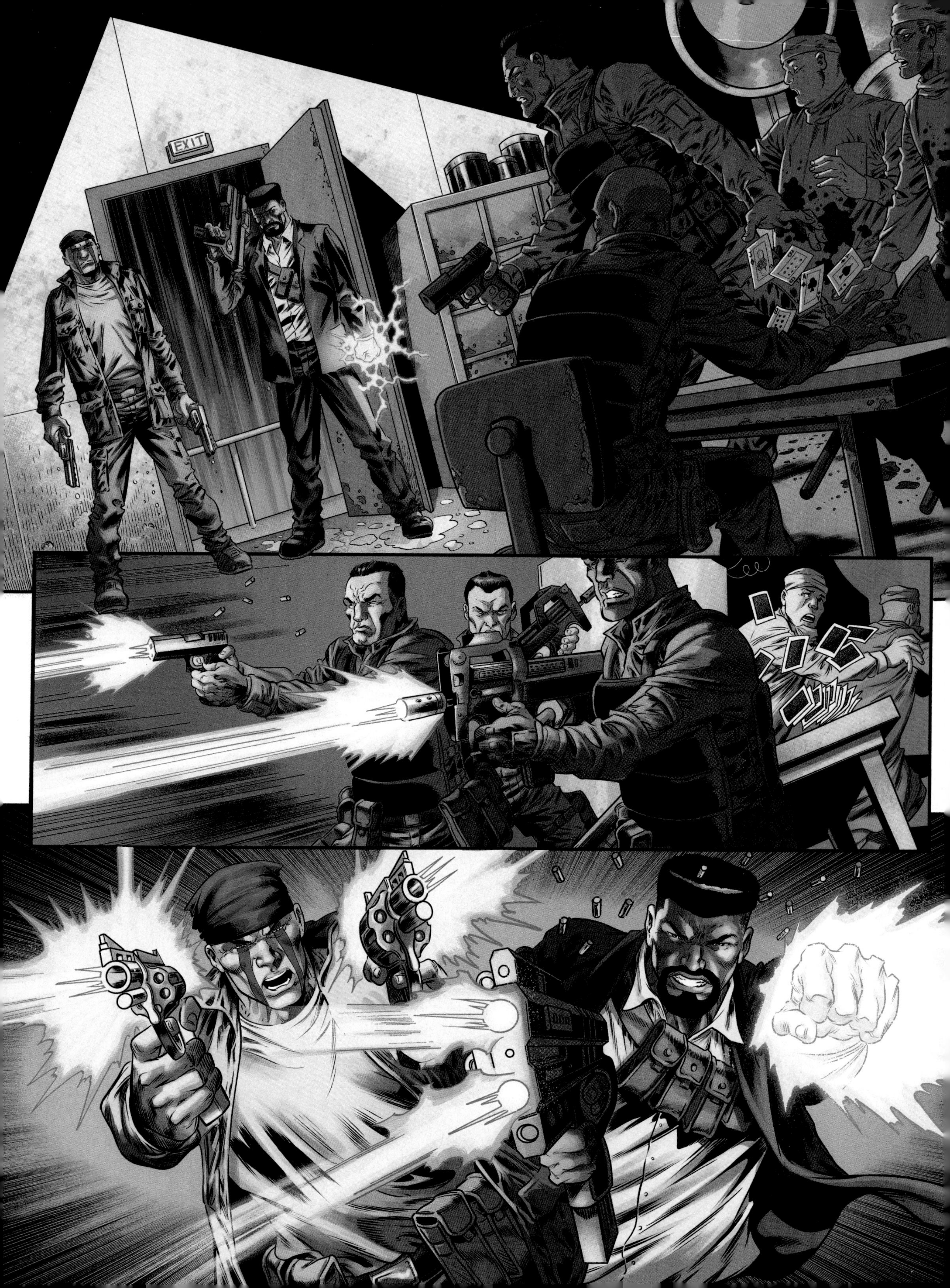
EXIT

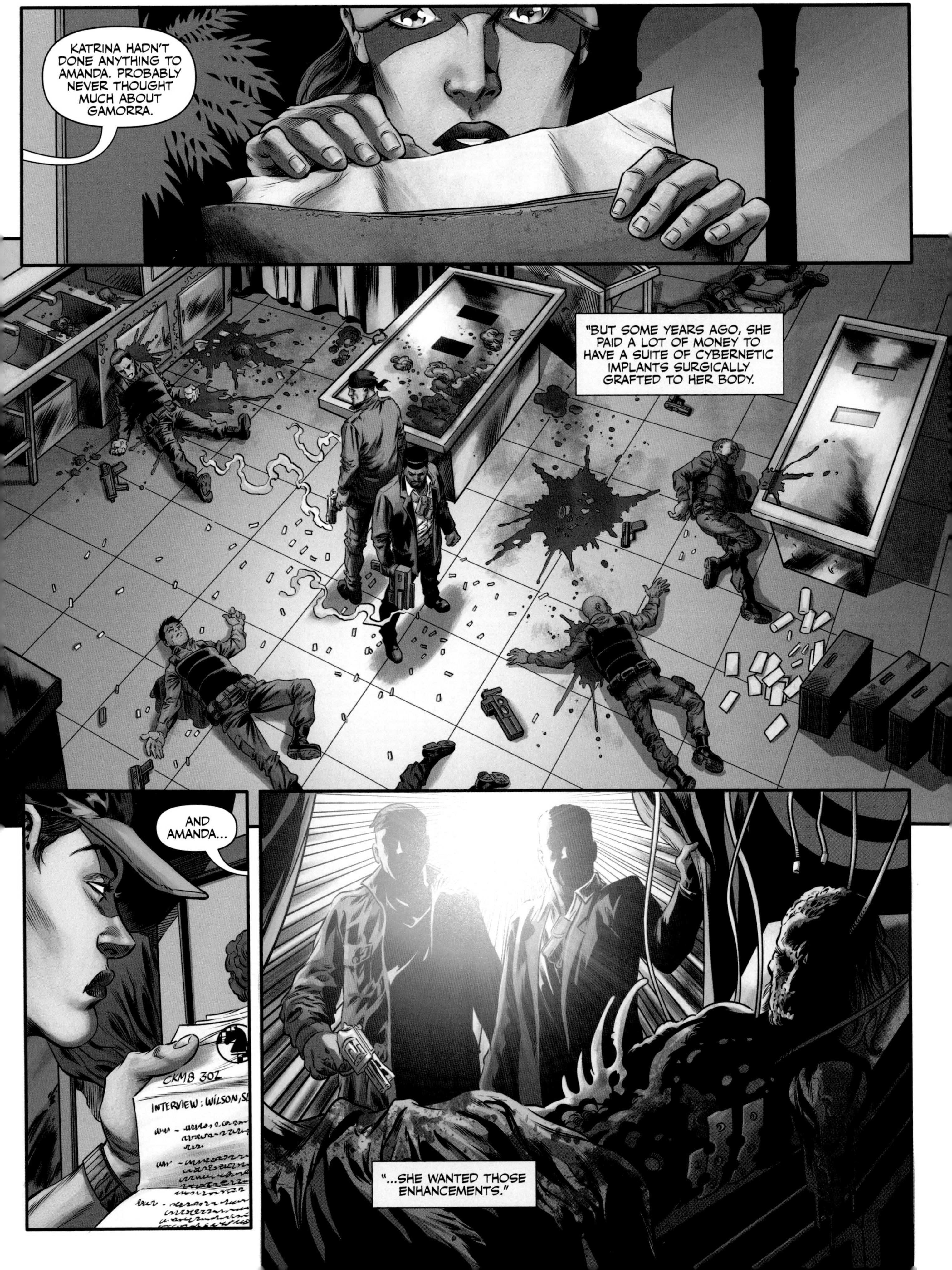
KATRINA HADN'T DONE ANYTHING TO AMANDA. PROBABLY NEVER THOUGHT MUCH ABOUT GAMORRA.
"BUT SOME YEARS AGO, SHE PAID A LOT OF MONEY TO HAVE A SUITE OF CYBERNETIC IMPLANTS SURGICALLY GRAFTED TO HER BODY.
AND AMANDA...
CKMB 302
"...SHE WANTED THOSE ENHANCEMENTS."

JESUS. WHAT... WHY DID SHE WANT THE...

YUMIKO GAMORRA.

HER FATHER WAS AN ASSHOLE AND A PEACOCK. BUT AT THE END OF THE DAY, HE WAS ABOUT *QUIET*.

HIS DAUGHTER IS A DIFFERENT STORY.

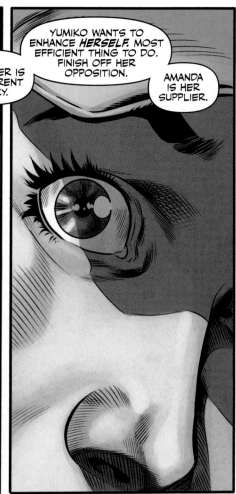

YUMIKO WANTS TO ENHANCE *HERSELF*. MOST EFFICIENT THING TO DO. FINISH OFF HER OPPOSITION.

AMANDA IS HER SUPPLIER.

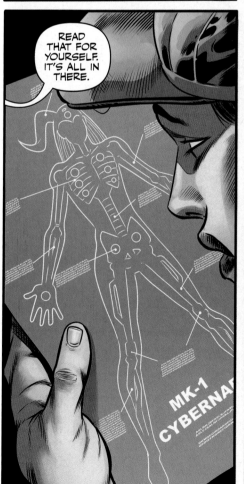

READ THAT FOR YOURSELF. IT'S ALL IN THERE.

MK-1 CYBERNA

BUT PLEASE READ FAST. IT'S IMPORTANT WE MOVE QUICKLY.

JUST A COUPLE MORE QUESTIONS.

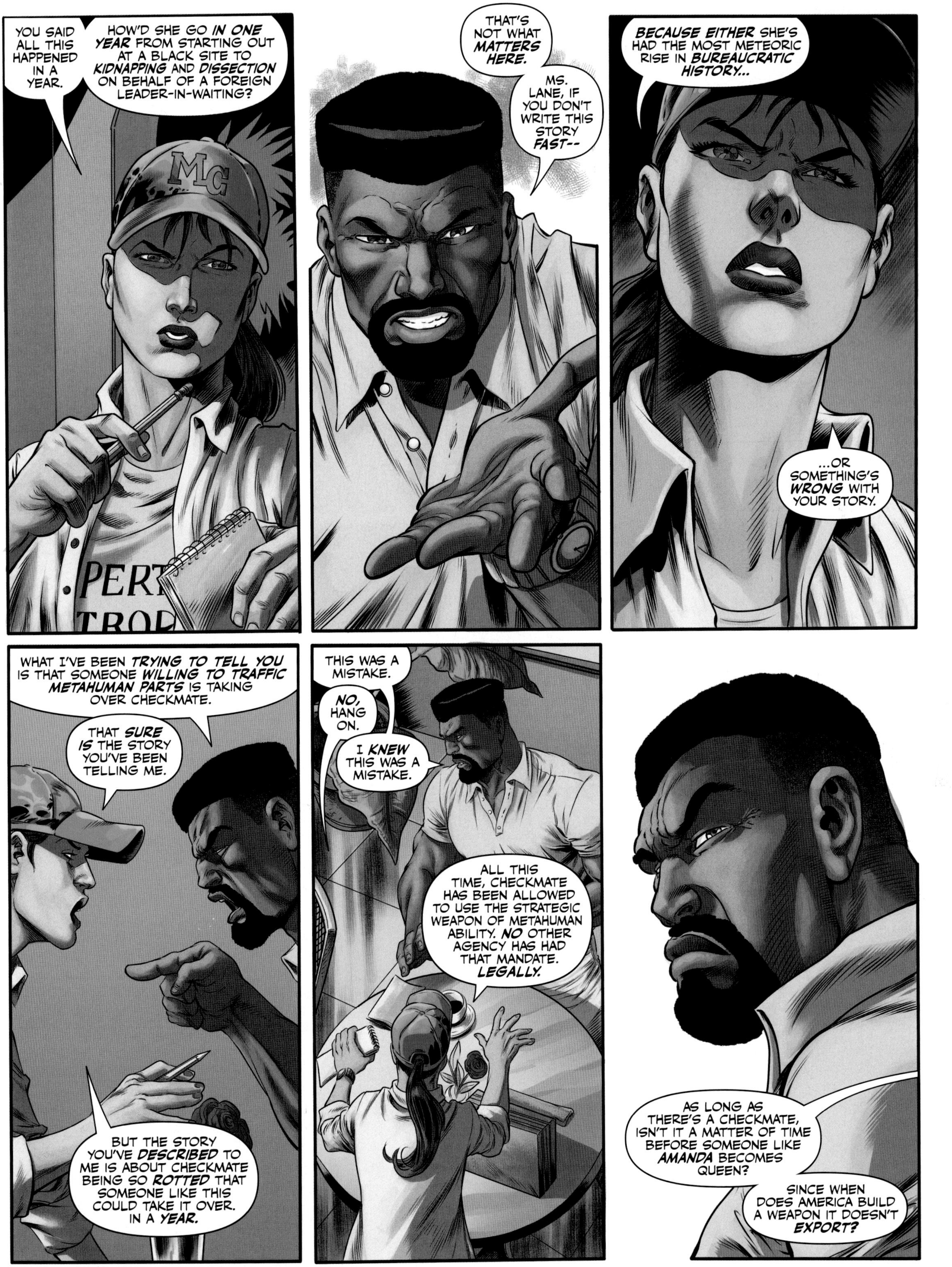

YOU SAID ALL THIS HAPPENED IN A YEAR.
HOW'D SHE GO IN ONE YEAR FROM STARTING OUT AT A BLACK SITE TO KIDNAPPING AND DISSECTION ON BEHALF OF A FOREIGN LEADER-IN-WAITING?
MC
PERT
TROP
THAT'S NOT WHAT MATTERS HERE.
MS. LANE, IF YOU DON'T WRITE THIS STORY FAST--
BECAUSE EITHER SHE'S HAD THE MOST METEORIC RISE IN BUREAUCRATIC HISTORY...
...OR SOMETHING'S WRONG WITH YOUR STORY.
WHAT I'VE BEEN TRYING TO TELL YOU IS THAT SOMEONE WILLING TO TRAFFIC METAHUMAN PARTS IS TAKING OVER CHECKMATE.
THAT SURE IS THE STORY YOU'VE BEEN TELLING ME.
BUT THE STORY YOU'VE DESCRIBED TO ME IS ABOUT CHECKMATE BEING SO ROTTED THAT SOMEONE LIKE THIS COULD TAKE IT OVER. IN A YEAR.
THIS WAS A MISTAKE.
NO, HANG ON.
I KNEW THIS WAS A MISTAKE.
ALL THIS TIME, CHECKMATE HAS BEEN ALLOWED TO USE THE STRATEGIC WEAPON OF METAHUMAN ABILITY. NO OTHER AGENCY HAS HAD THAT MANDATE. LEGALLY.
AS LONG AS THERE'S A CHECKMATE, ISN'T IT A MATTER OF TIME BEFORE SOMEONE LIKE AMANDA BECOMES QUEEN?
SINCE WHEN DOES AMERICA BUILD A WEAPON IT DOESN'T EXPORT?

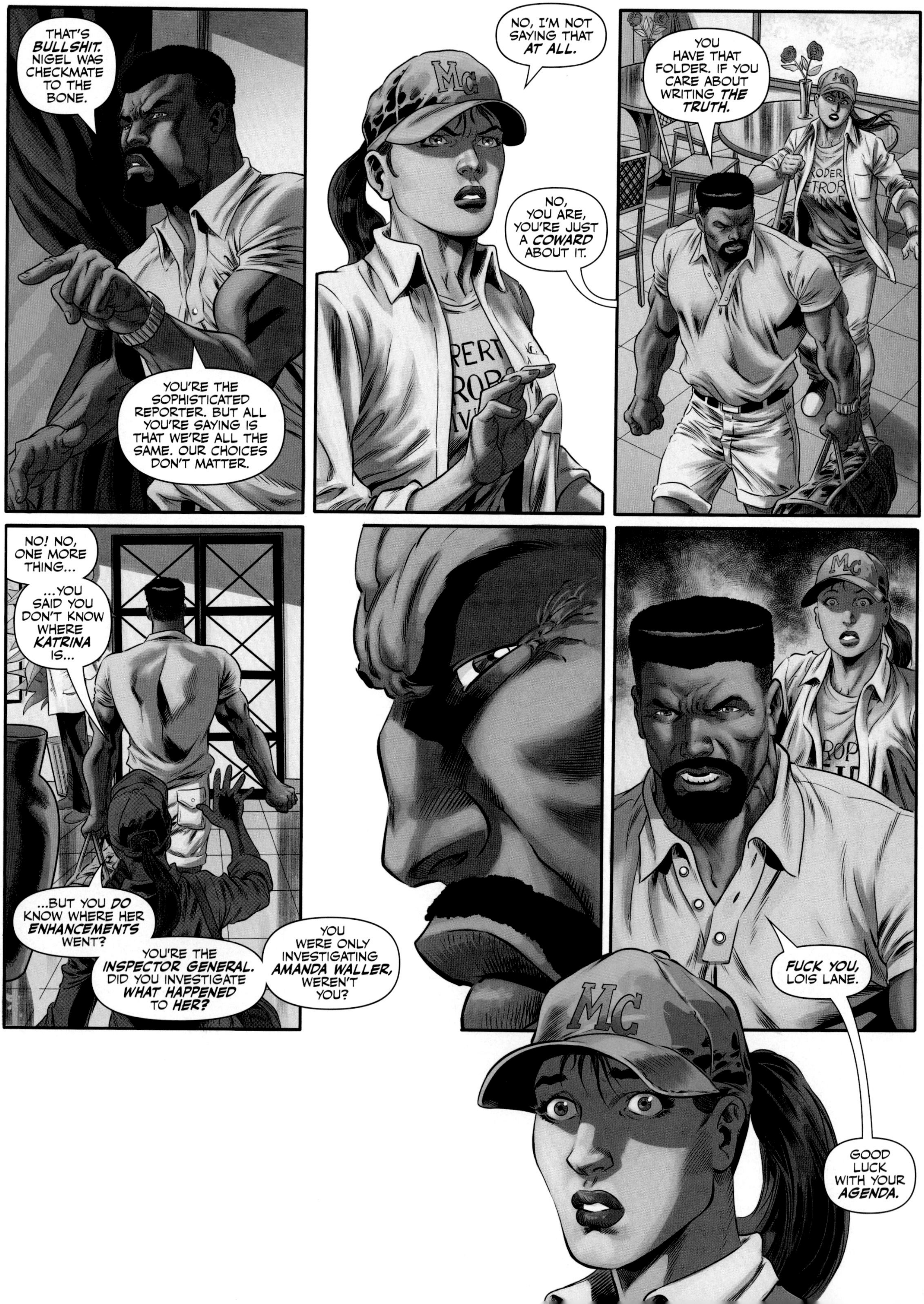
THAT'S BULLSHIT. NIGEL WAS CHECKMATE TO THE BONE.
YOU'RE THE SOPHISTICATED REPORTER. BUT ALL YOU'RE SAYING IS THAT WE'RE ALL THE SAME. OUR CHOICES DON'T MATTER.
NO, I'M NOT SAYING THAT AT ALL.
YOU HAVE THAT FOLDER. IF YOU CARE ABOUT WRITING THE TRUTH.
NO, YOU ARE, YOU'RE JUST A COWARD ABOUT IT.
NO! NO, ONE MORE THING...
...YOU SAID YOU DON'T KNOW WHERE KATRINA IS...
...BUT YOU DO KNOW WHERE HER ENHANCEMENTS WENT?
YOU'RE THE INSPECTOR GENERAL. DID YOU INVESTIGATE WHAT HAPPENED TO HER?
YOU WERE ONLY INVESTIGATING AMANDA WALLER, WEREN'T YOU?
FUCK YOU, LOIS LANE.
GOOD LUCK WITH YOUR AGENDA.

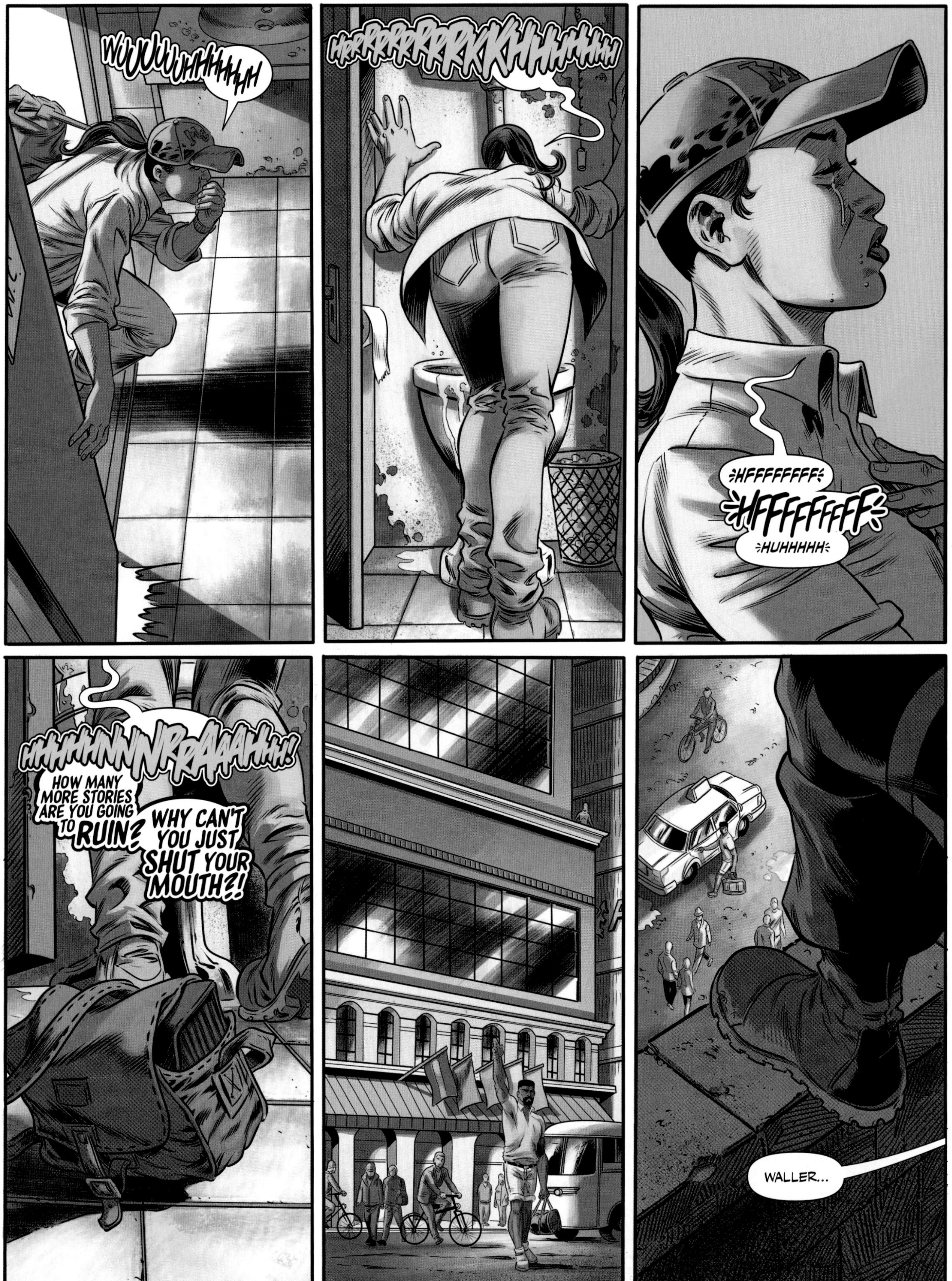
WUUUUUHHHHHHH
HRRRRRRRRRKKHHHHHHHH
HFFFFFFFF
HFFFFFFFF
HUHHHHH
HHHHHNNNRRAAAHHH!
HOW MANY MORE STORIES ARE YOU GOING TO RUIN?
WHY CAN'T YOU JUST SHUT YOUR MOUTH?!
WALLER...

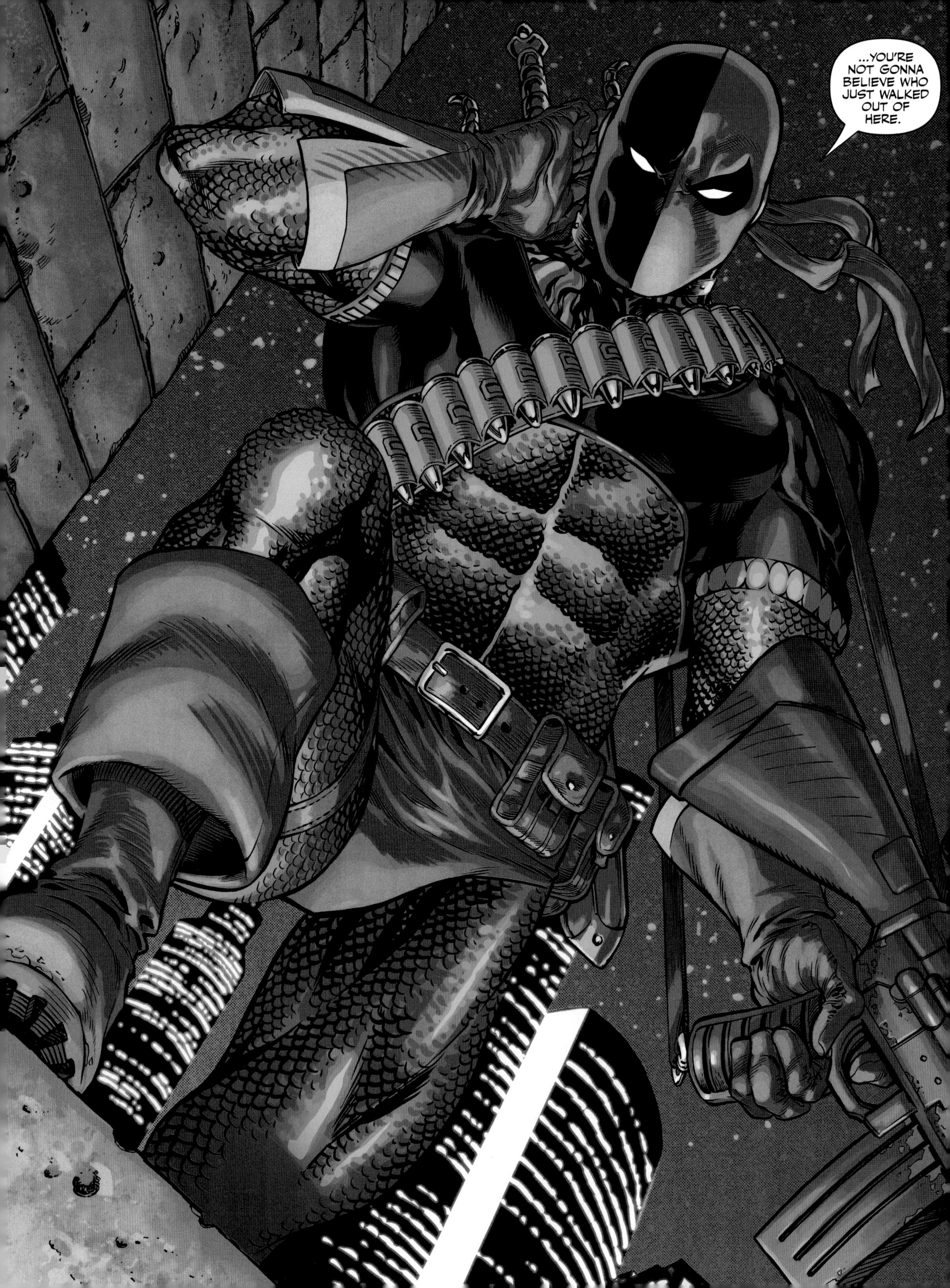
...YOU'RE NOT GONNA BELIEVE WHO JUST WALKED OUT OF HERE.

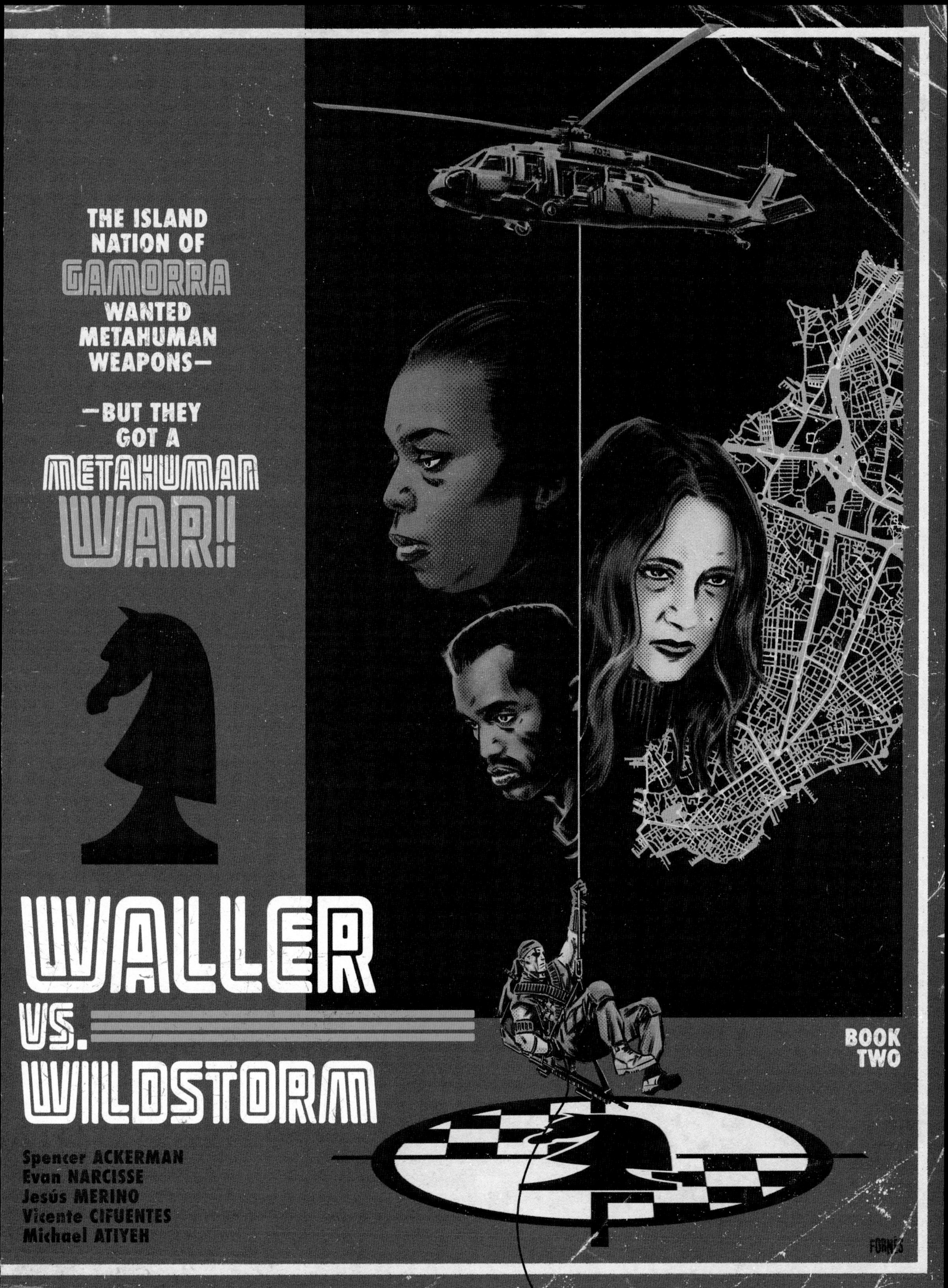
THE ISLAND NATION OF GAMORRA WANTED METAHUMAN WEAPONS—
—BUT THEY GOT A METAHUMAN WAR!!
WALLER VS. WILDSTORM
BOOK TWO
Spencer ACKERMAN
Evan NARCISSE
Jesús MERINO
Vicente CIFUENTES
Michael ATIYEH
FORNÉS

"GAMORRA'S NEW HERO HAS ARRIVED."

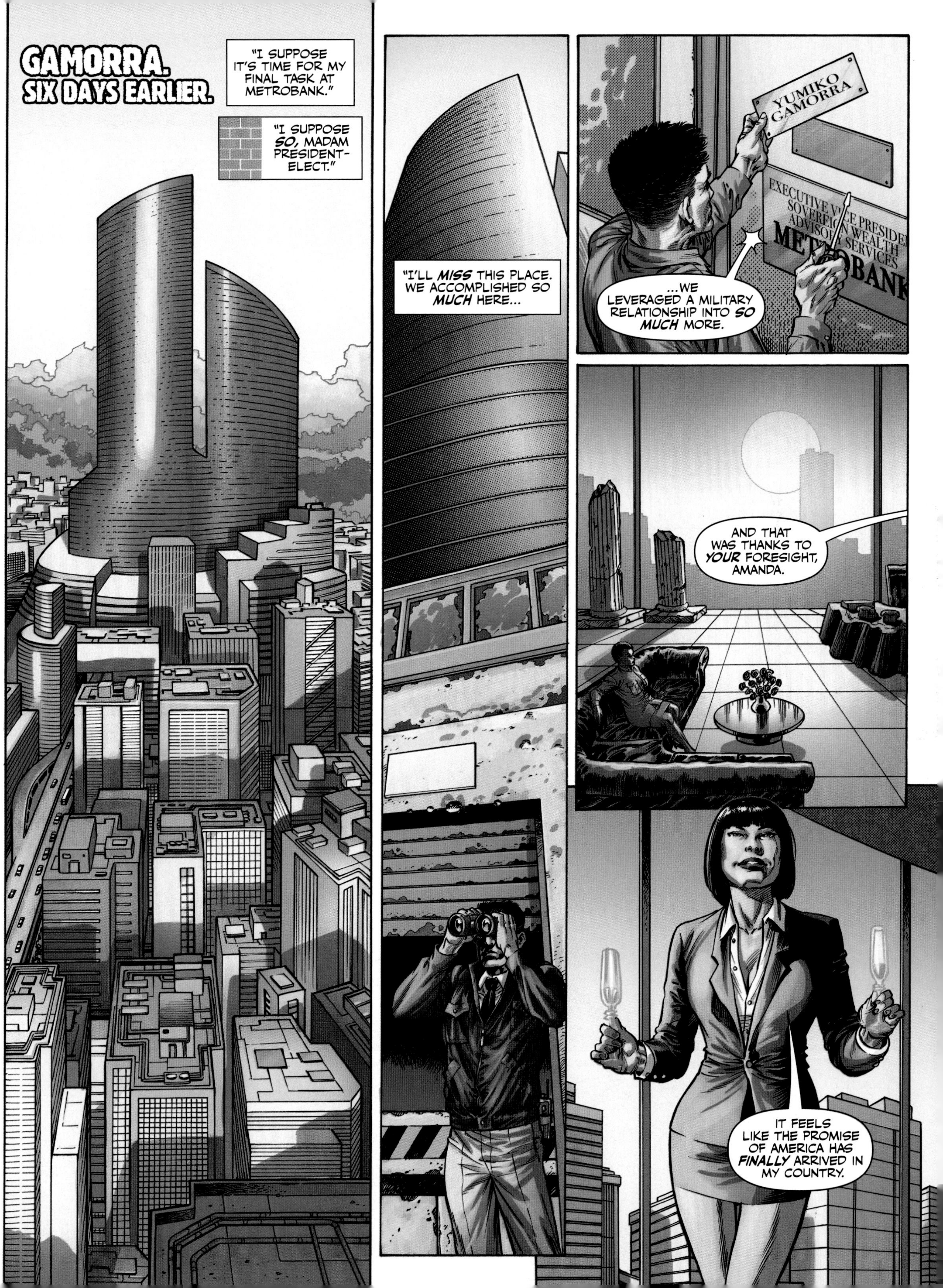
GAMORRA.
SIX DAYS EARLIER.
"I SUPPOSE IT'S TIME FOR MY FINAL TASK AT METROBANK."
"I SUPPOSE SO, MADAM PRESIDENT-ELECT."
"I'LL MISS THIS PLACE. WE ACCOMPLISHED SO MUCH HERE...
YUMIKO GAMORRA
EXECUTIVE VICE PRESIDENT SOVEREIGN WEALTH ADVISORY SERVICES
METROBANK
...WE LEVERAGED A MILITARY RELATIONSHIP INTO SO MUCH MORE.
AND THAT WAS THANKS TO YOUR FORESIGHT, AMANDA.
IT FEELS LIKE THE PROMISE OF AMERICA HAS FINALLY ARRIVED IN MY COUNTRY.

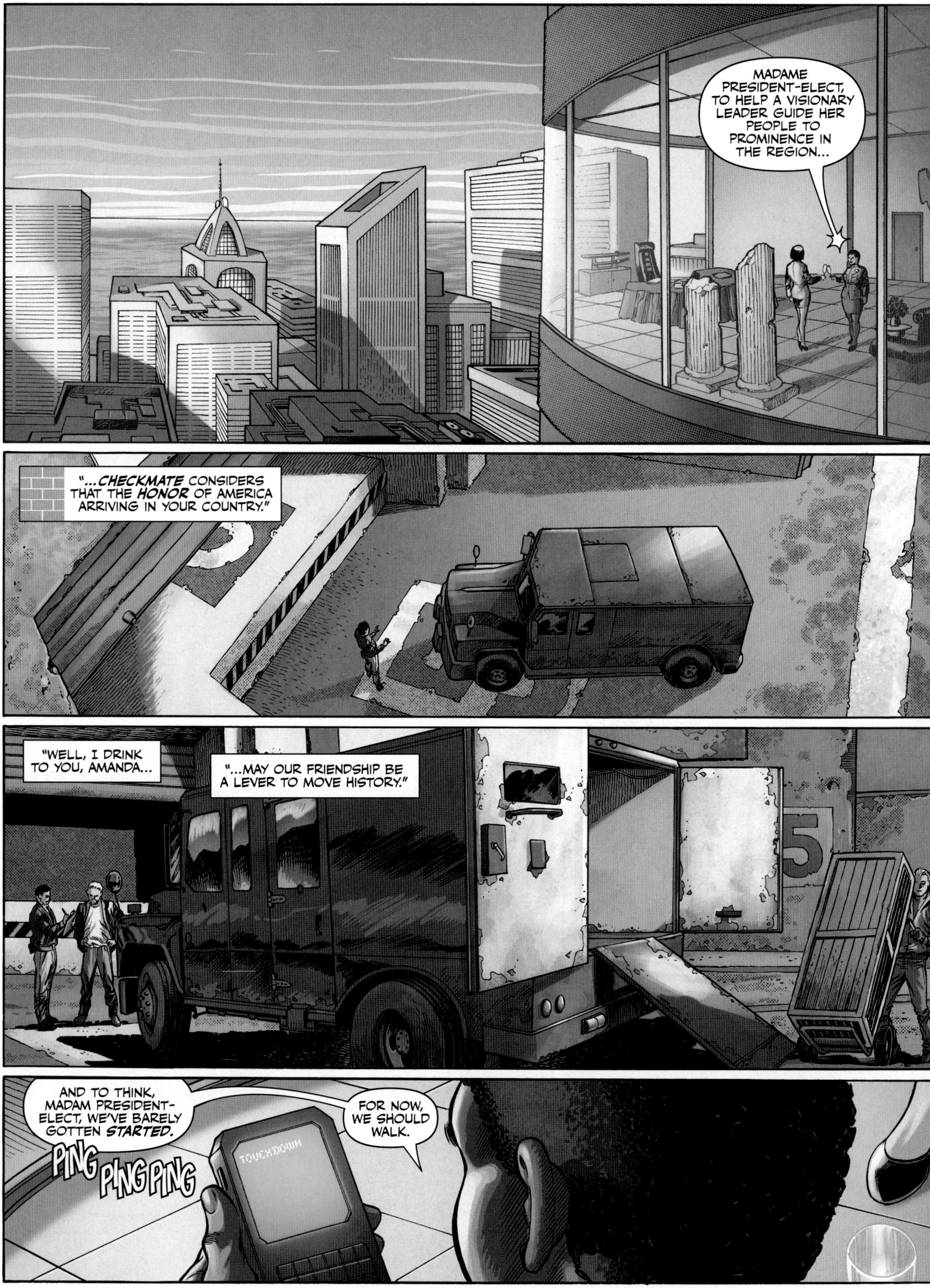

MADAME PRESIDENT-ELECT, TO HELP A VISIONARY LEADER GUIDE HER PEOPLE TO PROMINENCE IN THE REGION...
"...CHECKMATE CONSIDERS THAT THE HONOR OF AMERICA ARRIVING IN YOUR COUNTRY."
"WELL, I DRINK TO YOU, AMANDA...
"...MAY OUR FRIENDSHIP BE A LEVER TO MOVE HISTORY."
AND TO THINK, MADAM PRESIDENT-ELECT, WE'VE BARELY GOTTEN STARTED.
PING PING PING
TOUCHDOWN
FOR NOW, WE SHOULD WALK.

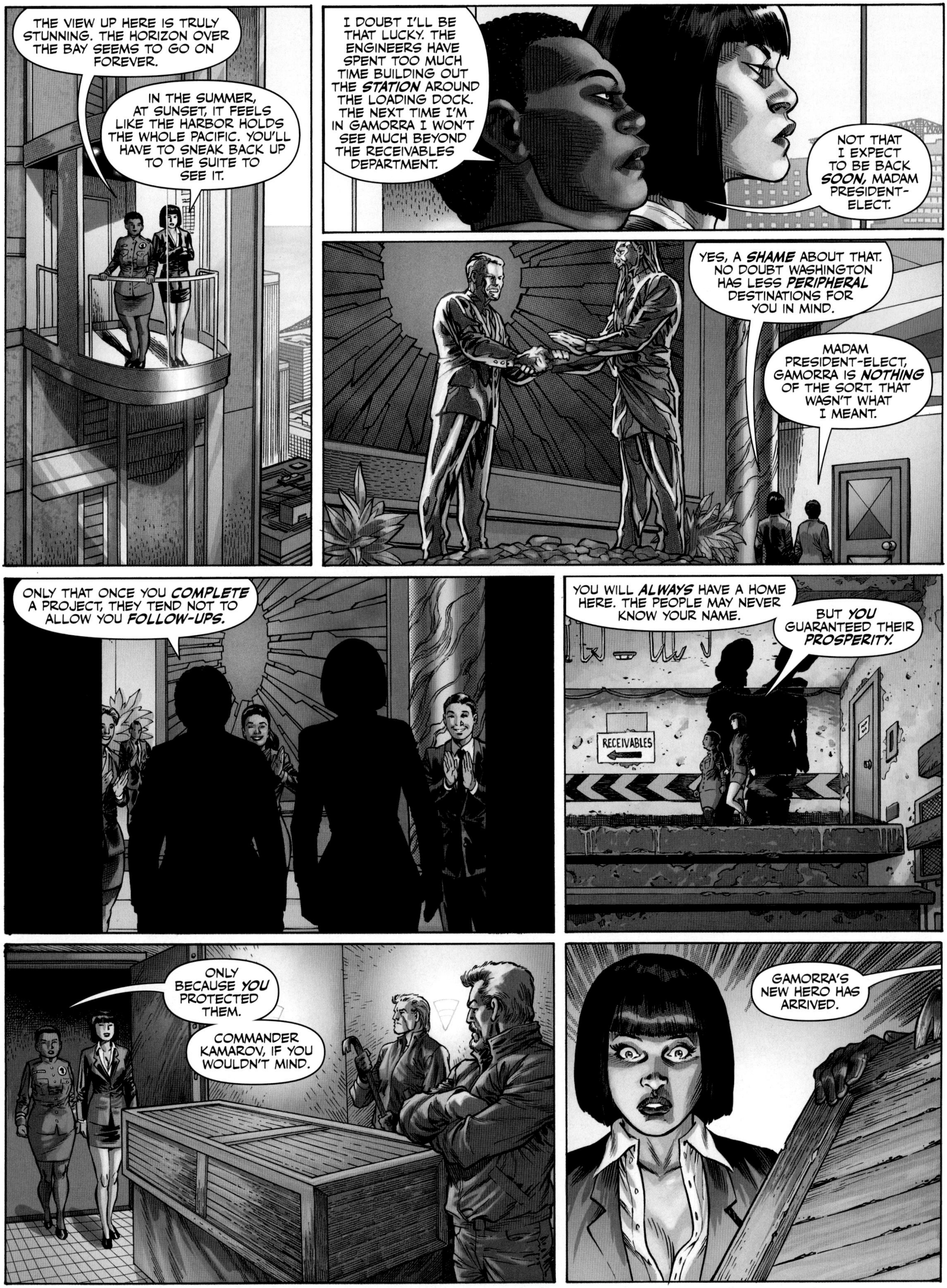
THE VIEW UP HERE IS TRULY STUNNING. THE HORIZON OVER THE BAY SEEMS TO GO ON FOREVER.
IN THE SUMMER, AT SUNSET, IT FEELS LIKE THE HARBOR HOLDS THE WHOLE PACIFIC. YOU'LL HAVE TO SNEAK BACK UP TO THE SUITE TO SEE IT.
I DOUBT I'LL BE THAT LUCKY. THE ENGINEERS HAVE SPENT TOO MUCH TIME BUILDING OUT THE STATION AROUND THE LOADING DOCK. THE NEXT TIME I'M IN GAMORRA I WON'T SEE MUCH BEYOND THE RECEIVABLES DEPARTMENT.
NOT THAT I EXPECT TO BE BACK SOON, MADAM PRESIDENT-ELECT.
YES, A SHAME ABOUT THAT. NO DOUBT WASHINGTON HAS LESS PERIPHERAL DESTINATIONS FOR YOU IN MIND.
MADAM PRESIDENT-ELECT, GAMORRA IS NOTHING OF THE SORT. THAT WASN'T WHAT I MEANT.
ONLY THAT ONCE YOU COMPLETE A PROJECT, THEY TEND NOT TO ALLOW YOU FOLLOW-UPS.
YOU WILL ALWAYS HAVE A HOME HERE. THE PEOPLE MAY NEVER KNOW YOUR NAME.
BUT YOU GUARANTEED THEIR PROSPERITY.
RECEIVABLES
ONLY BECAUSE YOU PROTECTED THEM.
COMMANDER KAMAROV, IF YOU WOULDN'T MIND.
GAMORRA'S NEW HERO HAS ARRIVED.

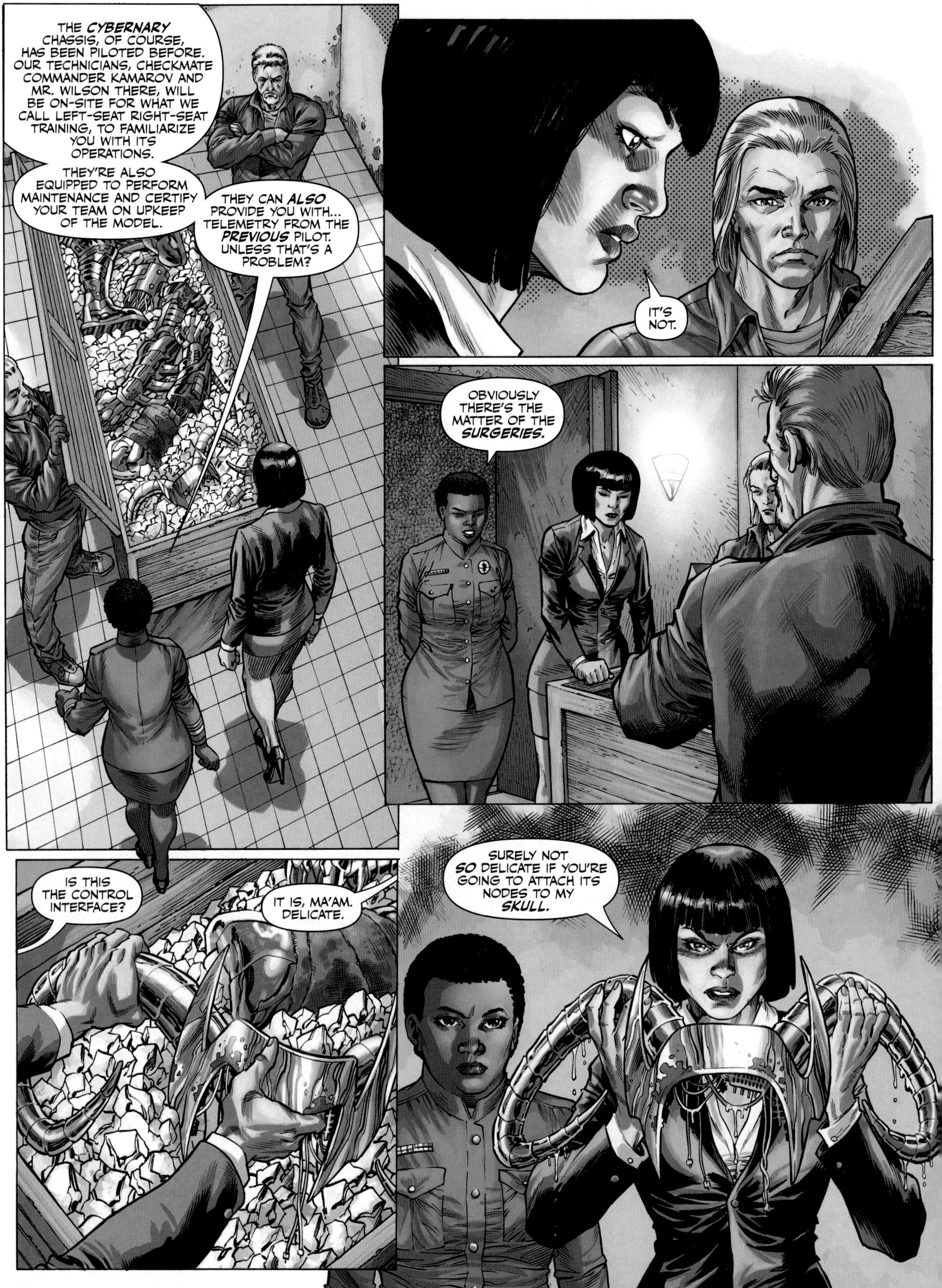
THE CYBERNARY CHASSIS, OF COURSE, HAS BEEN PILOTED BEFORE. OUR TECHNICIANS, CHECKMATE COMMANDER KAMAROV AND MR. WILSON THERE, WILL BE ON-SITE FOR WHAT WE CALL LEFT-SEAT RIGHT-SEAT TRAINING, TO FAMILIARIZE YOU WITH ITS OPERATIONS.
THEY'RE ALSO EQUIPPED TO PERFORM MAINTENANCE AND CERTIFY YOUR TEAM ON UPKEEP OF THE MODEL.
THEY CAN ALSO PROVIDE YOU WITH... TELEMETRY FROM THE PREVIOUS PILOT. UNLESS THAT'S A PROBLEM?
IT'S NOT.
OBVIOUSLY THERE'S THE MATTER OF THE SURGERIES.
IS THIS THE CONTROL INTERFACE?
IT IS, MA'AM. DELICATE.
SURELY NOT SO DELICATE IF YOU'RE GOING TO ATTACH ITS NODES TO MY SKULL.

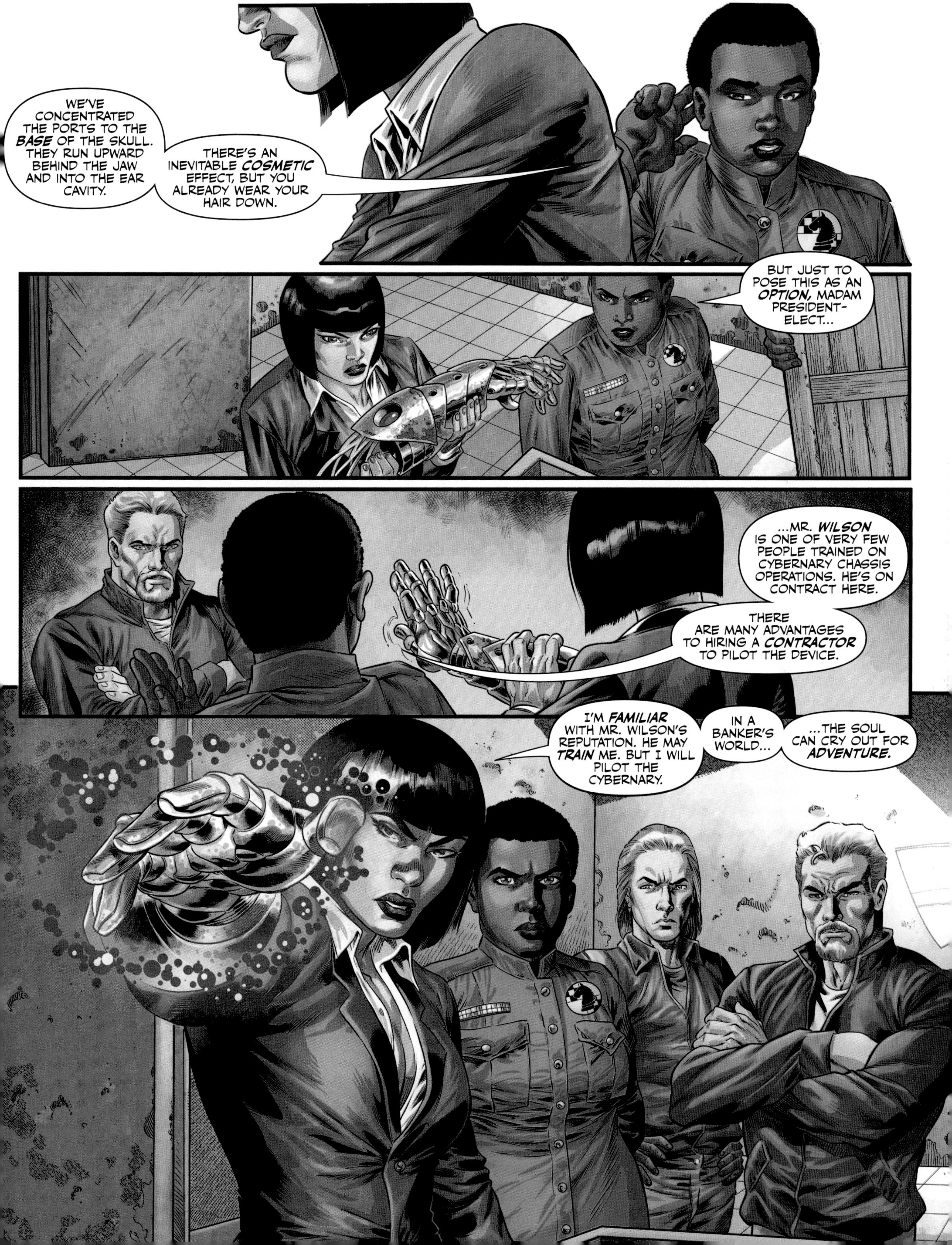
WE'VE CONCENTRATED THE PORTS TO THE BASE OF THE SKULL. THEY RUN UPWARD BEHIND THE JAW AND INTO THE EAR CAVITY.
THERE'S AN INEVITABLE COSMETIC EFFECT, BUT YOU ALREADY WEAR YOUR HAIR DOWN.
BUT JUST TO POSE THIS AS AN OPTION, MADAM PRESIDENT-ELECT...
...MR. WILSON IS ONE OF VERY FEW PEOPLE TRAINED ON CYBERNARY CHASSIS OPERATIONS. HE'S ON CONTRACT HERE.
THERE ARE MANY ADVANTAGES TO HIRING A CONTRACTOR TO PILOT THE DEVICE.
I'M FAMILIAR WITH MR. WILSON'S REPUTATION. HE MAY TRAIN ME. BUT I WILL PILOT THE CYBERNARY.
IN A BANKER'S WORLD...
...THE SOUL CAN CRY OUT FOR ADVENTURE.

DO YOU HAVE MY BRIEFING BOOK?

I DIDN'T STOP AT STATION AFTER GETTING OFF PLANE.

"THEN WE HAVE TO STOP OFF BEFORE FLYING BACK."

STRICTLY FORBIDDEN TO PASS

WHAT THE FUCK IS *THIS?* WE'VE BEEN *HIT!*

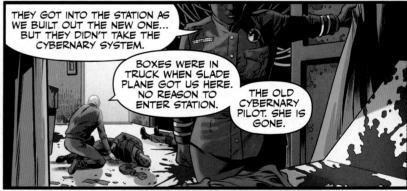

THEY GOT INTO THE STATION AS WE BUILT OUT THE NEW ONE... BUT THEY DIDN'T TAKE THE CYBERNARY SYSTEM.

BOXES WERE IN TRUCK WHEN SLADE PLANE GOT US HERE. NO REASON TO ENTER STATION.

THE OLD CYBERNARY PILOT. SHE IS GONE.

THEY TOOK THE *BODY* AFTER THE MEDICAL TEAM REMOVED THE CHASSIS.

JESUS.

NEW PLAN. YOU'RE STAYING HERE. GET INTO THE VENTS. THERE'S GOT TO BE A CAMERA OR AN INFRARED OR A MIC LEFT AROUND HERE.

GET ME SOMETHING I CAN *USE.*

PING PING PING

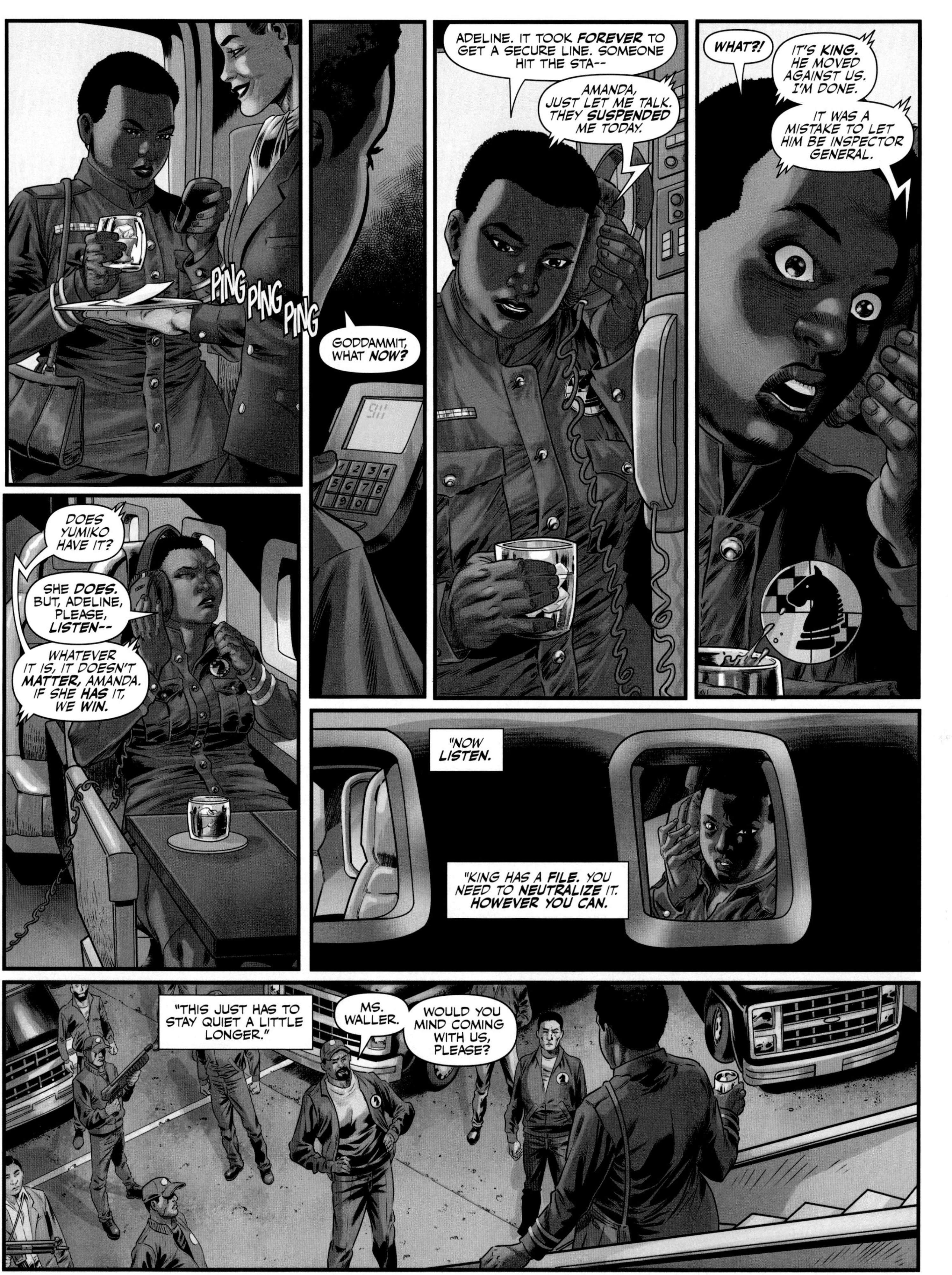
PING PING PING
GODDAMMIT, WHAT NOW?
ADELINE. IT TOOK FOREVER TO GET A SECURE LINE. SOMEONE HIT THE STA--
AMANDA, JUST LET ME TALK. THEY SUSPENDED ME TODAY.
WHAT?!
IT'S KING. HE MOVED AGAINST US. I'M DONE.
IT WAS A MISTAKE TO LET HIM BE INSPECTOR GENERAL.
DOES YUMIKO HAVE IT?
SHE DOES. BUT, ADELINE, PLEASE, LISTEN--
WHATEVER IT IS, IT DOESN'T MATTER, AMANDA. IF SHE HAS IT, WE WIN.
"NOW LISTEN.
"KING HAS A FILE. YOU NEED TO NEUTRALIZE IT. HOWEVER YOU CAN.
"THIS JUST HAS TO STAY QUIET A LITTLE LONGER."
MS. WALLER.
WOULD YOU MIND COMING WITH US, PLEASE?

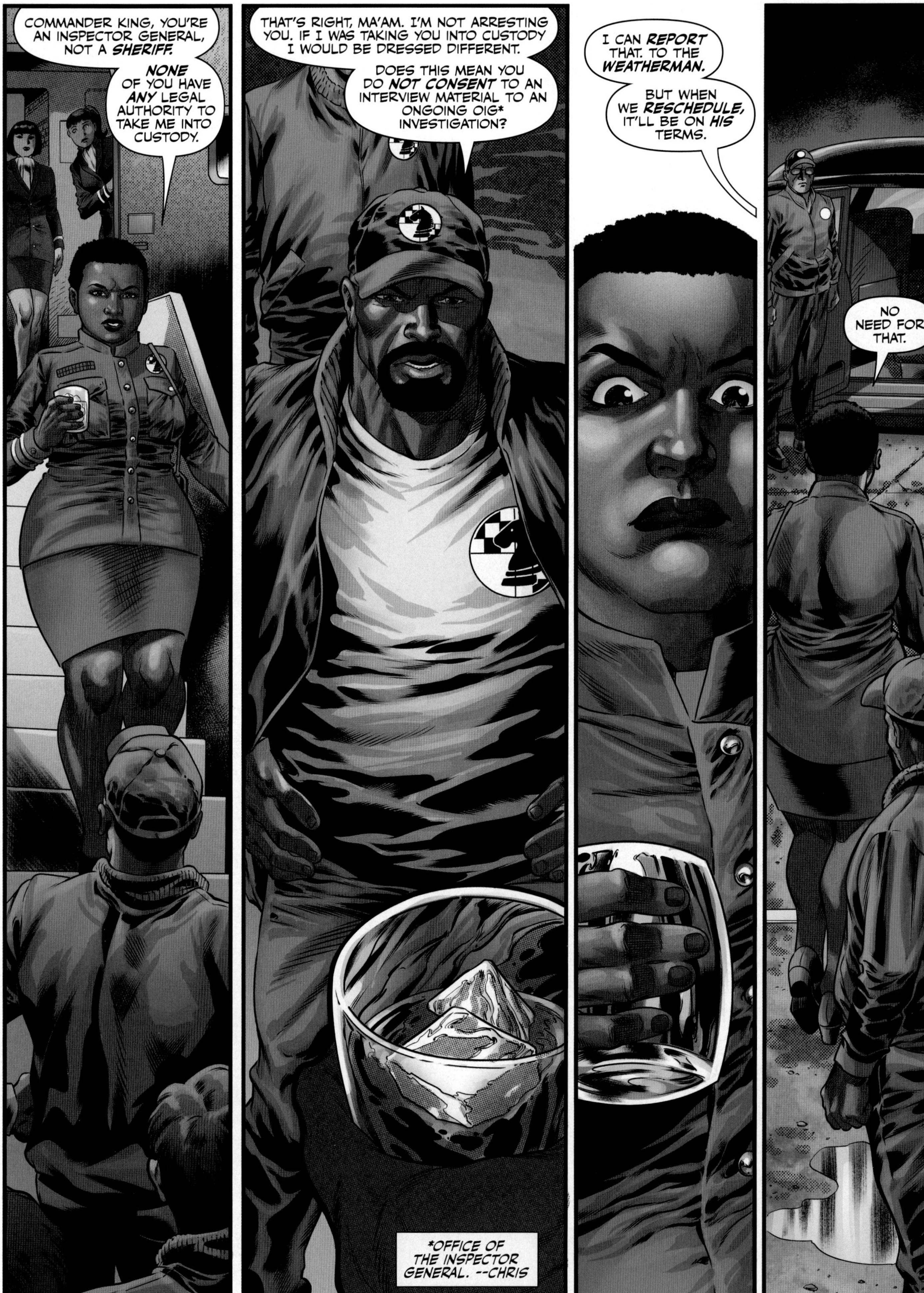

COMMANDER KING, YOU'RE AN INSPECTOR GENERAL, NOT A *SHERIFF.*
NONE OF YOU HAVE *ANY* LEGAL AUTHORITY TO TAKE ME INTO CUSTODY.
THAT'S RIGHT, MA'AM. I'M NOT ARRESTING YOU. IF I WAS TAKING YOU INTO CUSTODY I WOULD BE DRESSED DIFFERENT.
DOES THIS MEAN YOU DO *NOT CONSENT* TO AN INTERVIEW MATERIAL TO AN ONGOING OIG* INVESTIGATION?
*OFFICE OF THE INSPECTOR GENERAL. --CHRIS
I CAN *REPORT* THAT. TO THE *WEATHERMAN.*
BUT WHEN WE *RESCHEDULE,* IT'LL BE ON *HIS* TERMS.
NO NEED FOR THAT.

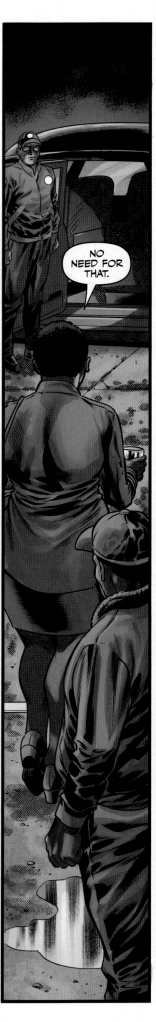

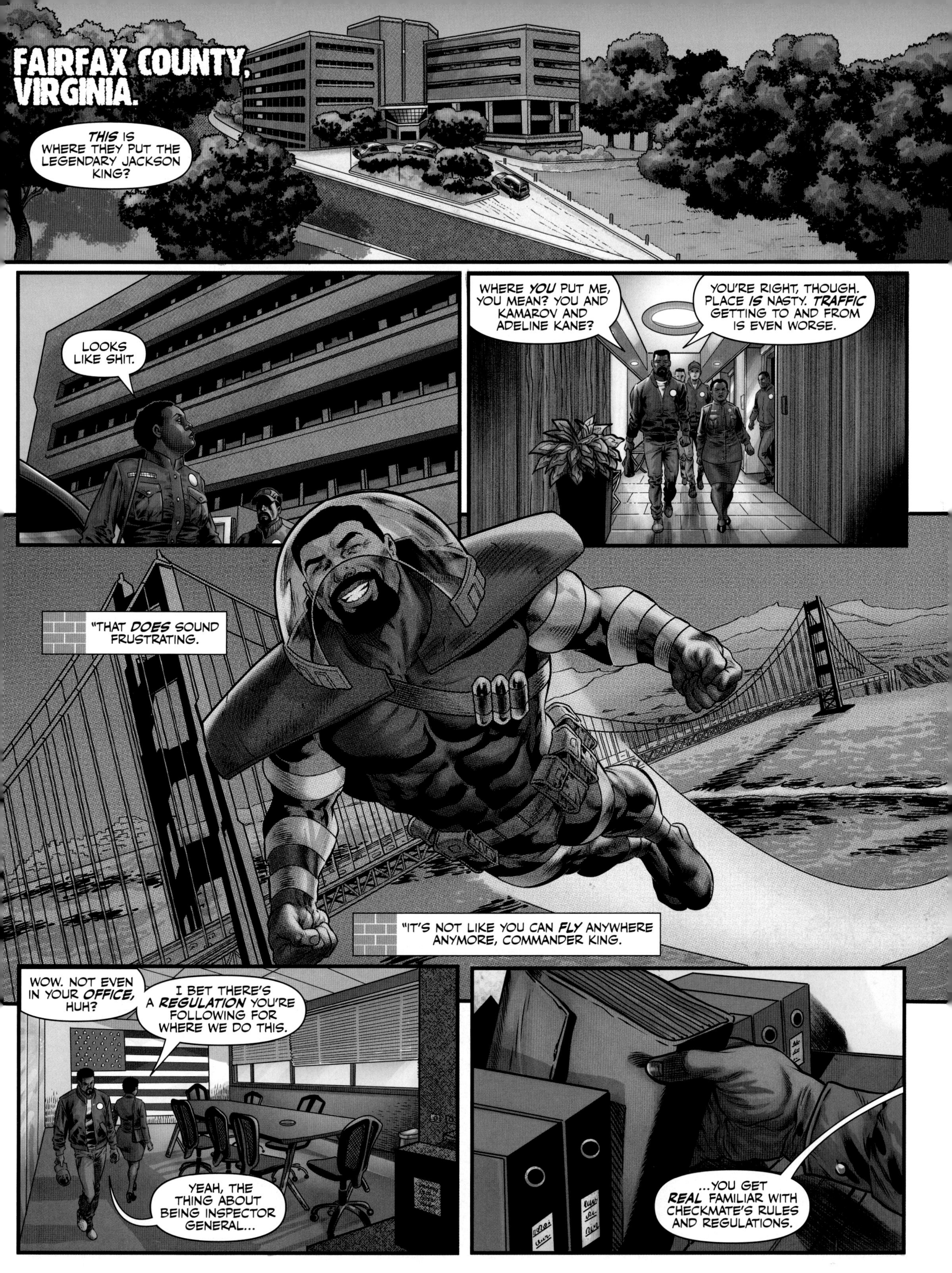
FAIRFAX COUNTY, VIRGINIA.
THIS IS WHERE THEY PUT THE LEGENDARY JACKSON KING?
LOOKS LIKE SHIT.
WHERE YOU PUT ME, YOU MEAN? YOU AND KAMAROV AND ADELINE KANE?
YOU'RE RIGHT, THOUGH. PLACE IS NASTY. TRAFFIC GETTING TO AND FROM IS EVEN WORSE.
"THAT DOES SOUND FRUSTRATING.
"IT'S NOT LIKE YOU CAN FLY ANYWHERE ANYMORE, COMMANDER KING.
WOW. NOT EVEN IN YOUR OFFICE, HUH?
I BET THERE'S A REGULATION YOU'RE FOLLOWING FOR WHERE WE DO THIS.
YEAH, THE THING ABOUT BEING INSPECTOR GENERAL...
...YOU GET REAL FAMILIAR WITH CHECKMATE'S RULES AND REGULATIONS.

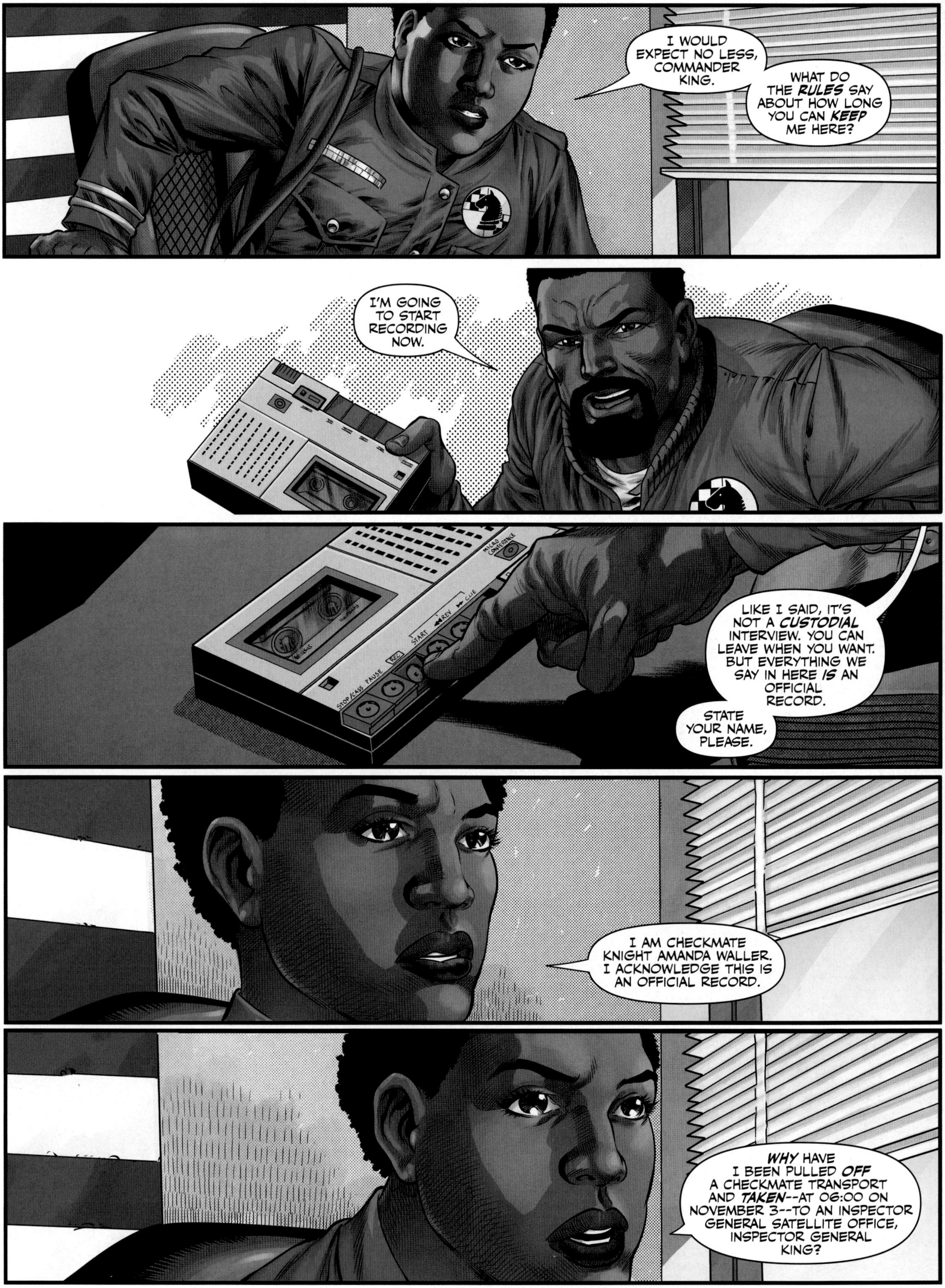
I WOULD EXPECT NO LESS, COMMANDER KING.
WHAT DO THE RULES SAY ABOUT HOW LONG YOU CAN KEEP ME HERE?
I'M GOING TO START RECORDING NOW.
LIKE I SAID, IT'S NOT A CUSTODIAL INTERVIEW. YOU CAN LEAVE WHEN YOU WANT. BUT EVERYTHING WE SAY IN HERE IS AN OFFICIAL RECORD.
STATE YOUR NAME, PLEASE.
I AM CHECKMATE KNIGHT AMANDA WALLER. I ACKNOWLEDGE THIS IS AN OFFICIAL RECORD.
WHY HAVE I BEEN PULLED OFF A CHECKMATE TRANSPORT AND TAKEN--AT 06:00 ON NOVEMBER 3--TO AN INSPECTOR GENERAL SATELLITE OFFICE, INSPECTOR GENERAL KING?

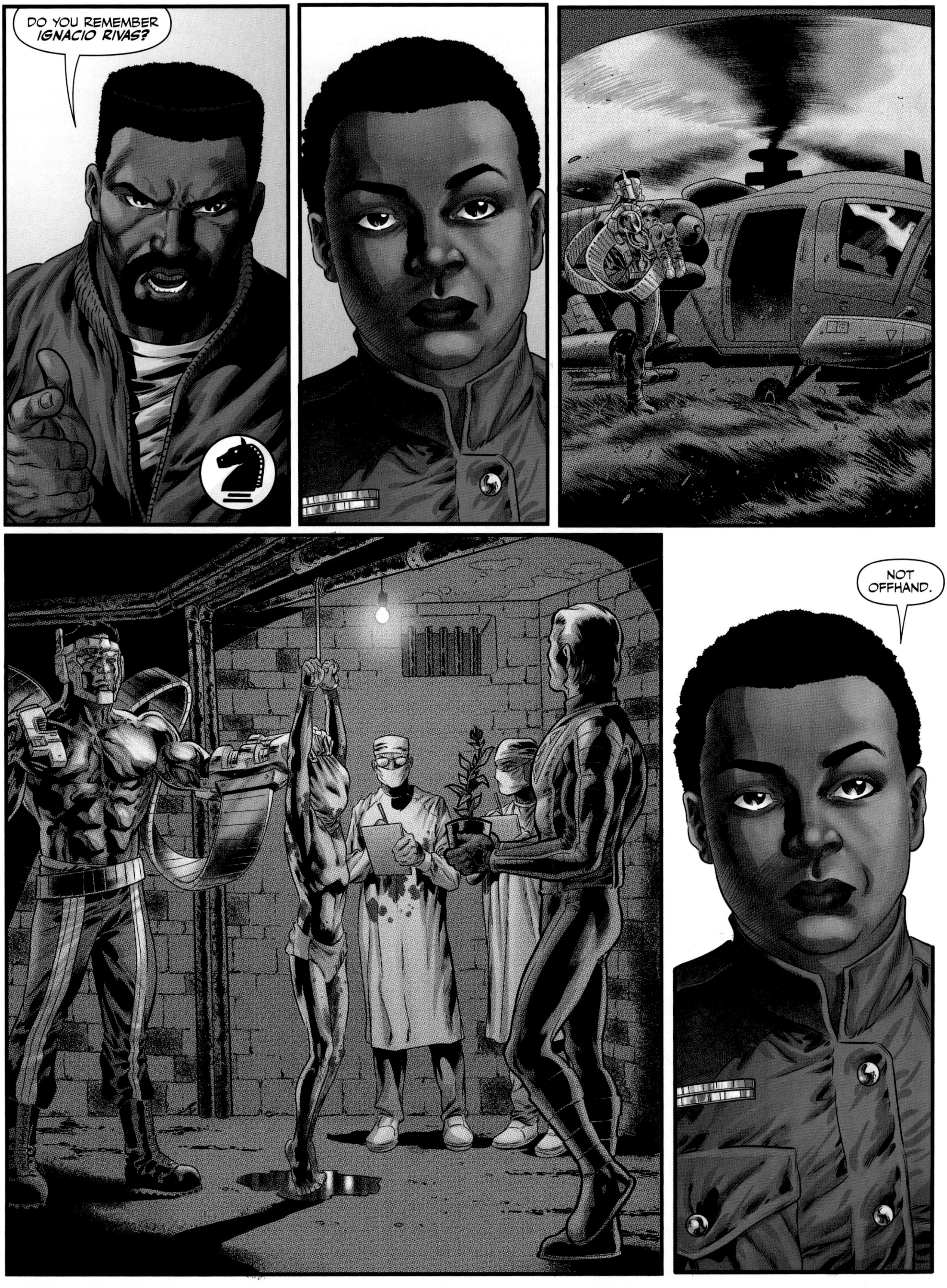
DO YOU REMEMBER IGNACIO RIVAS?
NOT OFFHAND.

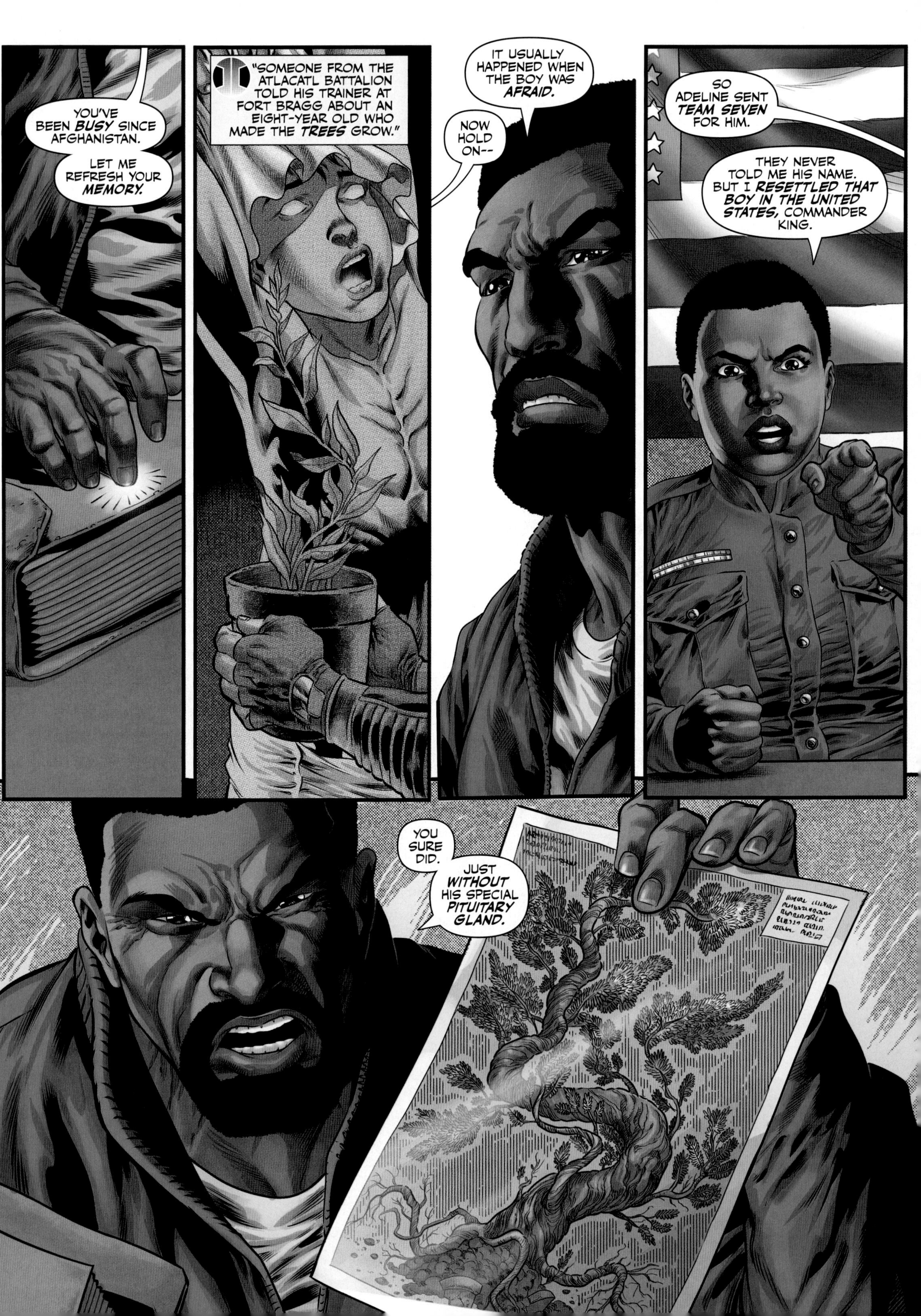
YOU'VE BEEN BUSY SINCE AFGHANISTAN.
LET ME REFRESH YOUR MEMORY.
"SOMEONE FROM THE ATLACATL BATTALION TOLD HIS TRAINER AT FORT BRAGG ABOUT AN EIGHT-YEAR OLD WHO MADE THE TREES GROW."
IT USUALLY HAPPENED WHEN THE BOY WAS AFRAID.
NOW HOLD ON--
SO ADELINE SENT TEAM SEVEN FOR HIM.
THEY NEVER TOLD ME HIS NAME. BUT I RESETTLED THAT BOY IN THE UNITED STATES, COMMANDER KING.
YOU SURE DID.
JUST WITHOUT HIS SPECIAL PITUITARY GLAND.

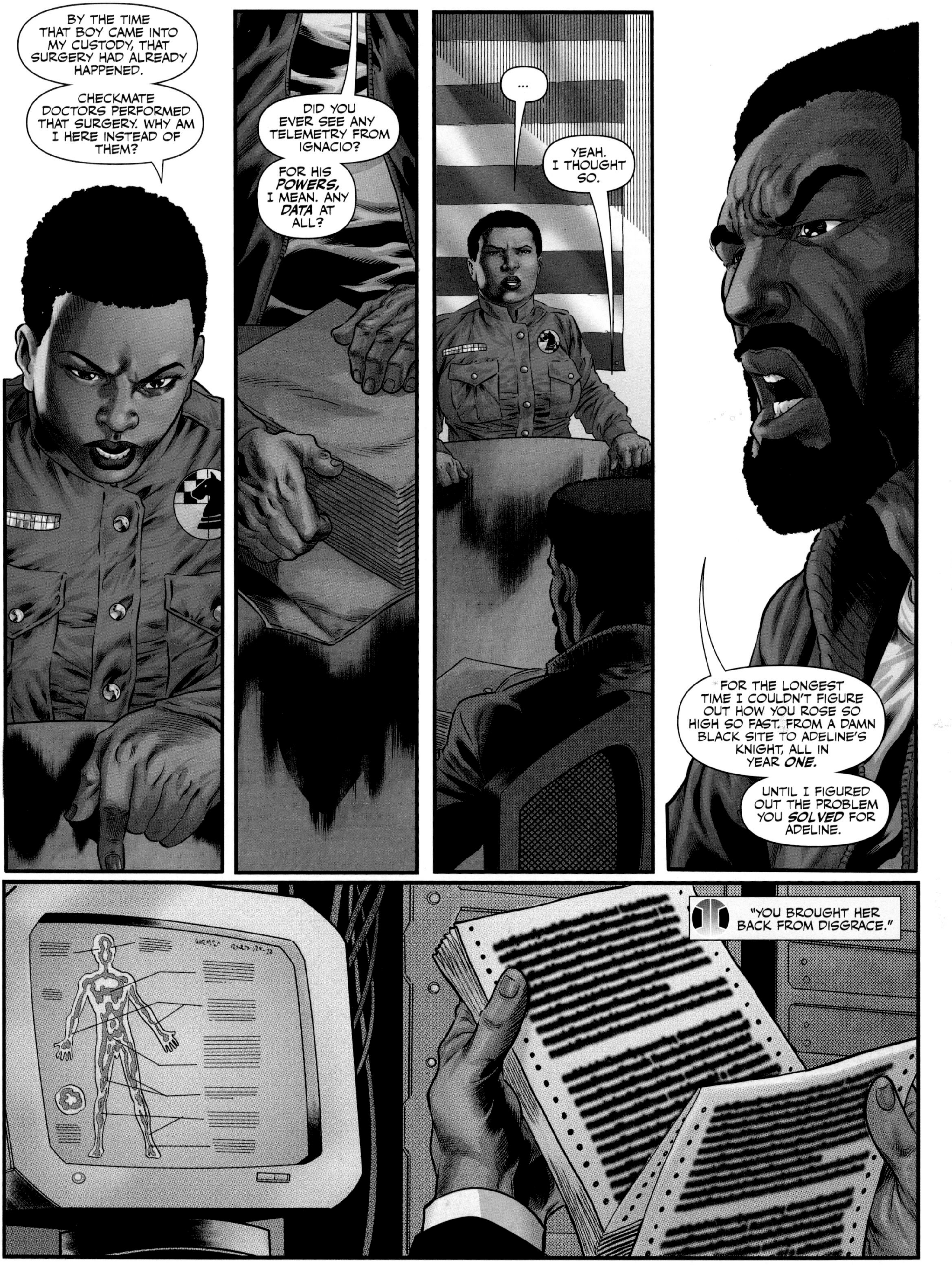
BY THE TIME THAT BOY CAME INTO MY CUSTODY, THAT SURGERY HAD ALREADY HAPPENED.
CHECKMATE DOCTORS PERFORMED THAT SURGERY. WHY AM I HERE INSTEAD OF THEM?
DID YOU EVER SEE ANY TELEMETRY FROM IGNACIO?
FOR HIS POWERS, I MEAN. ANY DATA AT ALL?
...
YEAH. I THOUGHT SO.
FOR THE LONGEST TIME I COULDN'T FIGURE OUT HOW YOU ROSE SO HIGH SO FAST. FROM A DAMN BLACK SITE TO ADELINE'S KNIGHT, ALL IN YEAR ONE.
UNTIL I FIGURED OUT THE PROBLEM YOU SOLVED FOR ADELINE.
"YOU BROUGHT HER BACK FROM DISGRACE."

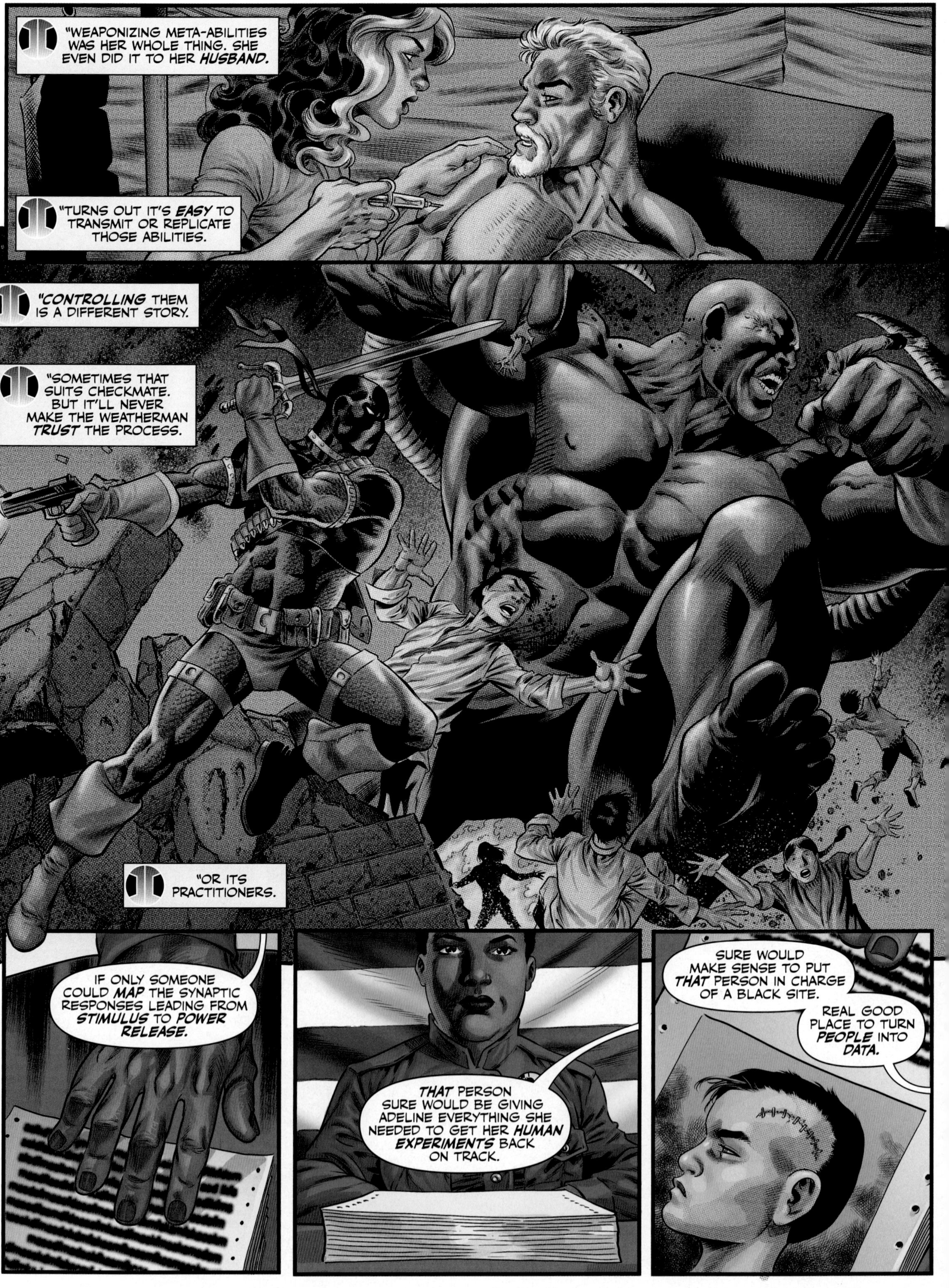
"WEAPONIZING META-ABILITIES WAS HER WHOLE THING. SHE EVEN DID IT TO HER HUSBAND.
"TURNS OUT IT'S EASY TO TRANSMIT OR REPLICATE THOSE ABILITIES.
"CONTROLLING THEM IS A DIFFERENT STORY.
"SOMETIMES THAT SUITS CHECKMATE. BUT IT'LL NEVER MAKE THE WEATHERMAN TRUST THE PROCESS.
"OR ITS PRACTITIONERS.
IF ONLY SOMEONE COULD MAP THE SYNAPTIC RESPONSES LEADING FROM STIMULUS TO POWER RELEASE.
THAT PERSON SURE WOULD BE GIVING ADELINE EVERYTHING SHE NEEDED TO GET HER HUMAN EXPERIMENTS BACK ON TRACK.
SURE WOULD MAKE SENSE TO PUT THAT PERSON IN CHARGE OF A BLACK SITE.
REAL GOOD PLACE TO TURN PEOPLE INTO DATA.

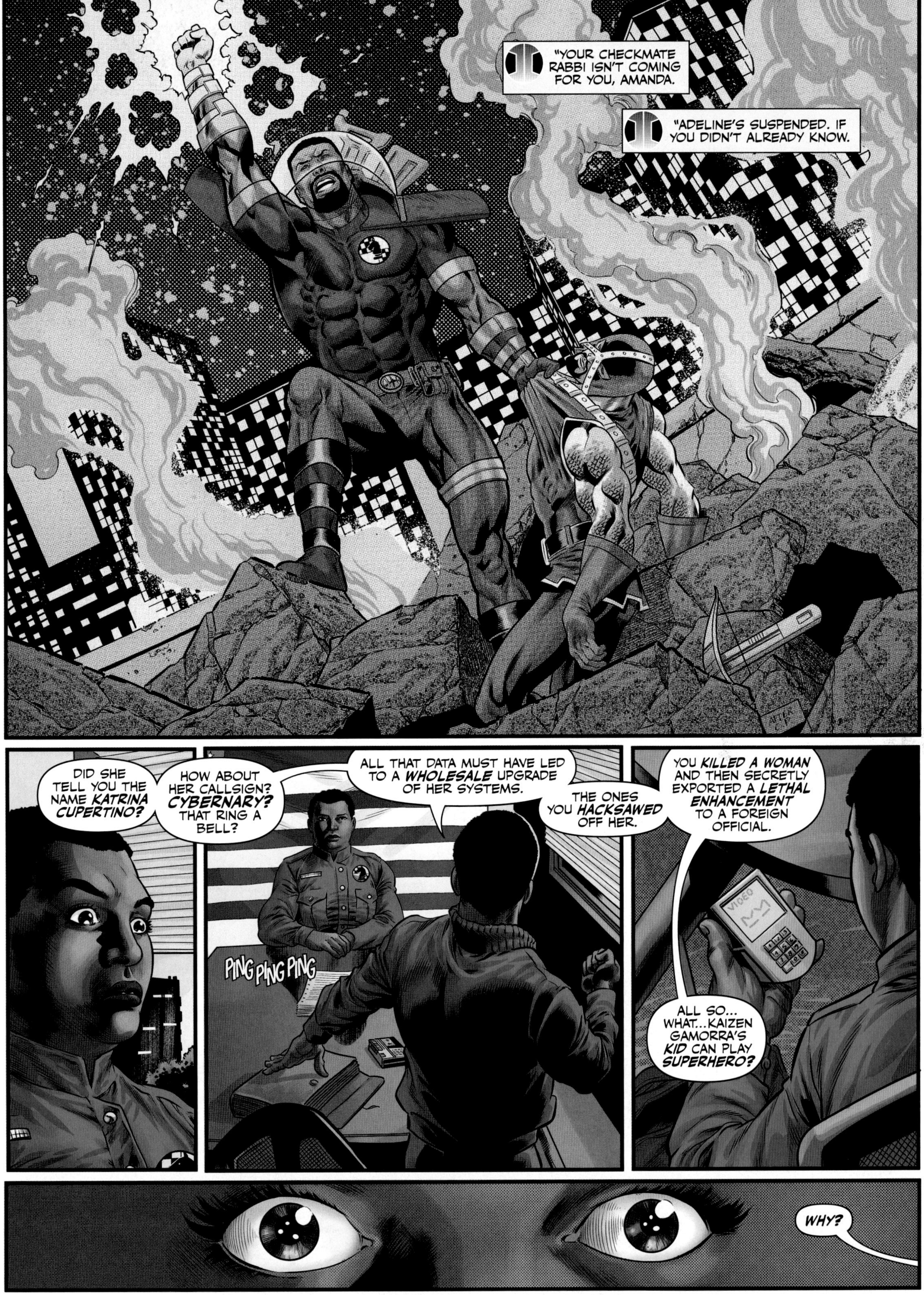
"YOUR CHECKMATE RABBI ISN'T COMING FOR YOU, AMANDA.
"ADELINE'S SUSPENDED. IF YOU DIDN'T ALREADY KNOW.
DID SHE TELL YOU THE NAME KATRINA CUPERTINO?
HOW ABOUT HER CALLSIGN? CYBERNARY? THAT RING A BELL?
ALL THAT DATA MUST HAVE LED TO A WHOLESALE UPGRADE OF HER SYSTEMS.
THE ONES YOU HACKSAWED OFF HER.
PING PING PING
YOU KILLED A WOMAN AND THEN SECRETLY EXPORTED A LETHAL ENHANCEMENT TO A FOREIGN OFFICIAL.
VIDEO
ALL SO... WHAT...KAIZEN GAMORRA'S KID CAN PLAY SUPERHERO?
WHY?

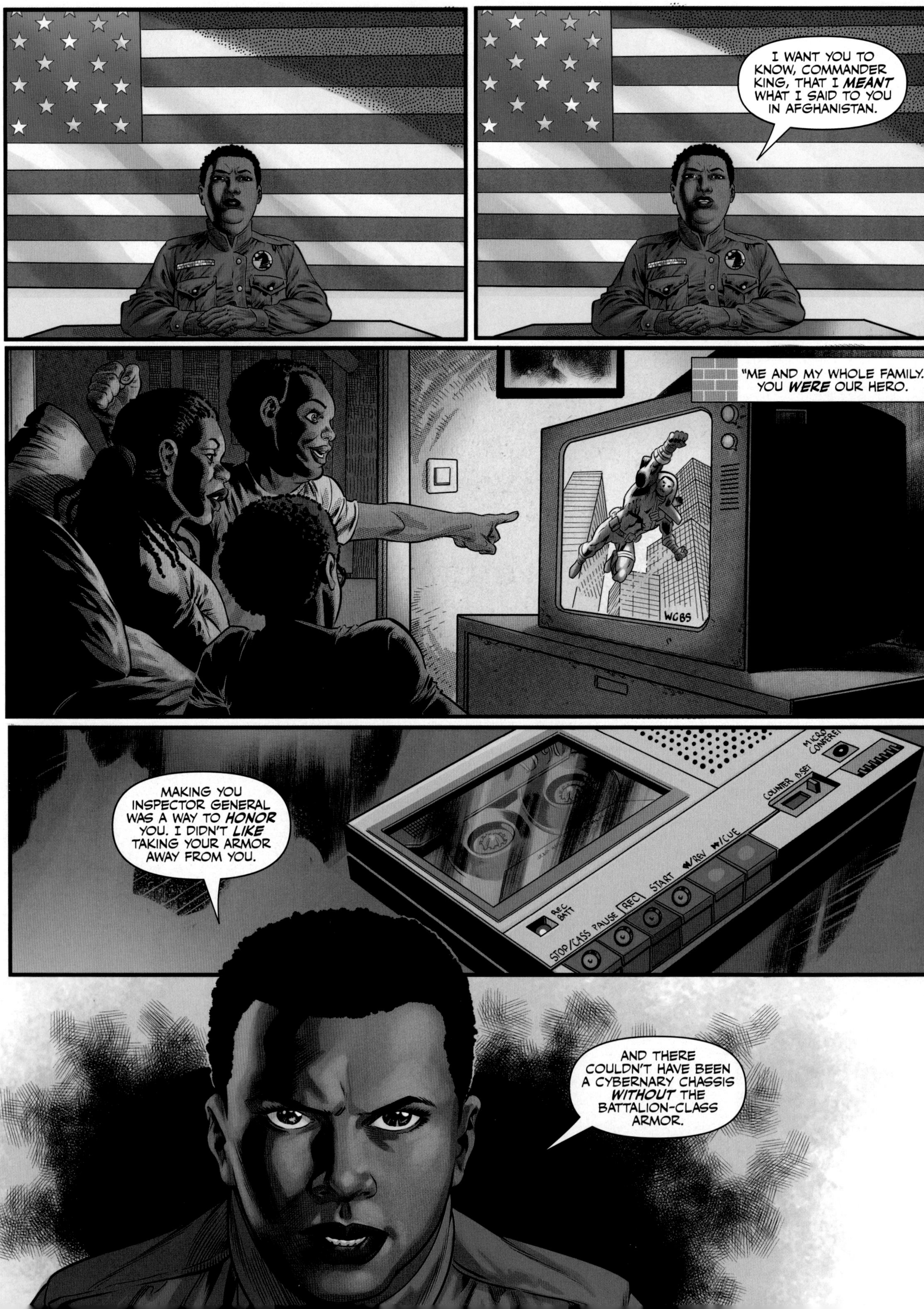
I WANT YOU TO KNOW, COMMANDER KING, THAT I MEANT WHAT I SAID TO YOU IN AFGHANISTAN.
"ME AND MY WHOLE FAMILY. YOU WERE OUR HERO.
WGBS
MAKING YOU INSPECTOR GENERAL WAS A WAY TO HONOR YOU. I DIDN'T LIKE TAKING YOUR ARMOR AWAY FROM YOU.
STOP/CASS PAUSE REC START REV CUE
COUNTER
AND THERE COULDN'T HAVE BEEN A CYBERNARY CHASSIS WITHOUT THE BATTALION-CLASS ARMOR.

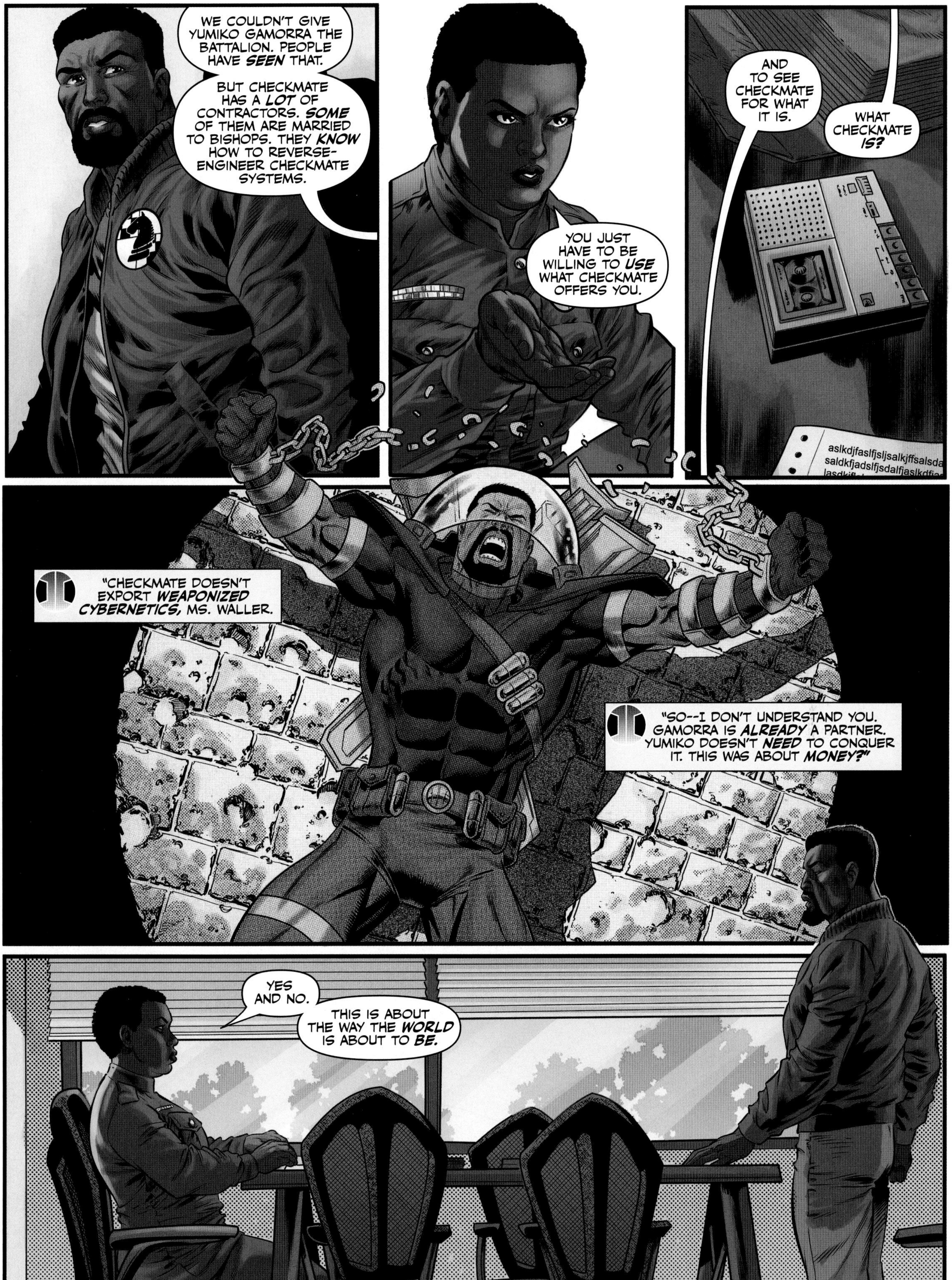
WE COULDN'T GIVE YUMIKO GAMORRA THE BATTALION. PEOPLE HAVE SEEN THAT.
BUT CHECKMATE HAS A LOT OF CONTRACTORS. SOME OF THEM ARE MARRIED TO BISHOPS. THEY KNOW HOW TO REVERSE-ENGINEER CHECKMATE SYSTEMS.
YOU JUST HAVE TO BE WILLING TO USE WHAT CHECKMATE OFFERS YOU.
AND TO SEE CHECKMATE FOR WHAT IT IS.
WHAT CHECKMATE IS?
"CHECKMATE DOESN'T EXPORT WEAPONIZED CYBERNETICS, MS. WALLER.
"SO--I DON'T UNDERSTAND YOU. GAMORRA IS ALREADY A PARTNER. YUMIKO DOESN'T NEED TO CONQUER IT. THIS WAS ABOUT MONEY?"
YES AND NO.
THIS IS ABOUT THE WAY THE WORLD IS ABOUT TO BE.

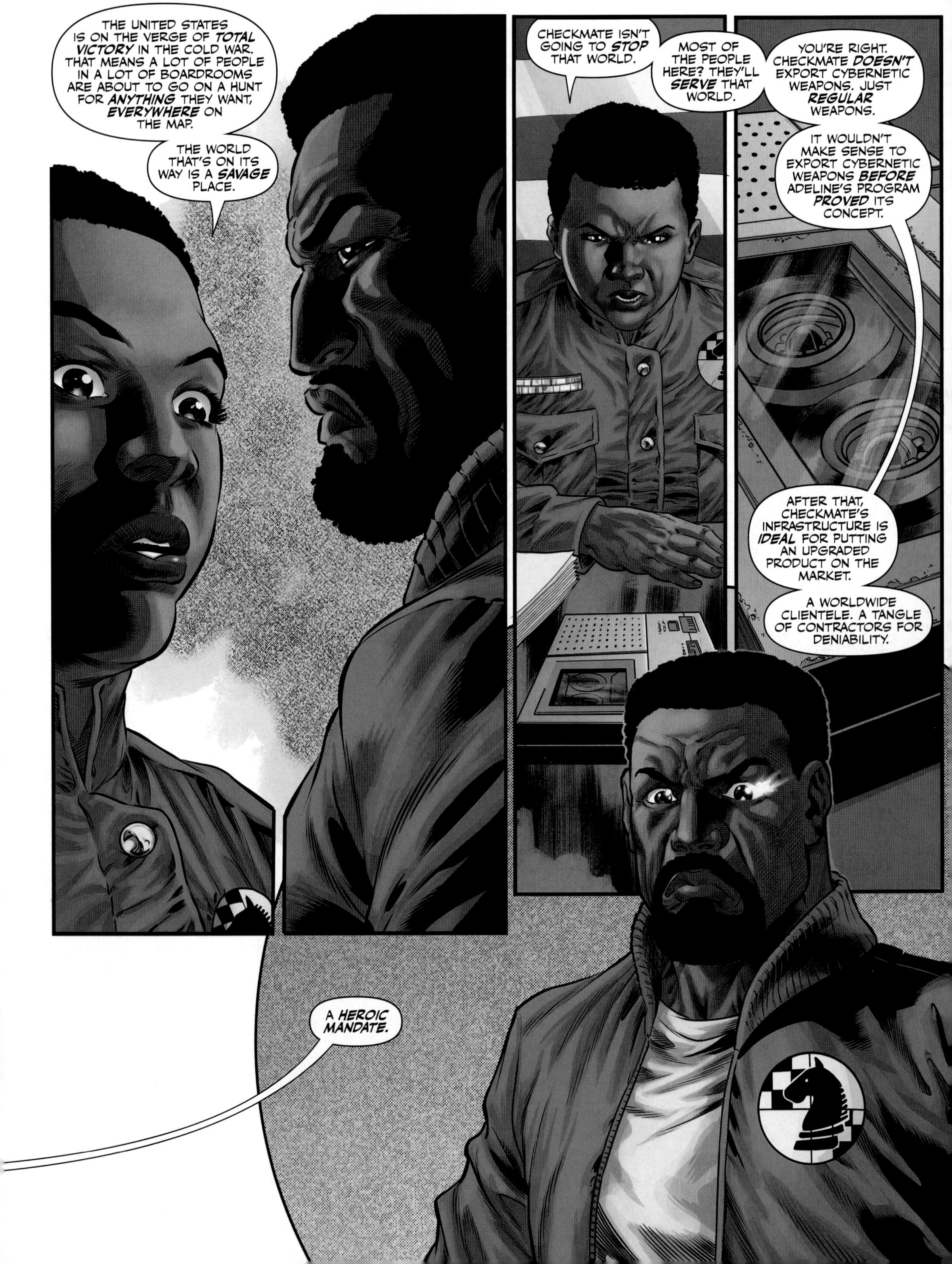
THE UNITED STATES IS ON THE VERGE OF *TOTAL VICTORY* IN THE COLD WAR. THAT MEANS A LOT OF PEOPLE IN A LOT OF BOARDROOMS ARE ABOUT TO GO ON A HUNT FOR *ANYTHING* THEY WANT, *EVERYWHERE* ON THE MAP.
THE WORLD THAT'S ON ITS WAY IS A *SAVAGE* PLACE.
CHECKMATE ISN'T GOING TO *STOP* THAT WORLD.
MOST OF THE PEOPLE HERE? THEY'LL *SERVE* THAT WORLD.
YOU'RE RIGHT. CHECKMATE *DOESN'T* EXPORT CYBERNETIC WEAPONS. JUST *REGULAR* WEAPONS.
IT WOULDN'T MAKE SENSE TO EXPORT CYBERNETIC WEAPONS *BEFORE* ADELINE'S PROGRAM *PROVED* ITS CONCEPT.
AFTER THAT, CHECKMATE'S INFRASTRUCTURE IS *IDEAL* FOR PUTTING AN UPGRADED PRODUCT ON THE MARKET.
A WORLDWIDE CLIENTELE. A TANGLE OF CONTRACTORS FOR DENIABILITY.
A *HEROIC MANDATE.*

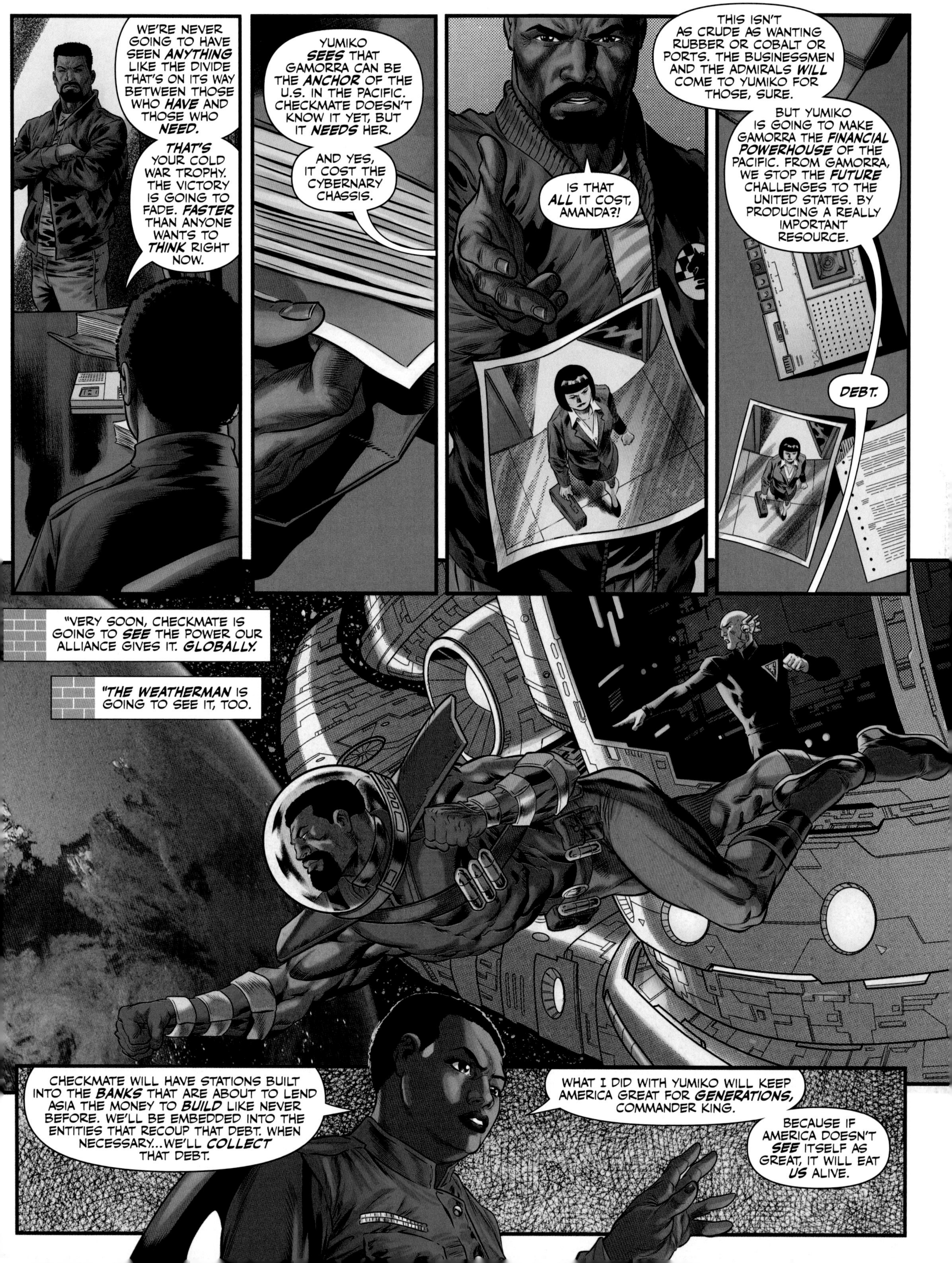
WE'RE NEVER GOING TO HAVE SEEN *ANYTHING* LIKE THE DIVIDE THAT'S ON ITS WAY BETWEEN THOSE WHO *HAVE* AND THOSE WHO *NEED.*
THAT'S YOUR COLD WAR TROPHY. THE VICTORY IS GOING TO FADE. *FASTER* THAN ANYONE WANTS TO *THINK* RIGHT NOW.
YUMIKO *SEES* THAT GAMORRA CAN BE THE *ANCHOR* OF THE U.S. IN THE PACIFIC. CHECKMATE DOESN'T KNOW IT YET, BUT IT *NEEDS* HER.
AND YES, IT COST THE CYBERNARY CHASSIS.
IS THAT *ALL* IT COST, AMANDA?!
THIS ISN'T AS CRUDE AS WANTING RUBBER OR COBALT OR PORTS. THE BUSINESSMEN AND THE ADMIRALS *WILL* COME TO YUMIKO FOR THOSE, SURE.
BUT YUMIKO IS GOING TO MAKE GAMORRA THE *FINANCIAL POWERHOUSE* OF THE PACIFIC. FROM GAMORRA, WE STOP THE *FUTURE* CHALLENGES TO THE UNITED STATES. BY PRODUCING A REALLY IMPORTANT RESOURCE.
DEBT.
"VERY SOON, CHECKMATE IS GOING TO *SEE* THE POWER OUR ALLIANCE GIVES IT. *GLOBALLY.*
"*THE WEATHERMAN* IS GOING TO SEE IT, TOO.
CHECKMATE WILL HAVE STATIONS BUILT INTO THE *BANKS* THAT ARE ABOUT TO LEND ASIA THE MONEY TO *BUILD* LIKE NEVER BEFORE. WE'LL BE EMBEDDED INTO THE ENTITIES THAT RECOUP THAT DEBT. WHEN NECESSARY...WE'LL *COLLECT* THAT DEBT.
WHAT I DID WITH YUMIKO WILL KEEP AMERICA GREAT FOR *GENERATIONS,* COMMANDER KING.
BECAUSE IF AMERICA DOESN'T *SEE* ITSELF AS GREAT, IT WILL EAT *US* ALIVE.

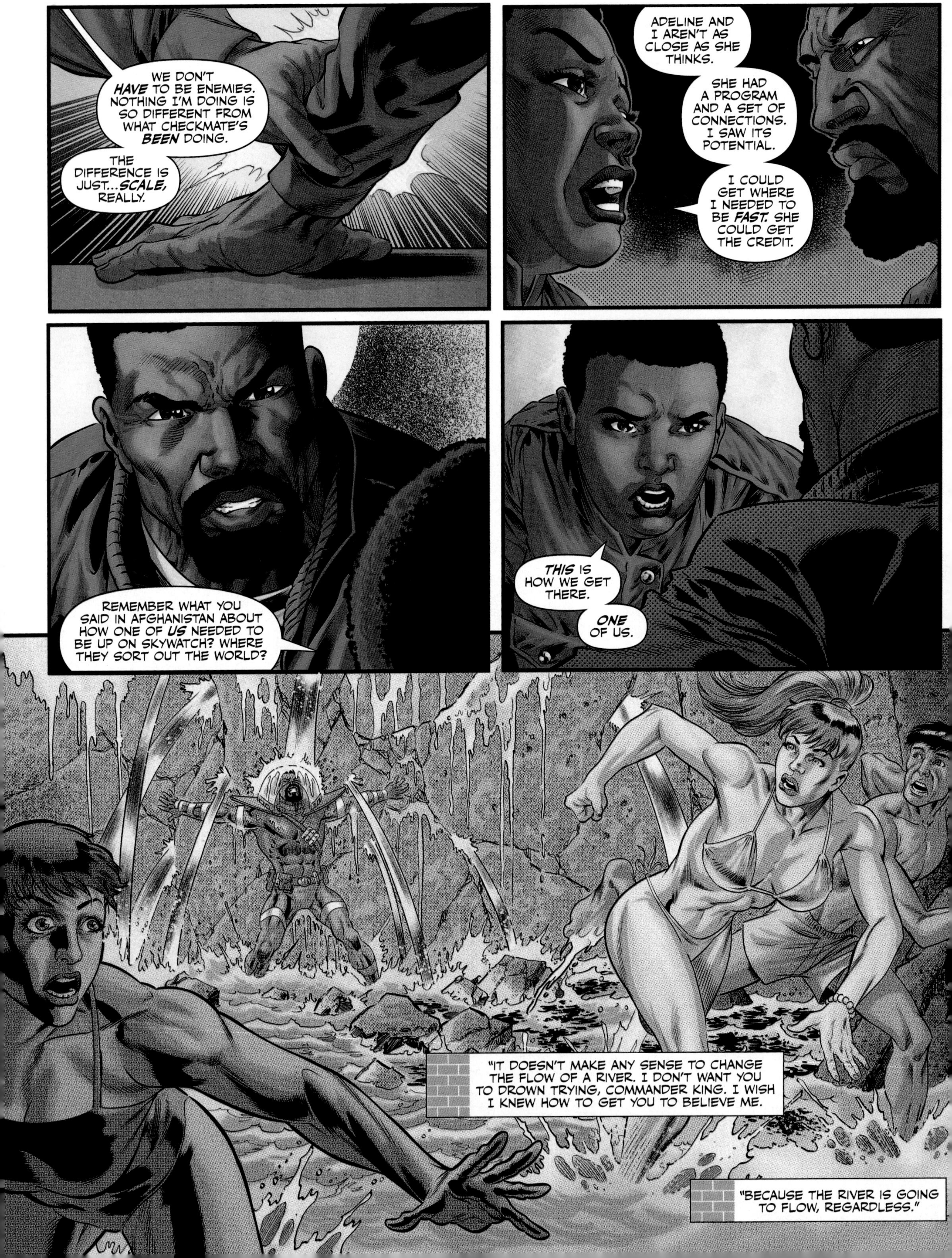
WE DON'T HAVE TO BE ENEMIES. NOTHING I'M DOING IS SO DIFFERENT FROM WHAT CHECKMATE'S BEEN DOING.
THE DIFFERENCE IS JUST...SCALE, REALLY.
ADELINE AND I AREN'T AS CLOSE AS SHE THINKS.
SHE HAD A PROGRAM AND A SET OF CONNECTIONS. I SAW ITS POTENTIAL.
I COULD GET WHERE I NEEDED TO BE FAST. SHE COULD GET THE CREDIT.
REMEMBER WHAT YOU SAID IN AFGHANISTAN ABOUT HOW ONE OF US NEEDED TO BE UP ON SKYWATCH? WHERE THEY SORT OUT THE WORLD?
THIS IS HOW WE GET THERE.
ONE OF US.
"IT DOESN'T MAKE ANY SENSE TO CHANGE THE FLOW OF A RIVER. I DON'T WANT YOU TO DROWN TRYING, COMMANDER KING. I WISH I KNEW HOW TO GET YOU TO BELIEVE ME.
"BECAUSE THE RIVER IS GOING TO FLOW, REGARDLESS."

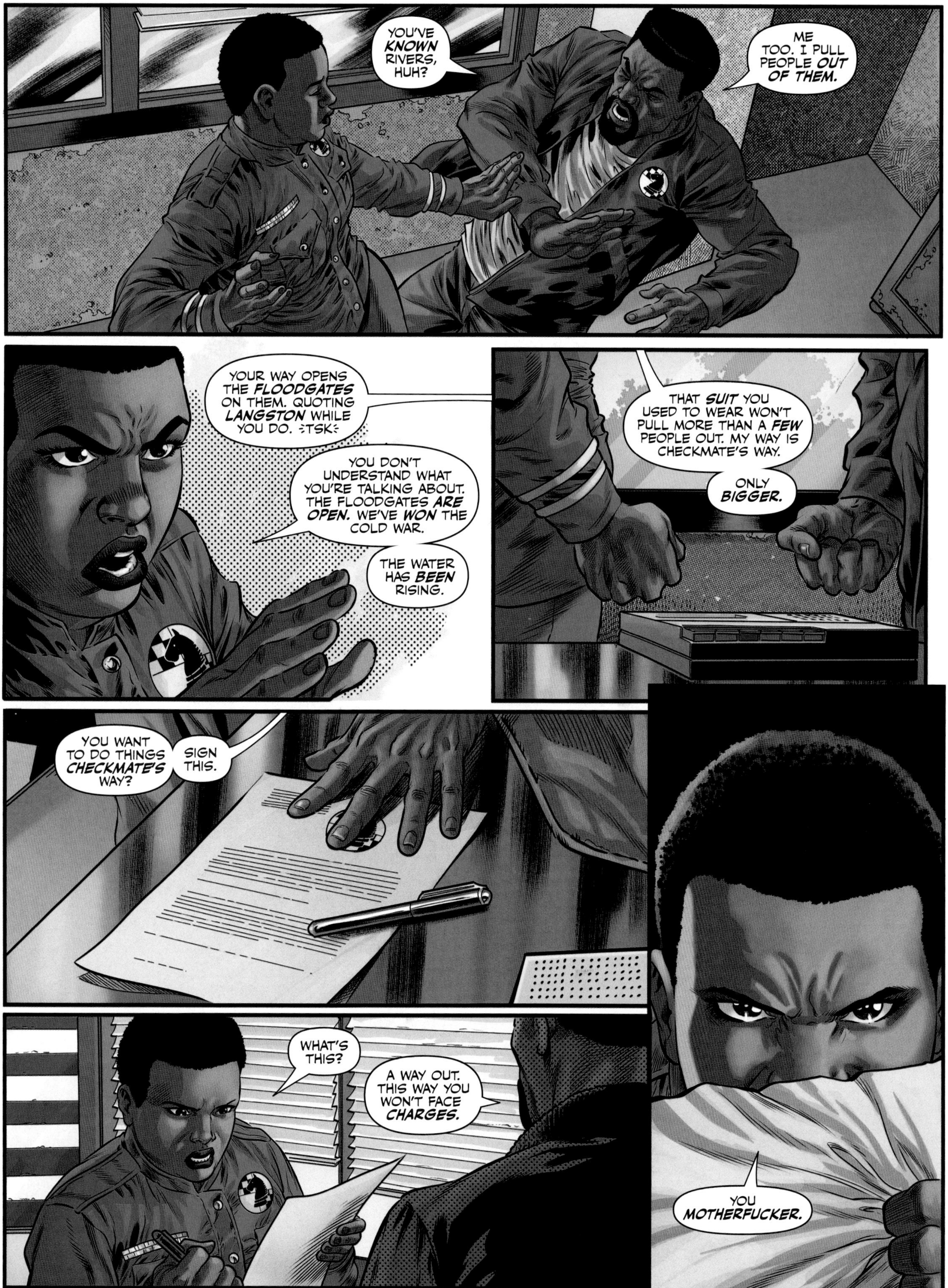
YOU'VE KNOWN RIVERS, HUH?
ME TOO. I PULL PEOPLE OUT OF THEM.
YOUR WAY OPENS THE FLOODGATES ON THEM. QUOTING LANGSTON WHILE YOU DO. ≈TSK≈
YOU DON'T UNDERSTAND WHAT YOU'RE TALKING ABOUT. THE FLOODGATES ARE OPEN. WE'VE WON THE COLD WAR.
THE WATER HAS BEEN RISING.
THAT SUIT YOU USED TO WEAR WON'T PULL MORE THAN A FEW PEOPLE OUT. MY WAY IS CHECKMATE'S WAY.
ONLY BIGGER.
YOU WANT TO DO THINGS CHECKMATE'S WAY?
SIGN THIS.
WHAT'S THIS?
A WAY OUT. THIS WAY YOU WON'T FACE CHARGES.
YOU MOTHERFUCKER.

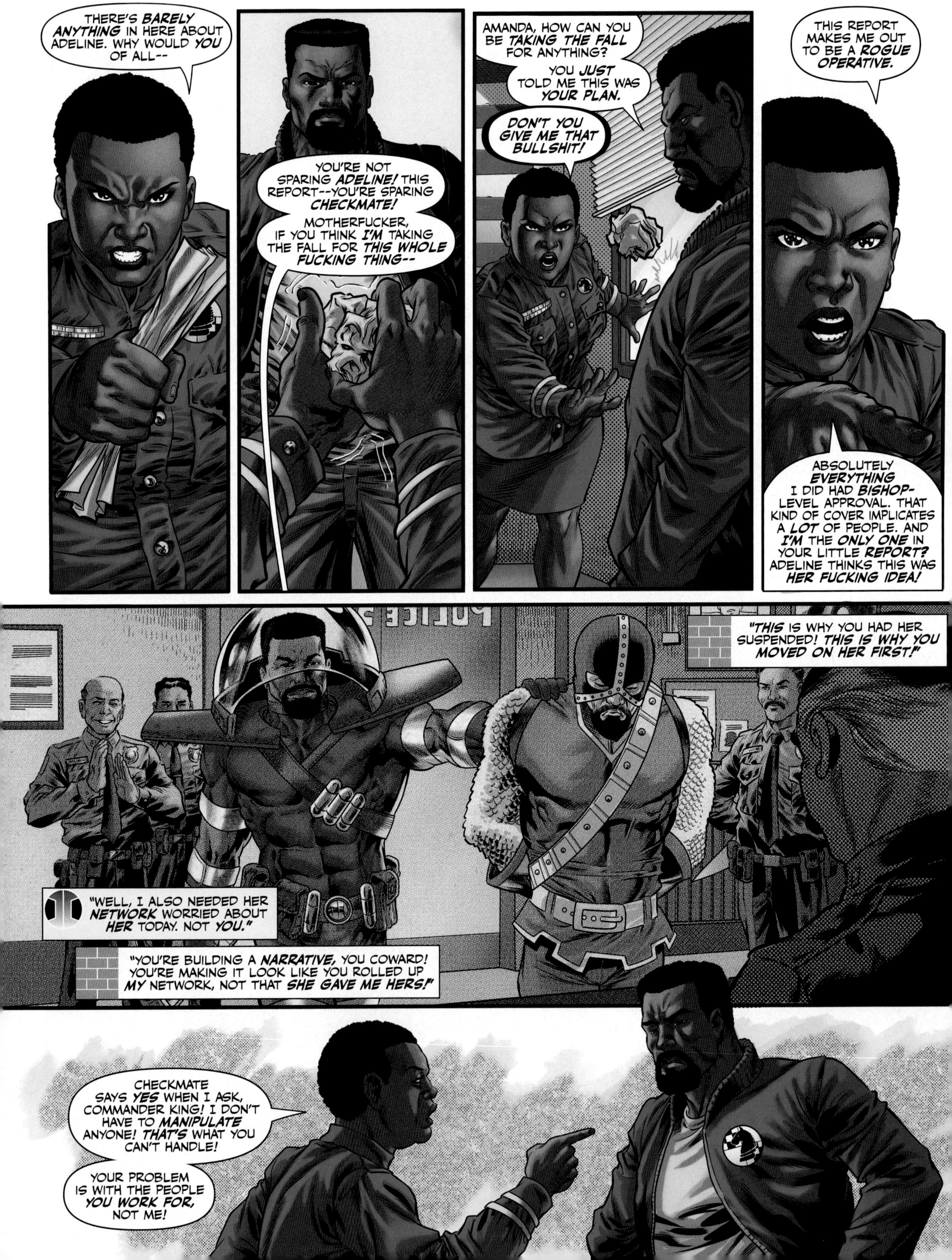

THERE'S BARELY ANYTHING IN HERE ABOUT ADELINE. WHY WOULD YOU OF ALL--
YOU'RE NOT SPARING ADELINE! THIS REPORT--YOU'RE SPARING CHECKMATE!
MOTHERFUCKER, IF YOU THINK I'M TAKING THE FALL FOR THIS WHOLE FUCKING THING--
AMANDA, HOW CAN YOU BE TAKING THE FALL FOR ANYTHING?
YOU JUST TOLD ME THIS WAS YOUR PLAN.
DON'T YOU GIVE ME THAT BULLSHIT!
THIS REPORT MAKES ME OUT TO BE A ROGUE OPERATIVE.
ABSOLUTELY EVERYTHING I DID HAD BISHOP-LEVEL APPROVAL. THAT KIND OF COVER IMPLICATES A LOT OF PEOPLE. AND I'M THE ONLY ONE IN YOUR LITTLE REPORT? ADELINE THINKS THIS WAS HER FUCKING IDEA!
"THIS IS WHY YOU HAD HER SUSPENDED! THIS IS WHY YOU MOVED ON HER FIRST!"
"WELL, I ALSO NEEDED HER NETWORK WORRIED ABOUT HER TODAY. NOT YOU."
"YOU'RE BUILDING A NARRATIVE, YOU COWARD! YOU'RE MAKING IT LOOK LIKE YOU ROLLED UP MY NETWORK, NOT THAT SHE GAVE ME HERS!"
CHECKMATE SAYS YES WHEN I ASK, COMMANDER KING! I DON'T HAVE TO MANIPULATE ANYONE! THAT'S WHAT YOU CAN'T HANDLE!
YOUR PROBLEM IS WITH THE PEOPLE YOU WORK FOR, NOT ME!

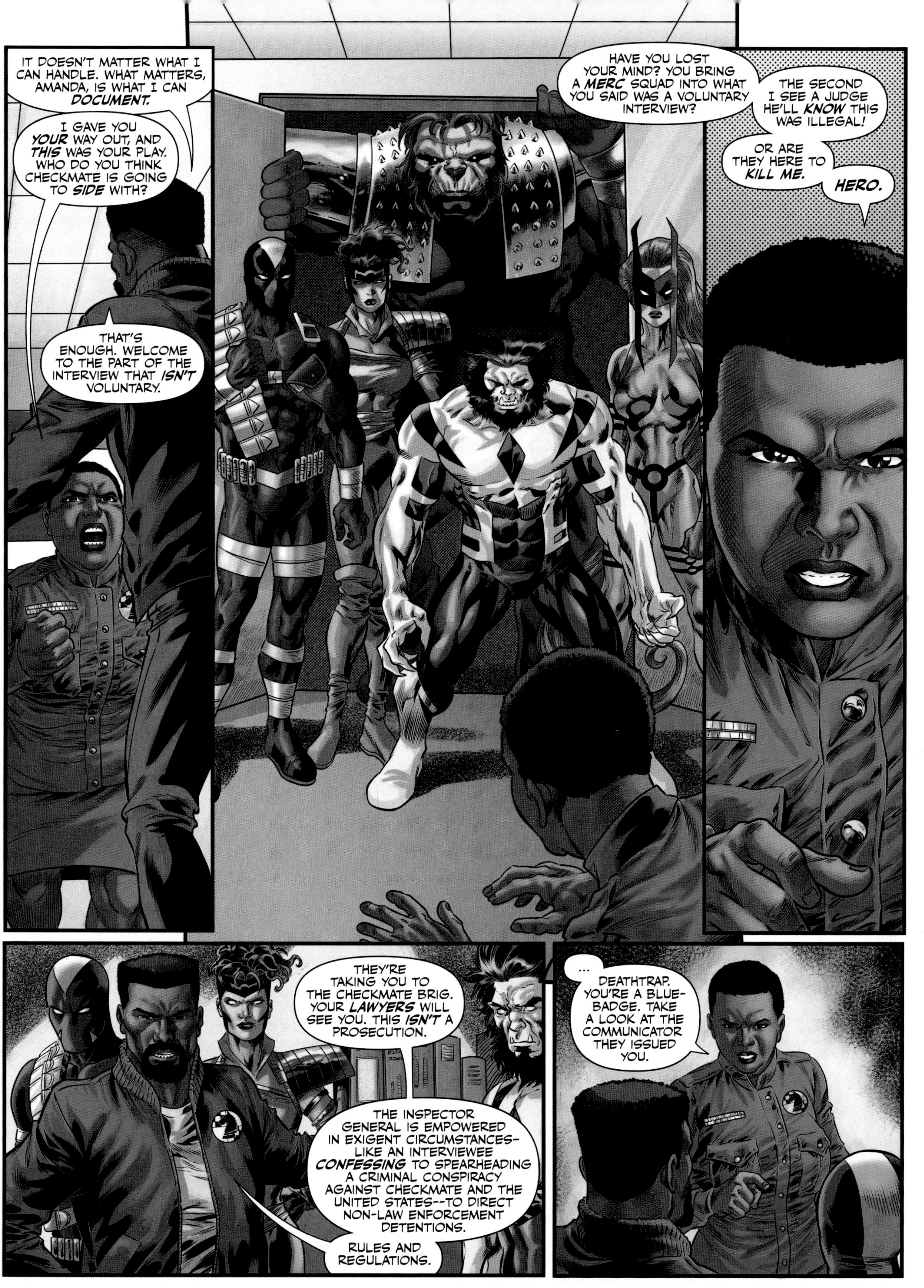

IT DOESN'T MATTER WHAT I CAN HANDLE. WHAT MATTERS, AMANDA, IS WHAT I CAN *DOCUMENT.*
I GAVE YOU *YOUR* WAY OUT, AND *THIS* WAS YOUR PLAY. WHO DO YOU THINK CHECKMATE IS GOING TO *SIDE* WITH?
THAT'S ENOUGH. WELCOME TO THE PART OF THE INTERVIEW THAT *ISN'T* VOLUNTARY.
HAVE YOU LOST YOUR MIND? YOU BRING A *MERC* SQUAD INTO WHAT YOU SAID WAS A VOLUNTARY INTERVIEW?
THE SECOND I SEE A JUDGE HE'LL *KNOW* THIS WAS ILLEGAL!
OR ARE THEY HERE TO *KILL ME.*
HERO.
THEY'RE TAKING YOU TO THE CHECKMATE BRIG. YOUR *LAWYERS* WILL SEE YOU. THIS *ISN'T* A PROSECUTION.
THE INSPECTOR GENERAL IS EMPOWERED IN EXIGENT CIRCUMSTANCES-LIKE AN INTERVIEWEE *CONFESSING* TO SPEARHEADING A CRIMINAL CONSPIRACY AGAINST CHECKMATE AND THE UNITED STATES--TO DIRECT NON-LAW ENFORCEMENT DETENTIONS.
RULES AND REGULATIONS.
... DEATHTRAP. YOU'RE A BLUE-BADGE. TAKE A LOOK AT THE COMMUNICATOR THEY ISSUED YOU.

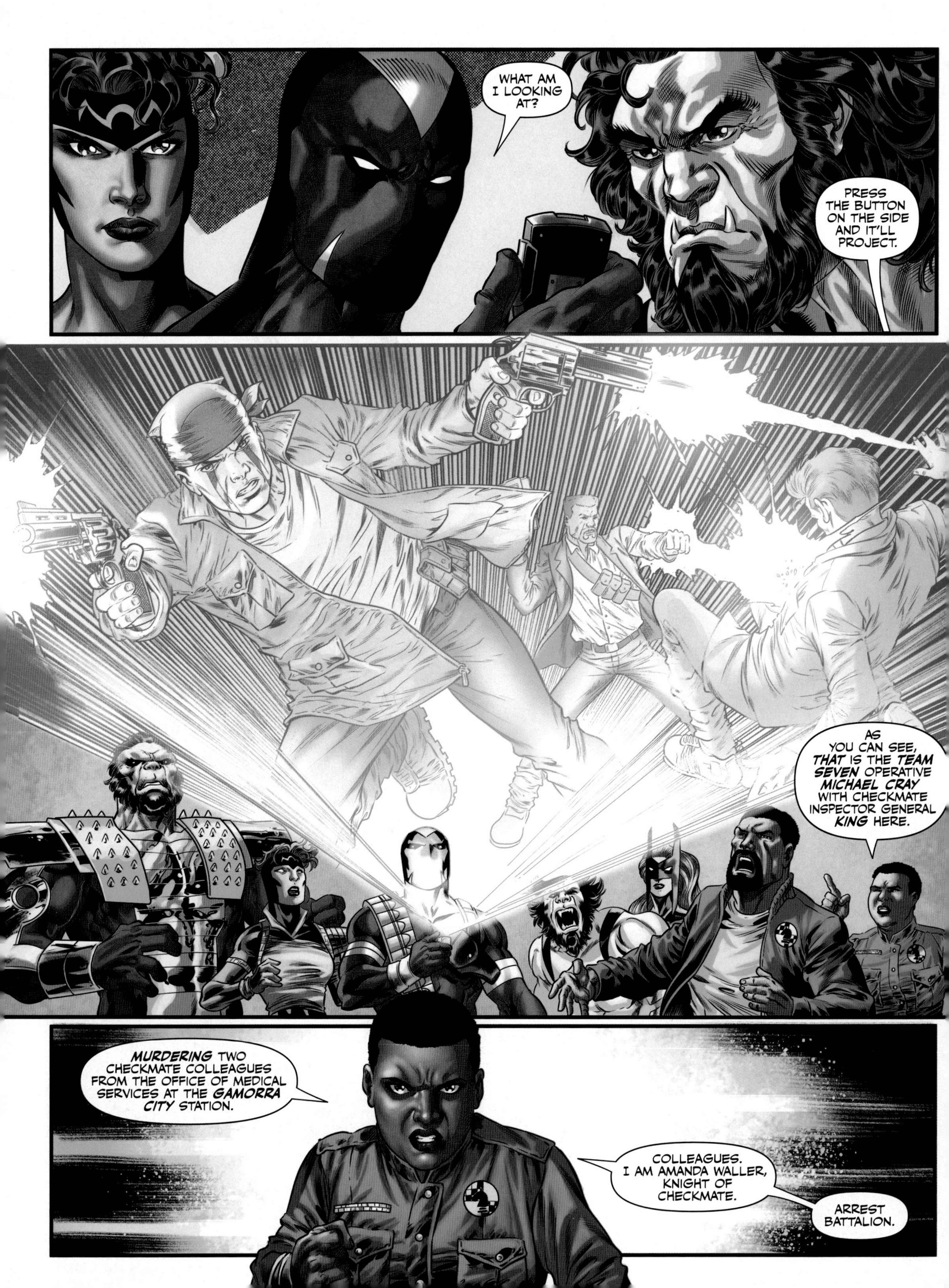
WHAT AM I LOOKING AT?
PRESS THE BUTTON ON THE SIDE AND IT'LL PROJECT.
AS YOU CAN SEE, THAT IS THE TEAM SEVEN OPERATIVE MICHAEL CRAY WITH CHECKMATE INSPECTOR GENERAL KING HERE.
MURDERING TWO CHECKMATE COLLEAGUES FROM THE OFFICE OF MEDICAL SERVICES AT THE GAMORRA CITY STATION.
COLLEAGUES. I AM AMANDA WALLER, KNIGHT OF CHECKMATE.
ARREST BATTALION.

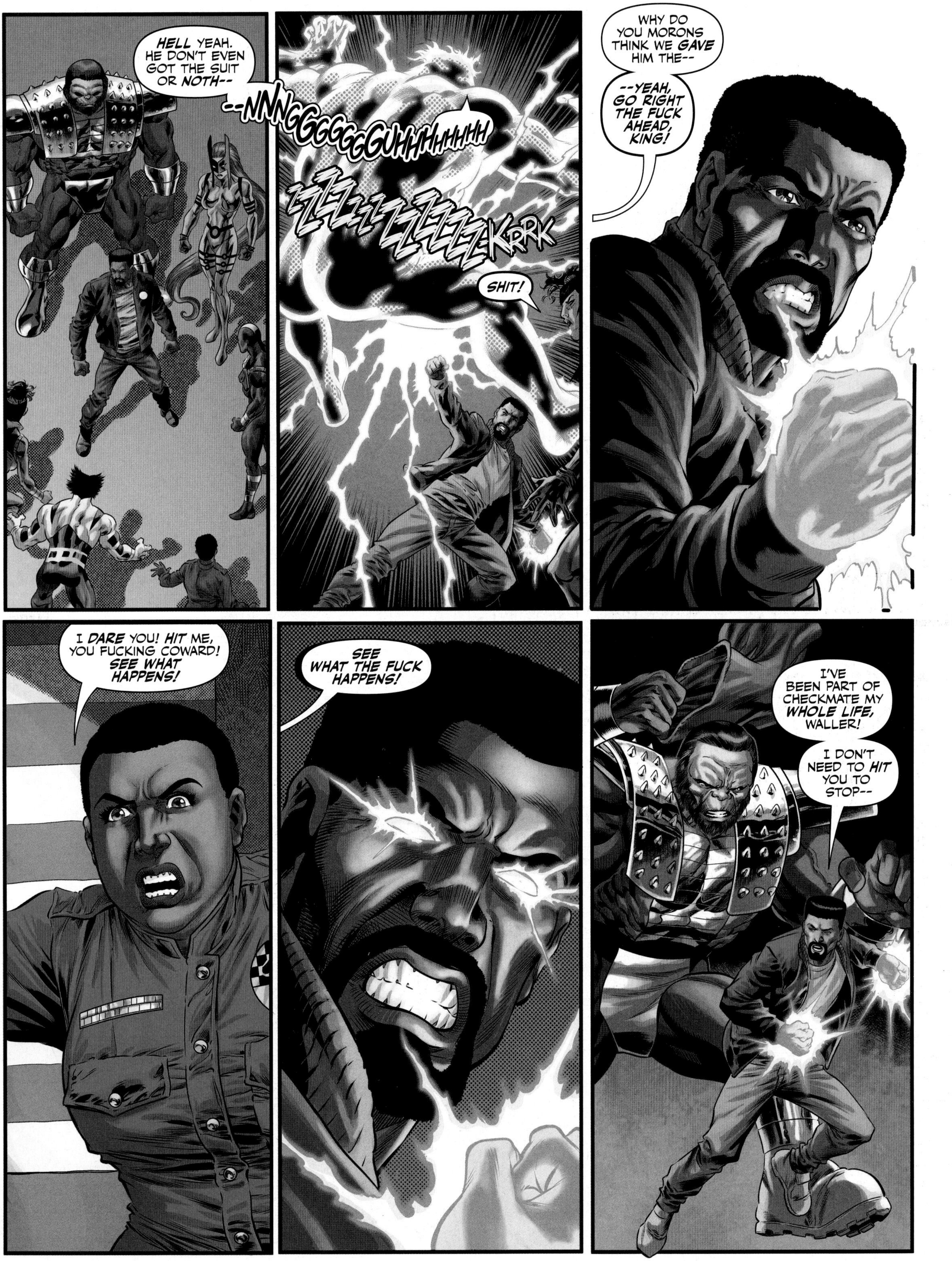

HELL YEAH. HE DON'T EVEN GOT THE SUIT OR NOTH--
--NNNGGGGGGGUHHHHHHHH
ZZZZZZZZZZZZZZZZKRRK
SHIT!
WHY DO YOU MORONS THINK WE GAVE HIM THE--
--YEAH, GO RIGHT THE FUCK AHEAD, KING!
I DARE YOU! HIT ME, YOU FUCKING COWARD! SEE WHAT HAPPENS!
SEE WHAT THE FUCK HAPPENS!
I'VE BEEN PART OF CHECKMATE MY WHOLE LIFE, WALLER!
I DON'T NEED TO HIT YOU TO STOP--

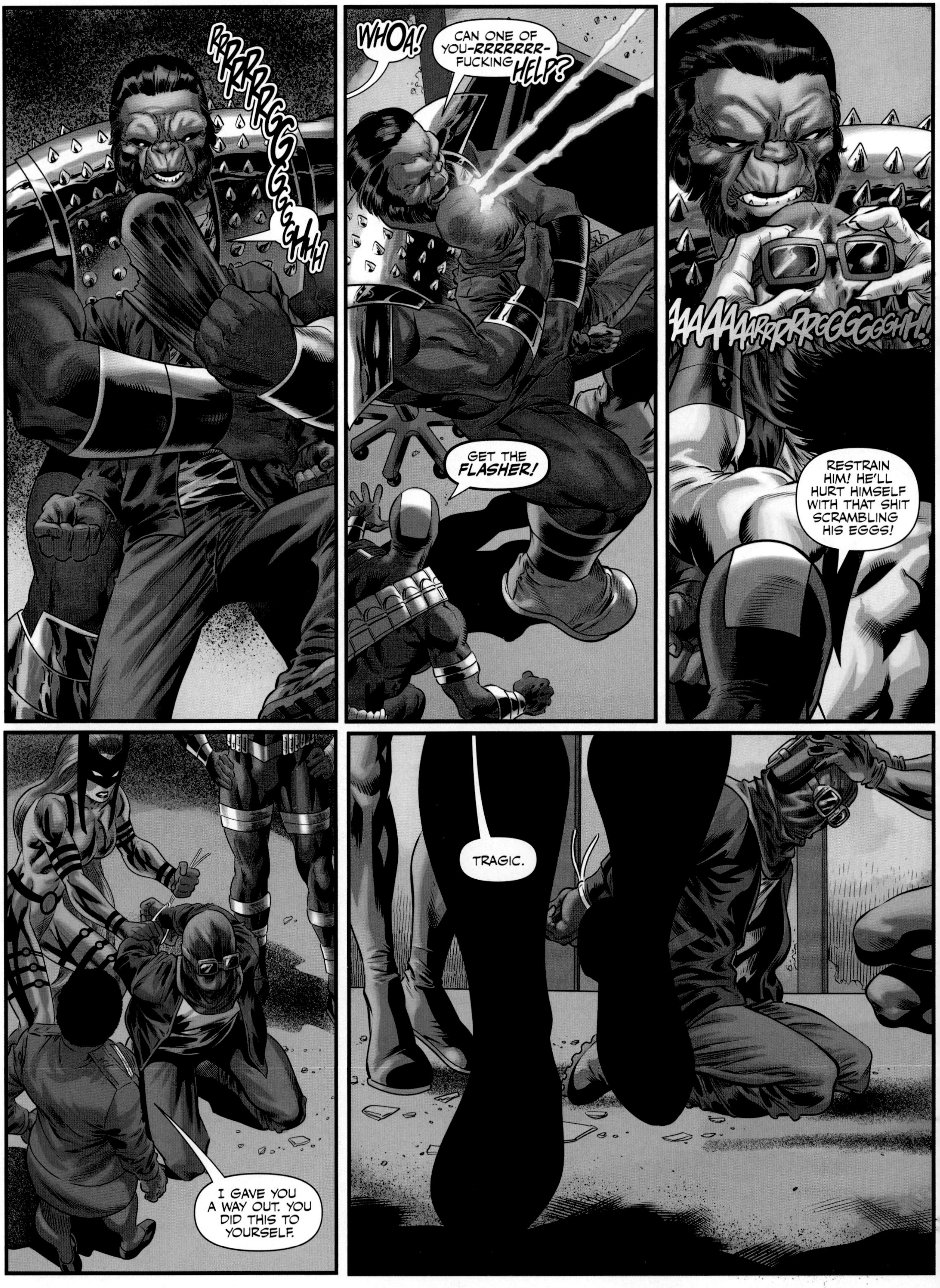
RRRRRRRGGGGGGHHH
WHOA!
CAN ONE OF YOU-RRRRRRR-FUCKING HELP?
GET THE FLASHER!
AAAAAARRRRRGGGGGHH!
RESTRAIN HIM! HE'LL HURT HIMSELF WITH THAT SHIT SCRAMBLING HIS EGGS!
I GAVE YOU A WAY OUT. YOU DID THIS TO YOURSELF.
TRAGIC.

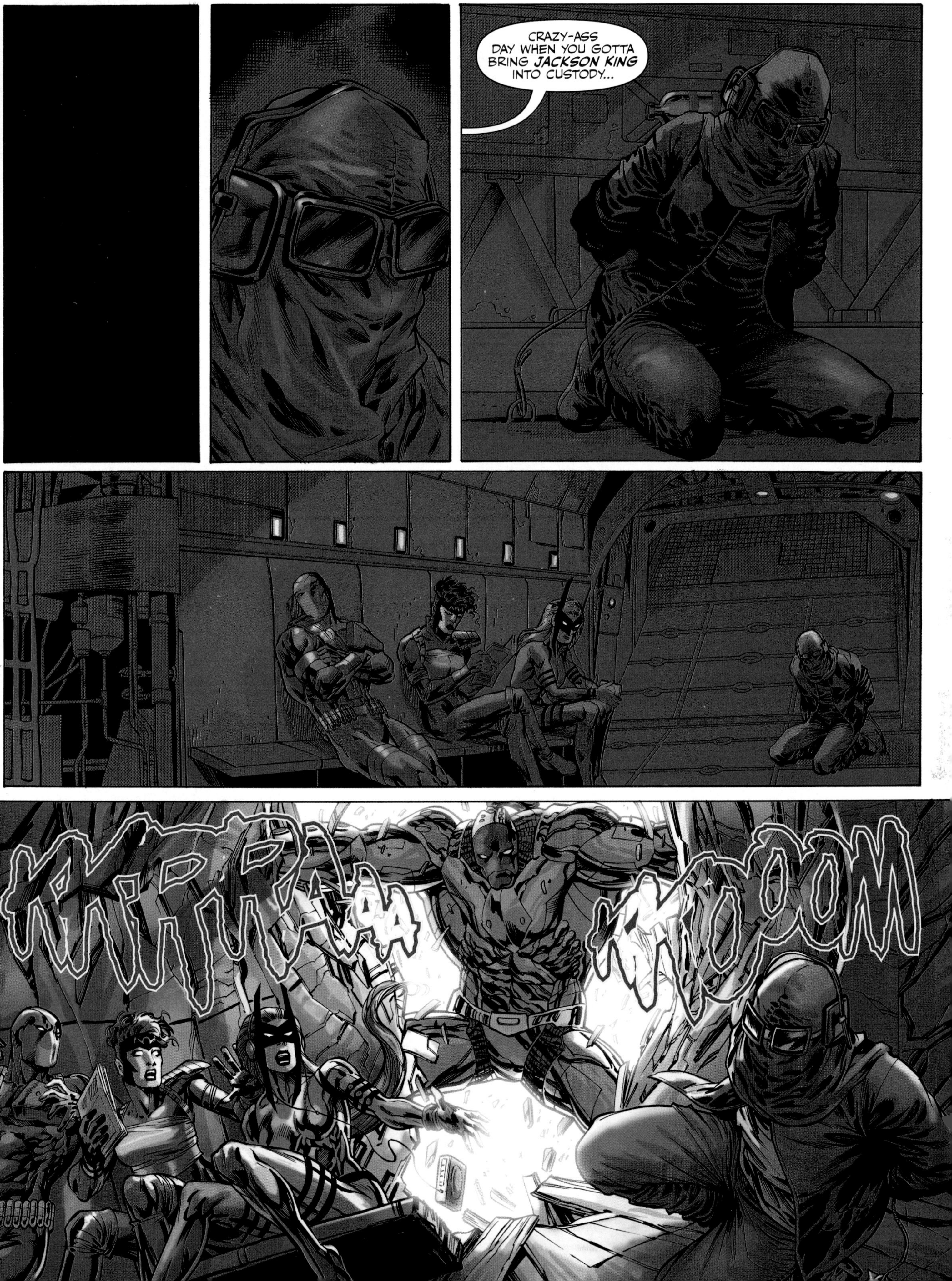
CRAZY-ASS DAY WHEN YOU GOTTA BRING JACKSON KING INTO CUSTODY...

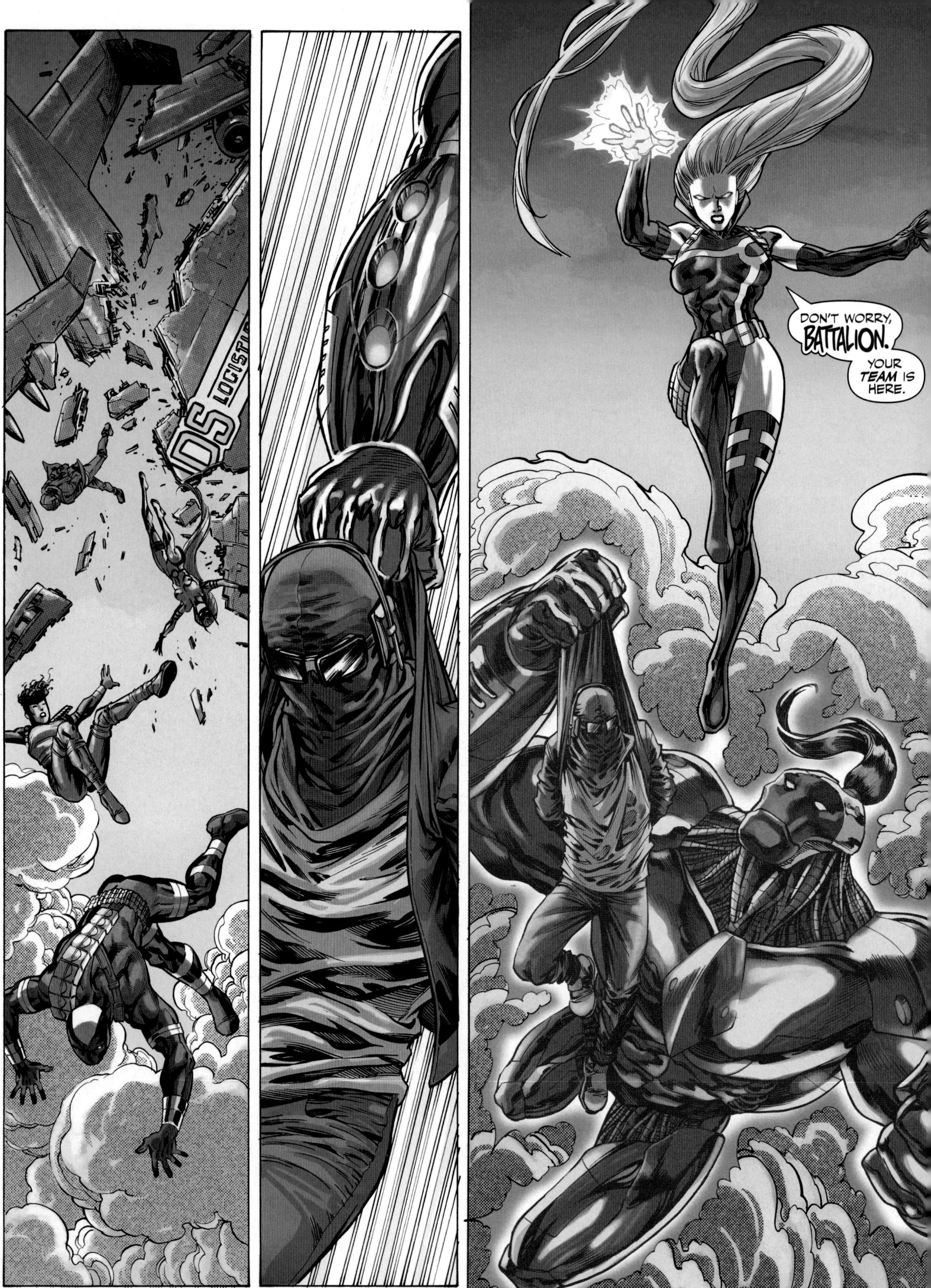
DON'T WORRY, BATTALION. YOUR TEAM IS HERE.

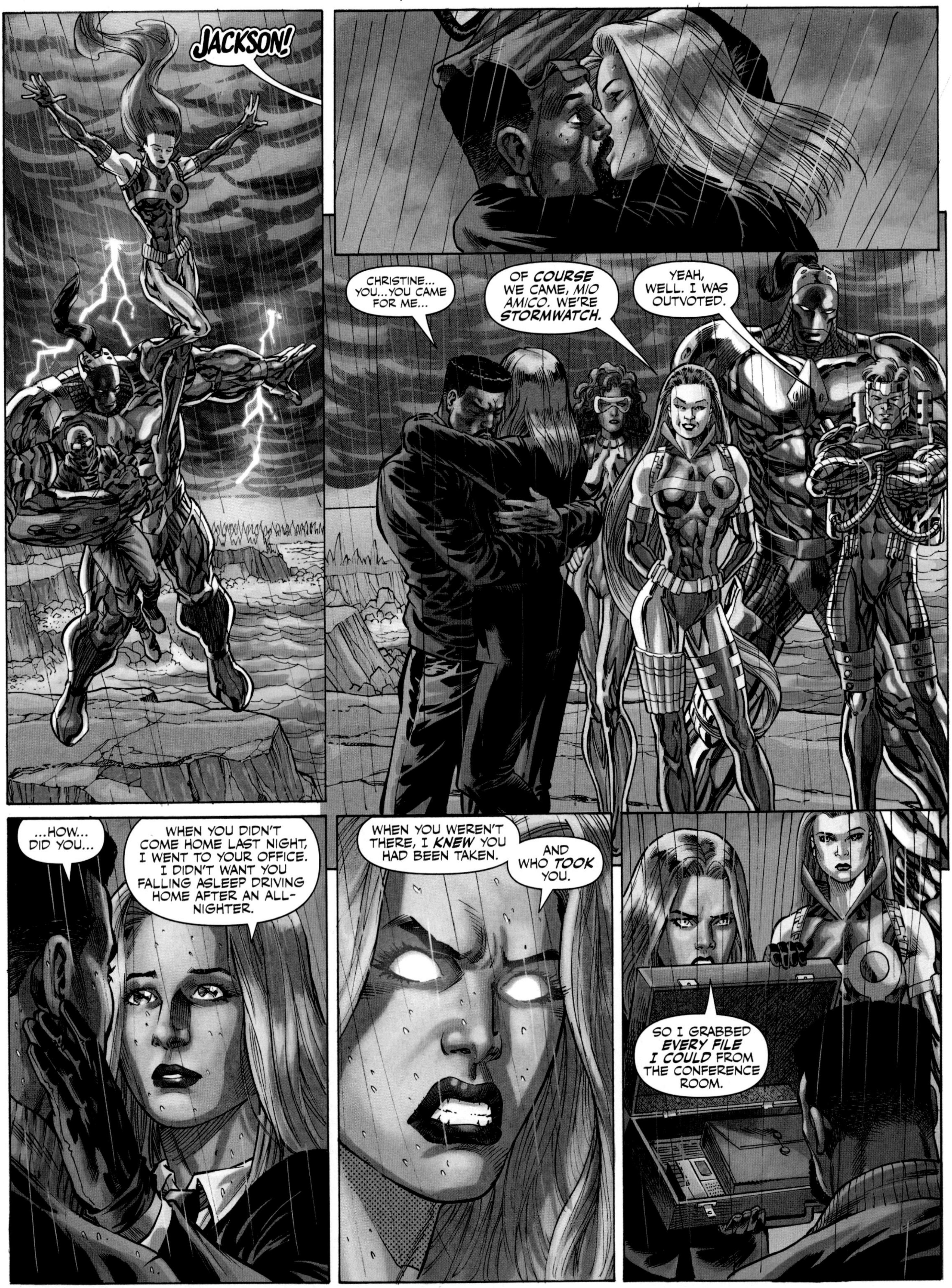

JACKSON!
CHRISTINE... YOU...YOU CAME FOR ME...
OF COURSE WE CAME, MIO AMICO. WE'RE STORMWATCH.
YEAH, WELL. I WAS OUTVOTED.
...HOW... DID YOU...
WHEN YOU DIDN'T COME HOME LAST NIGHT, I WENT TO YOUR OFFICE. I DIDN'T WANT YOU FALLING ASLEEP DRIVING HOME AFTER AN ALL-NIGHTER.
WHEN YOU WEREN'T THERE, I KNEW YOU HAD BEEN TAKEN.
AND WHO TOOK YOU.
SO I GRABBED EVERY FILE I COULD FROM THE CONFERENCE ROOM.

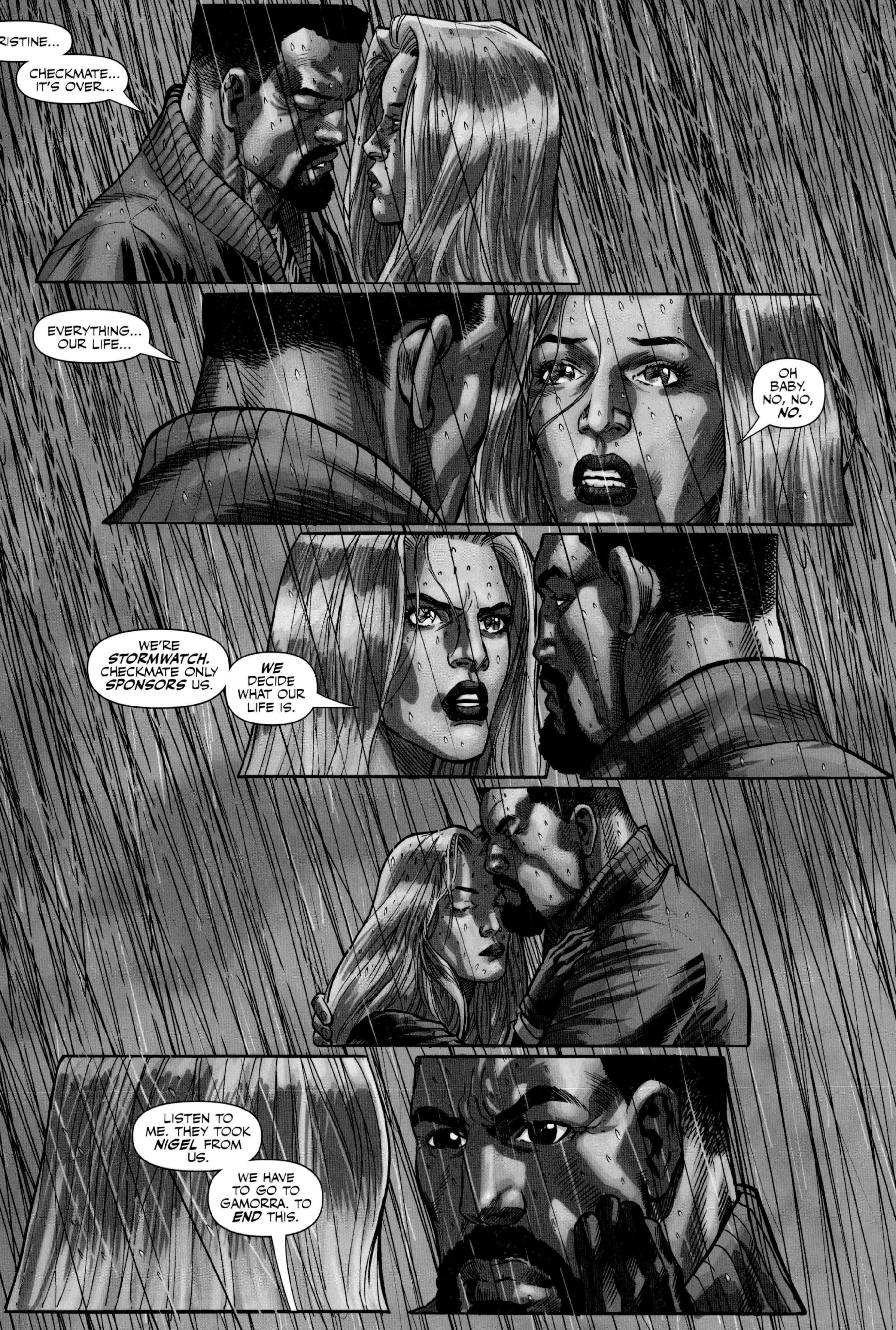
CHRISTINE...
CHECKMATE... IT'S OVER...
EVERYTHING... OUR LIFE...
OH BABY. NO, NO, **NO.**
WE'RE ***STORMWATCH.*** CHECKMATE ONLY ***SPONSORS*** US.
WE DECIDE WHAT OUR LIFE IS.
LISTEN TO ME. THEY TOOK ***NIGEL*** FROM US.
WE HAVE TO GO TO GAMORRA. TO ***END*** THIS.

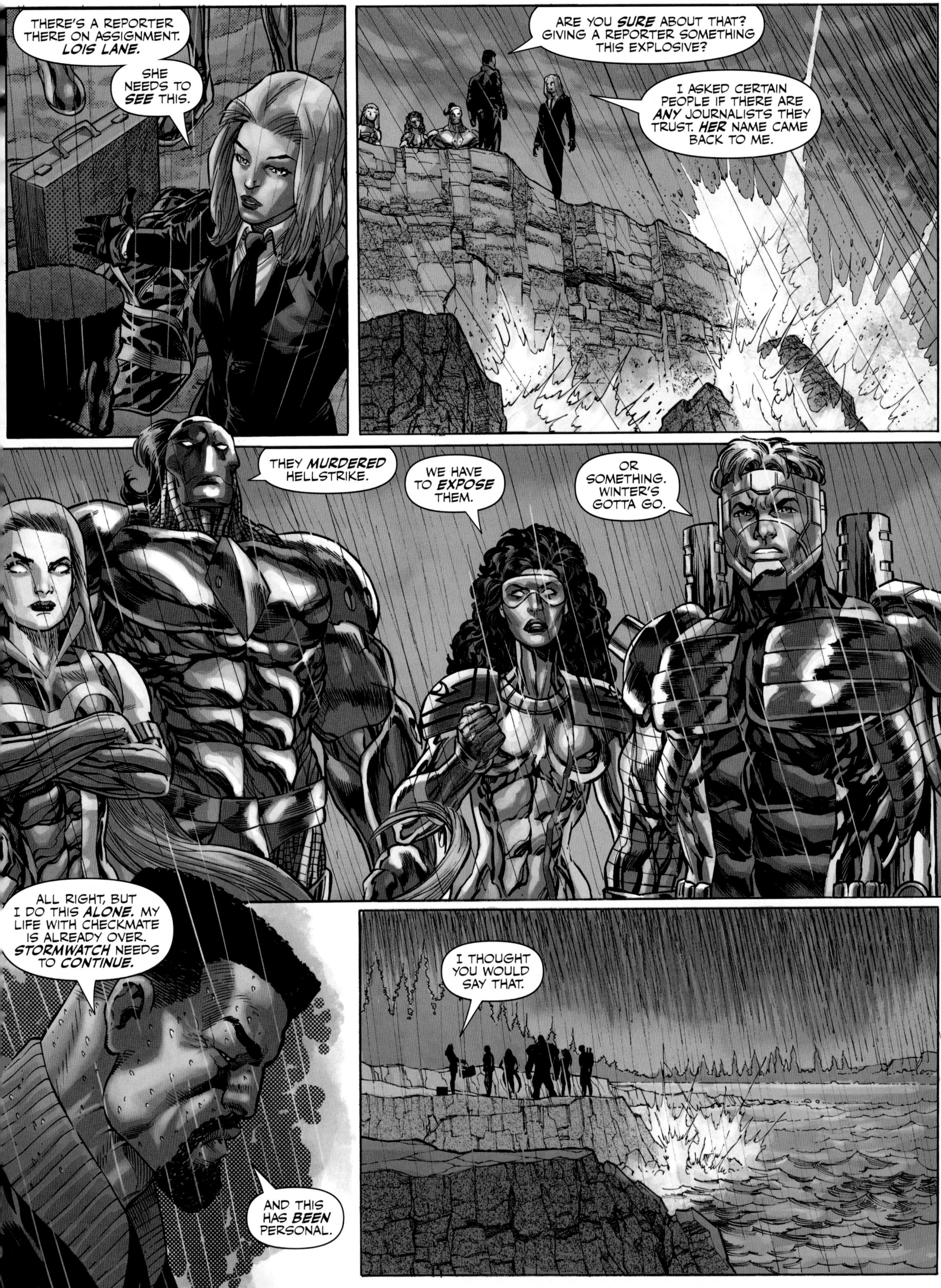
THERE'S A REPORTER THERE ON ASSIGNMENT. **LOIS LANE.**
SHE NEEDS TO **SEE** THIS.
ARE YOU **SURE** ABOUT THAT? GIVING A REPORTER SOMETHING THIS EXPLOSIVE?
I ASKED CERTAIN PEOPLE IF THERE ARE **ANY** JOURNALISTS THEY TRUST. **HER** NAME CAME BACK TO ME.
THEY **MURDERED** HELLSTRIKE.
WE HAVE TO **EXPOSE** THEM.
OR SOMETHING. WINTER'S GOTTA GO.
ALL RIGHT, BUT I DO THIS **ALONE.** MY LIFE WITH CHECKMATE IS ALREADY OVER. **STORMWATCH** NEEDS TO **CONTINUE.**
AND THIS HAS **BEEN** PERSONAL.
I THOUGHT YOU WOULD SAY THAT.

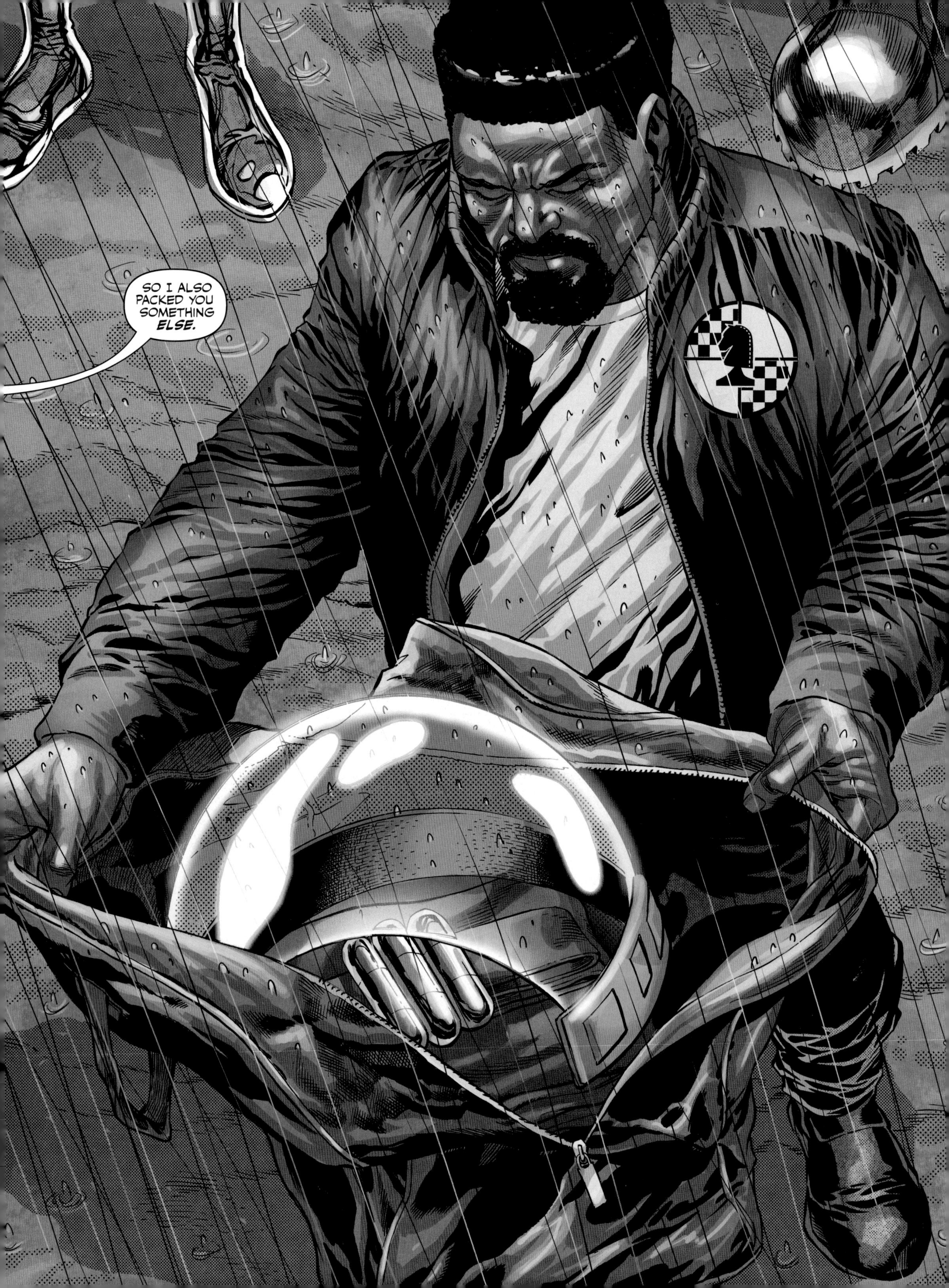
SO I ALSO PACKED YOU SOMETHING *ELSE.*

WALLER VS WILDSTORM

BOOK THREE

SPENCER ACKERMAN
EVAN NARCISSE
JESÚS MERINO
VICENTE CIFUENTES
MICHAEL ATIYEH

FORNÉS

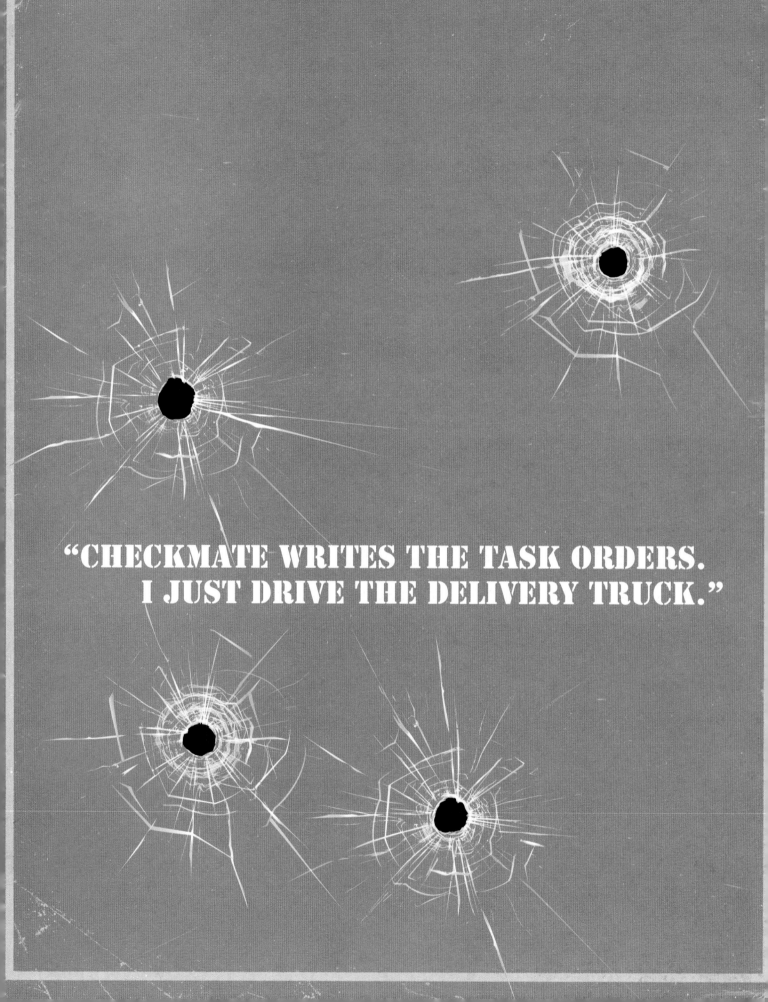

"CHECKMATE WRITES THE TASK ORDERS.
I JUST DRIVE THE DELIVERY TRUCK."

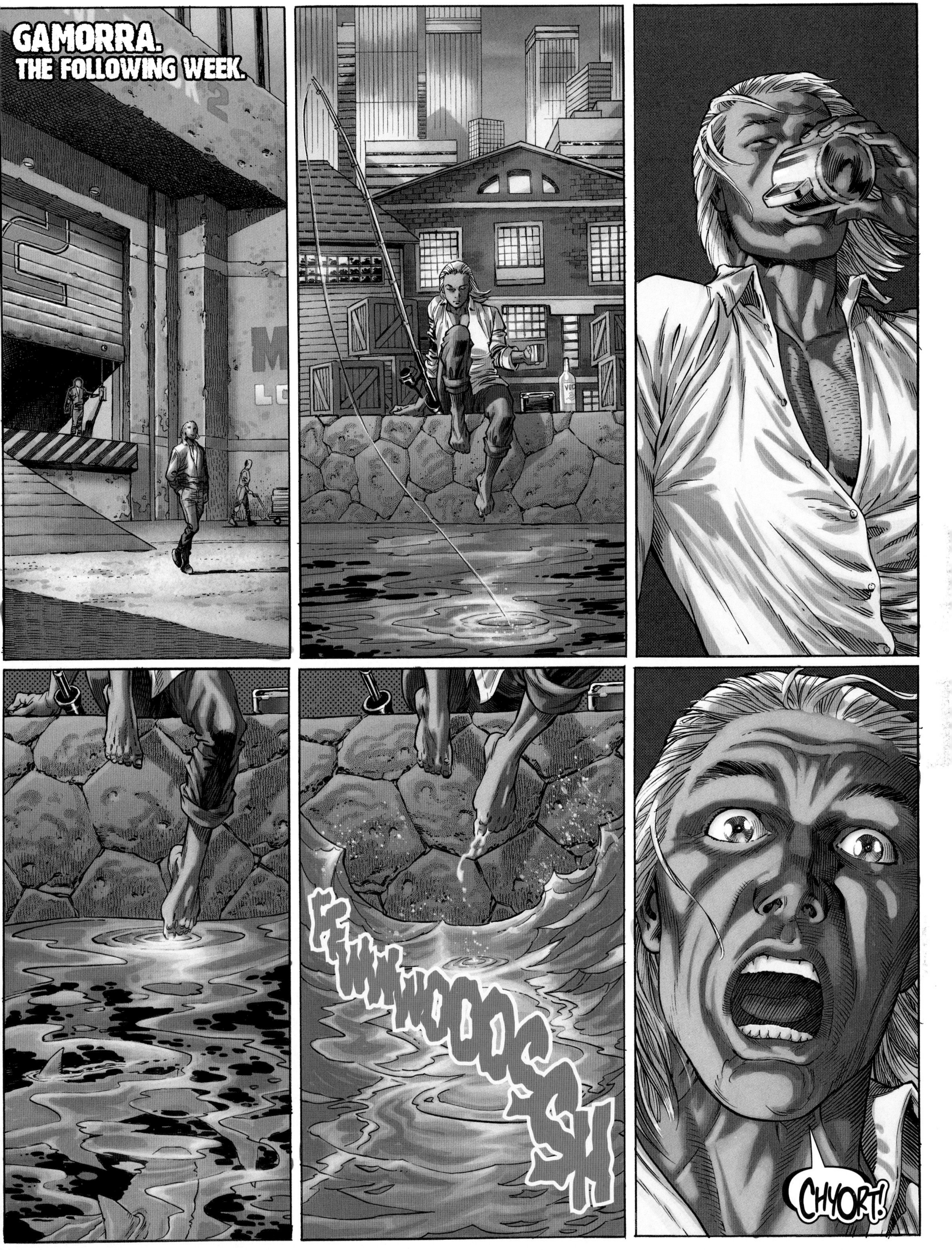
GAMORRA.
THE FOLLOWING WEEK.
FWWHOOOSH
CHYORT!

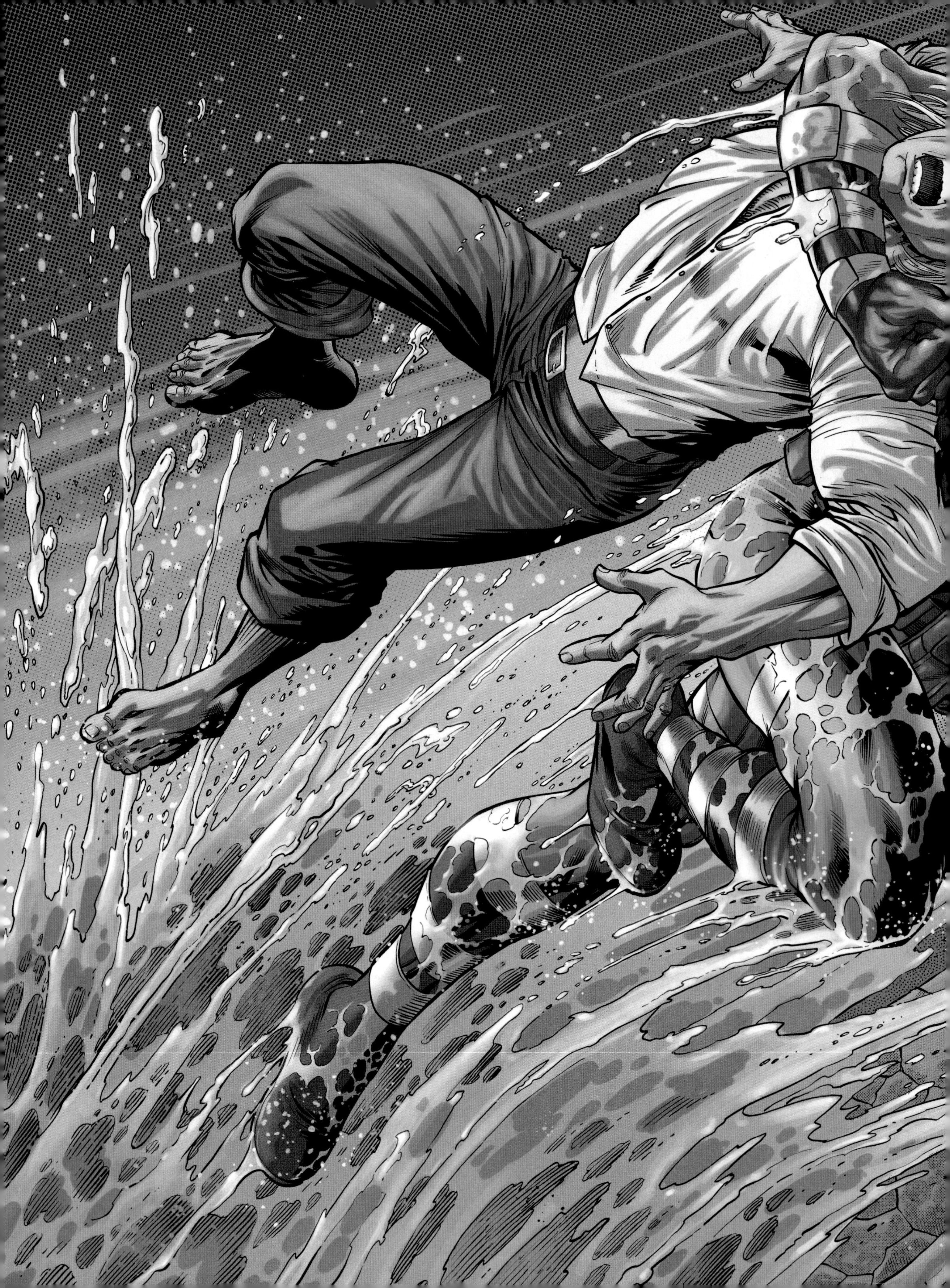

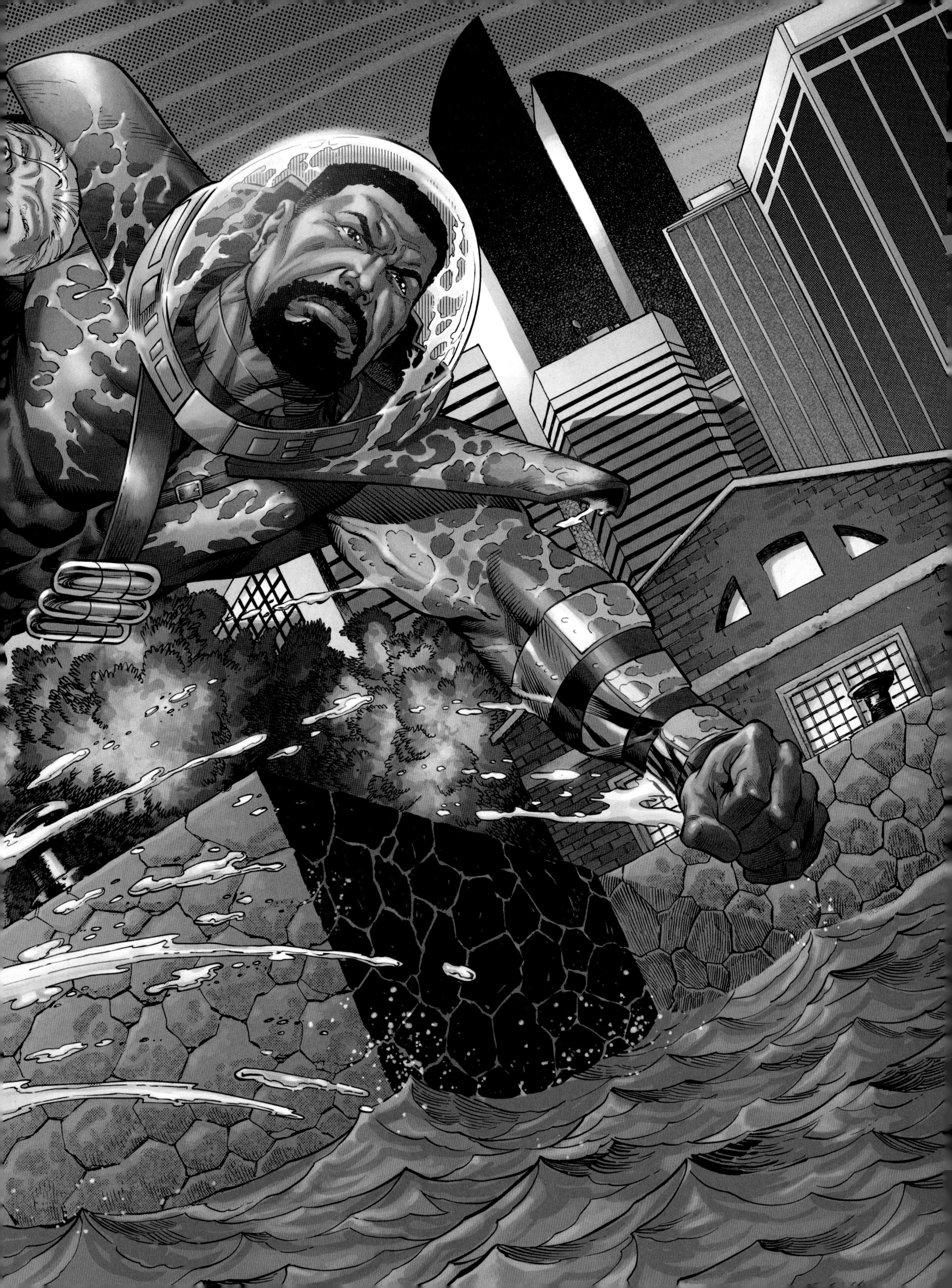

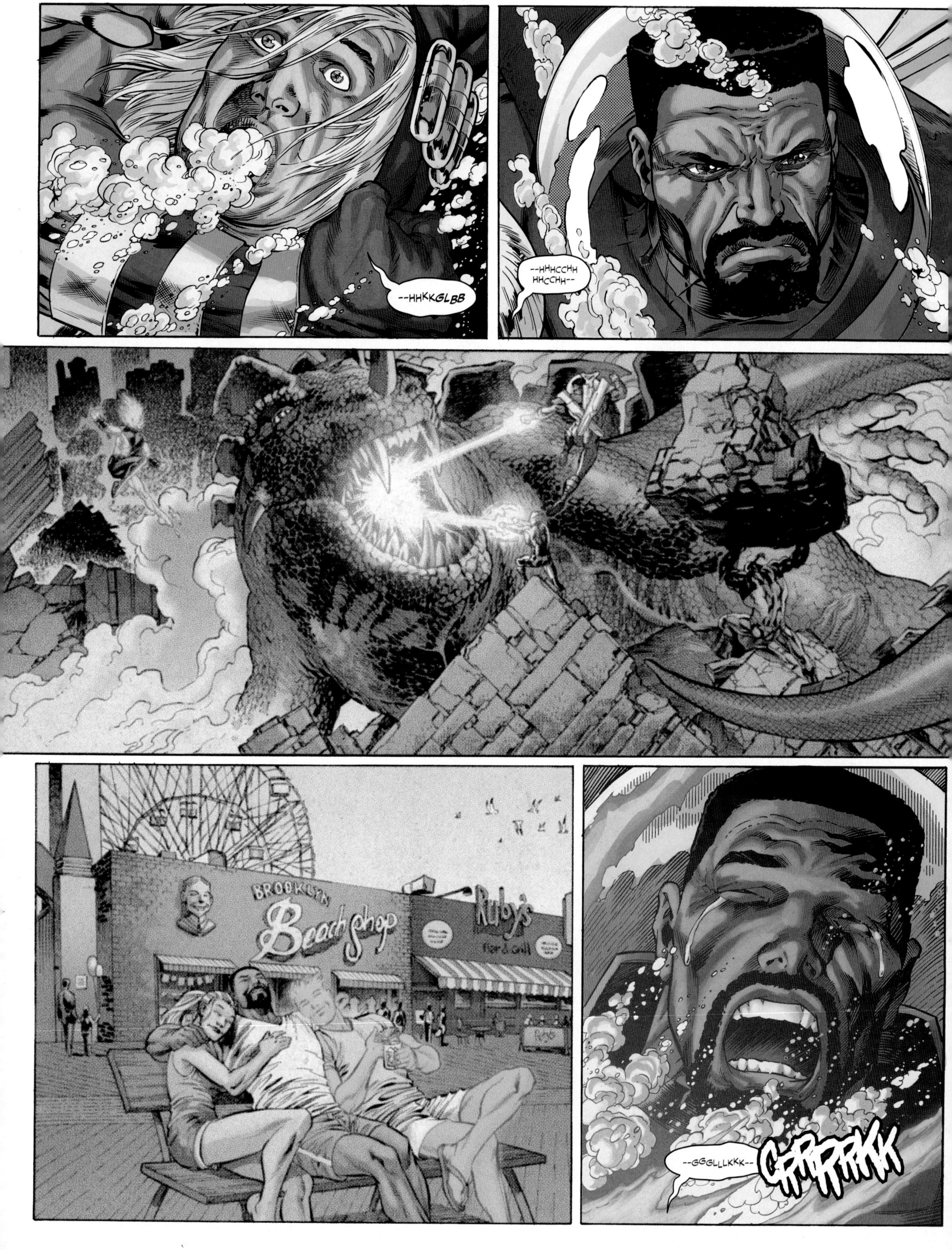
--HHKKGLBB
--HHHCCHH HHCCHH--
BROOKLYN
Beach shop
Ruby's
Bar & Grill
--GGGLLLKKK--
GRRRRKK

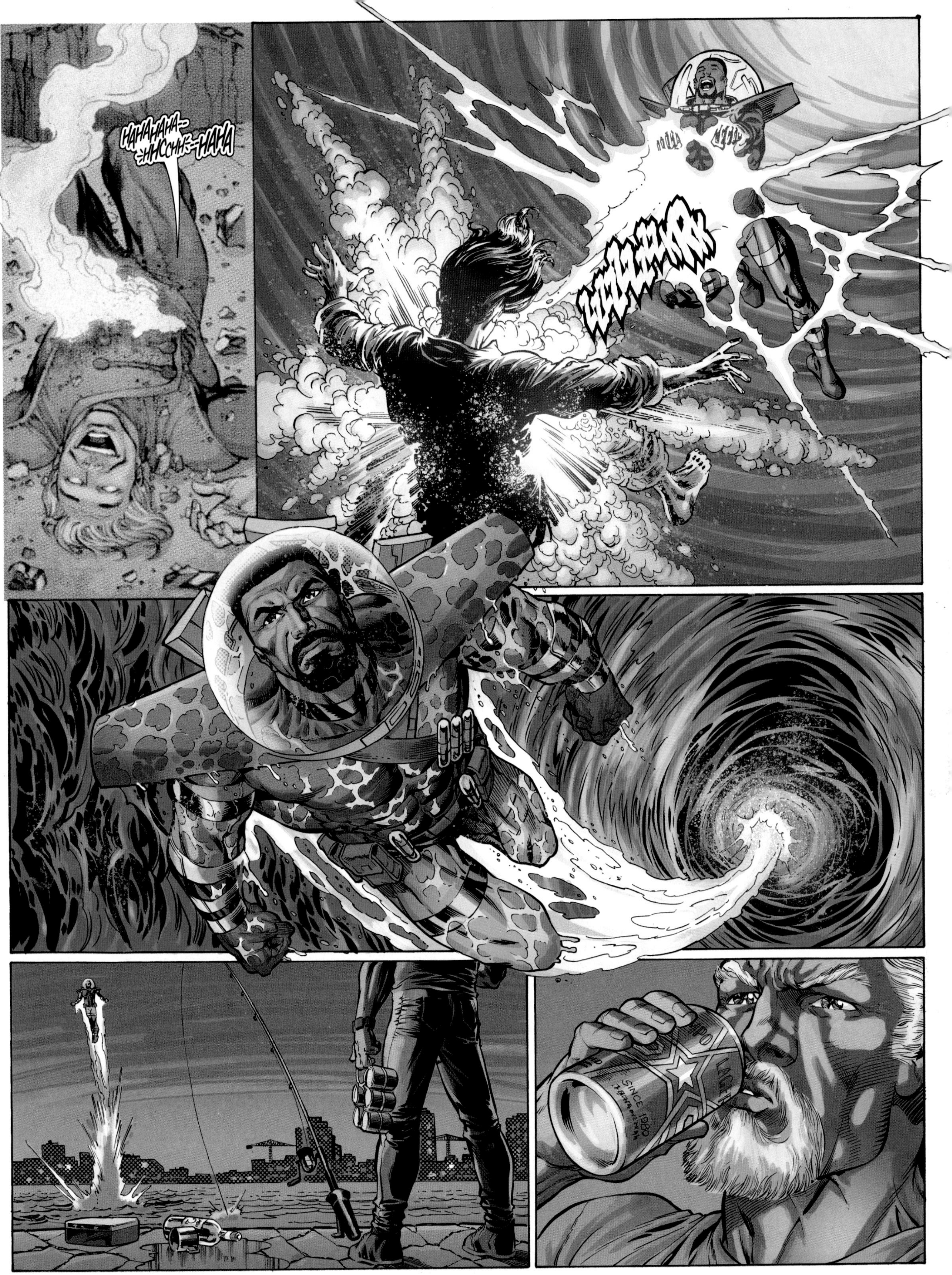
HAHAHAHA-
-HHCCHH--HAHA
SINCE 1980

GAMORRA CITY 3 KM
CUPERTINO HUMAN RESOURCES INC
HEY, EXCUSE ME? FORGET ABOUT THE HOTEL...
...CAN YOU LET ME OUT *HERE?*
HI! SORRY TO BOTHER YOU. DO YOU *WORK* HERE?
MY NAME IS *LOIS LANE* AND I'M A REPORTER FOR THE *DAILY PLANET!*
YEAH? GOOD FOR YOU.

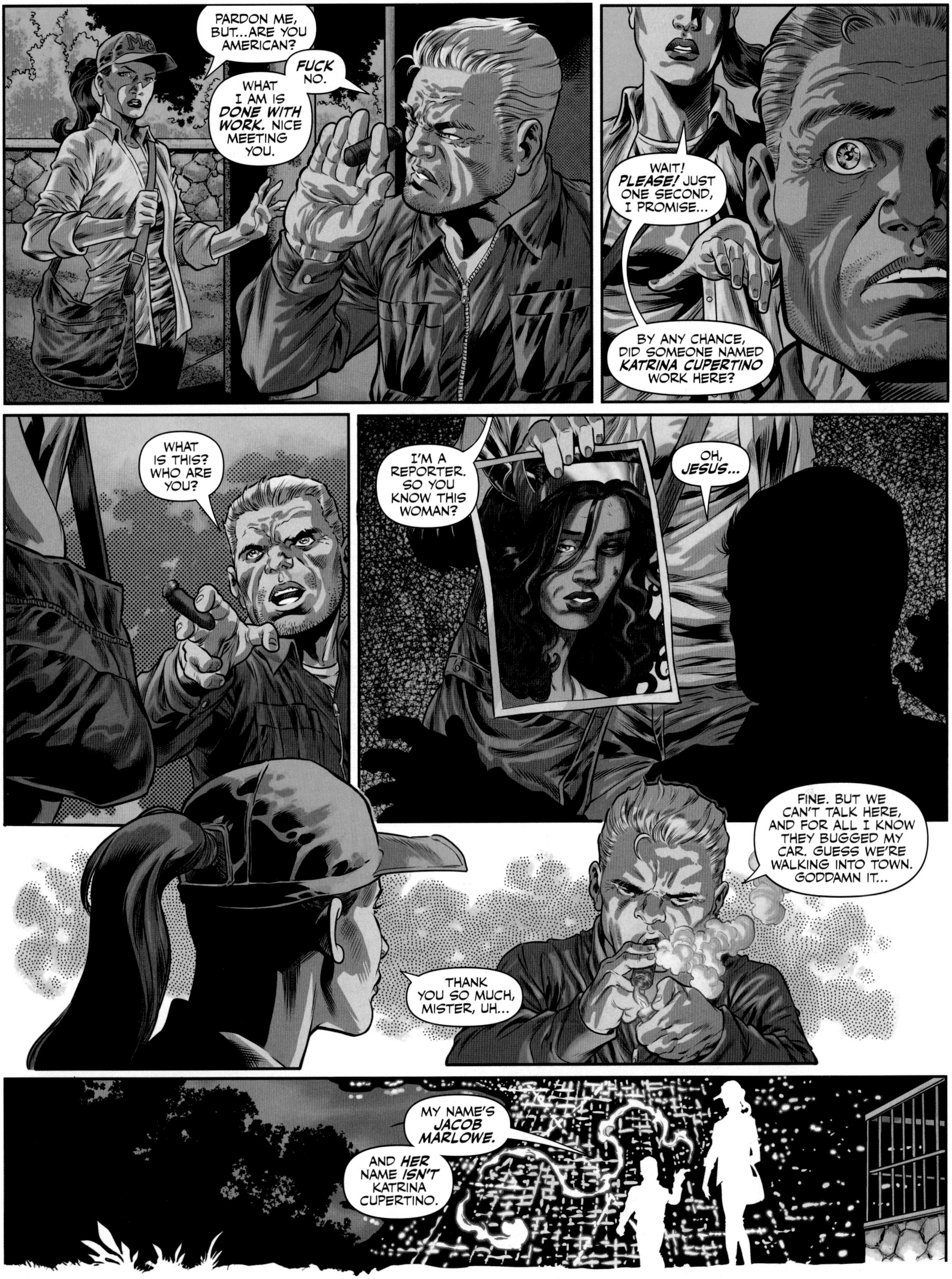
PARDON ME, BUT...ARE YOU AMERICAN?
FUCK NO.
WHAT I AM IS DONE WITH WORK. NICE MEETING YOU.
WAIT! PLEASE! JUST ONE SECOND, I PROMISE...
BY ANY CHANCE, DID SOMEONE NAMED KATRINA CUPERTINO WORK HERE?
WHAT IS THIS? WHO ARE YOU?
I'M A REPORTER. SO YOU KNOW THIS WOMAN?
OH, JESUS...
FINE. BUT WE CAN'T TALK HERE, AND FOR ALL I KNOW THEY BUGGED MY CAR. GUESS WE'RE WALKING INTO TOWN. GODDAMN IT...
THANK YOU SO MUCH, MISTER, UH...
MY NAME'S JACOB MARLOWE.
AND HER NAME ISN'T KATRINA CUPERTINO.

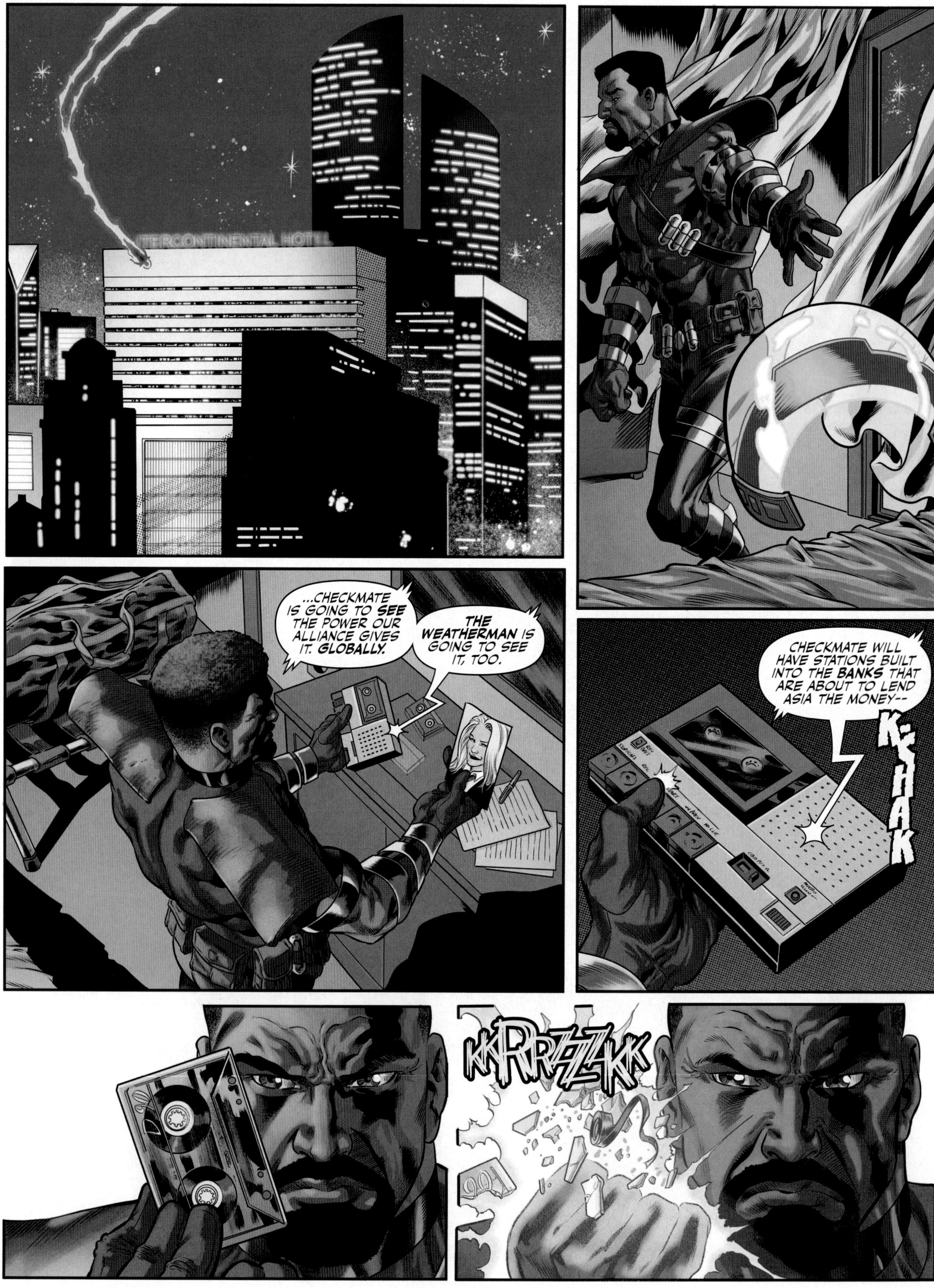
TERCONTINENTAL HOTEL
...CHECKMATE IS GOING TO SEE THE POWER OUR ALLIANCE GIVES IT. GLOBALLY.
THE WEATHERMAN IS GOING TO SEE IT, TOO.
CHECKMATE WILL HAVE STATIONS BUILT INTO THE BANKS THAT ARE ABOUT TO LEND ASIA THE MONEY--
K-SHAK
KRRZZAKK

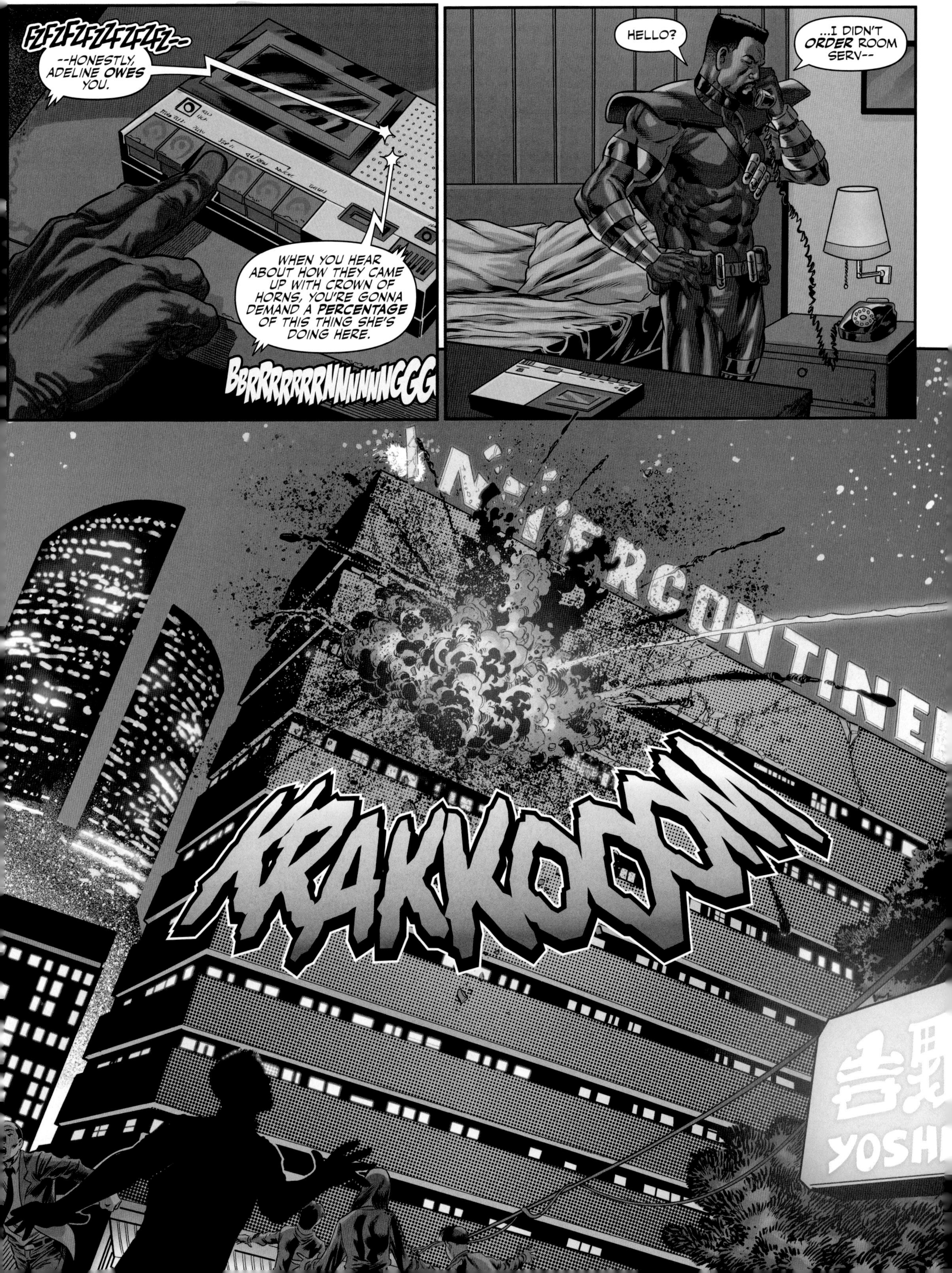
FZFZFZFZZFZFZFZ--
--HONESTLY, ADELINE OWES YOU.
WHEN YOU HEAR ABOUT HOW THEY CAME UP WITH CROWN OF HORNS, YOU'RE GONNA DEMAND A PERCENTAGE OF THIS THING SHE'S DOING HERE.
BBRRRRRRRNNNNNNGGG
HELLO?
...I DIDN'T ORDER ROOM SERV--
RCONTINE
KRAKKOOM
YOSH

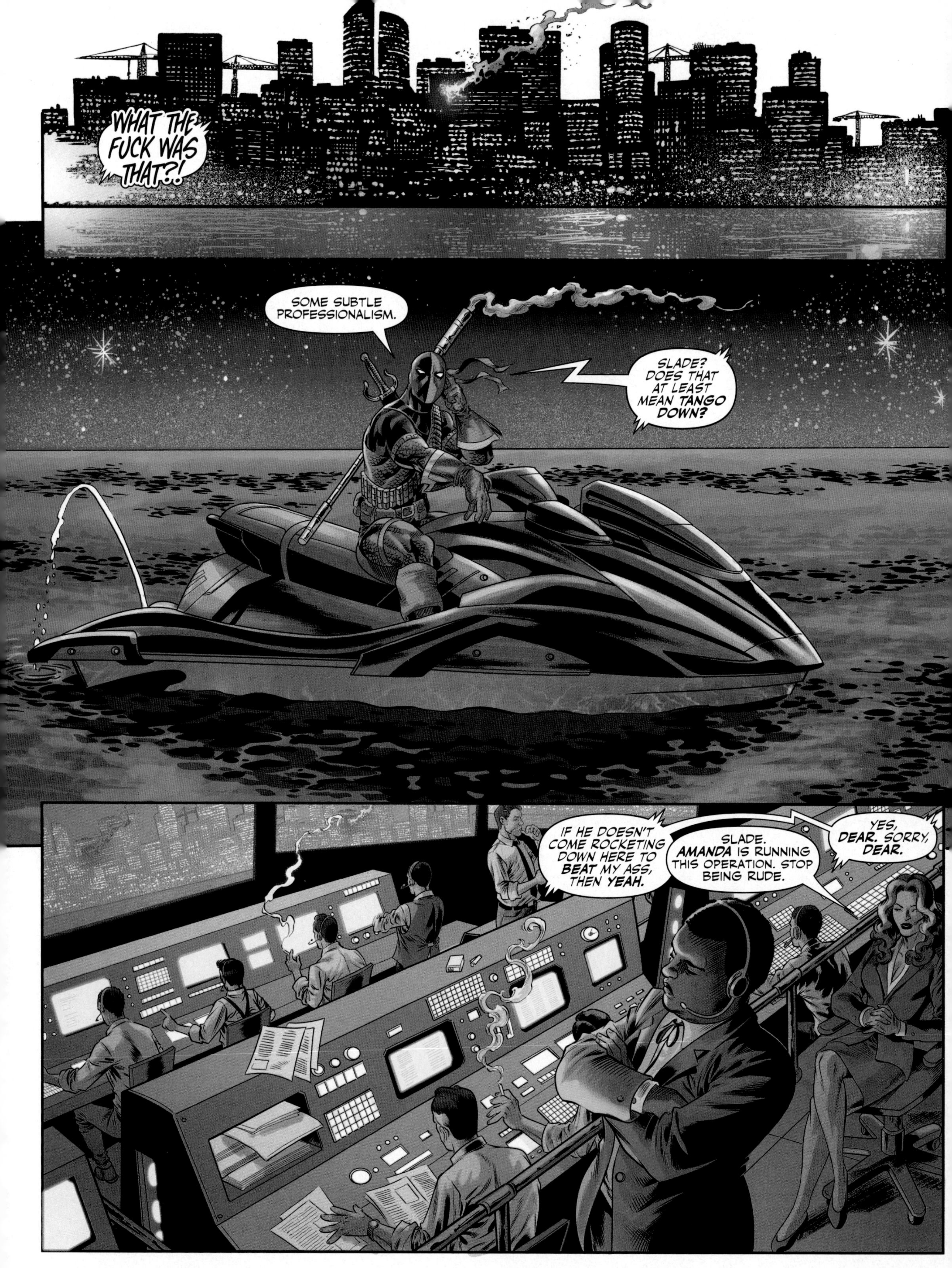
WHAT THE FUCK WAS THAT?!
SOME SUBTLE PROFESSIONALISM.
SLADE? DOES THAT AT LEAST MEAN TANGO DOWN?
IF HE DOESN'T COME ROCKETING DOWN HERE TO BEAT MY ASS, THEN YEAH.
SLADE. AMANDA IS RUNNING THIS OPERATION. STOP BEING RUDE.
YES, DEAR. SORRY, DEAR.

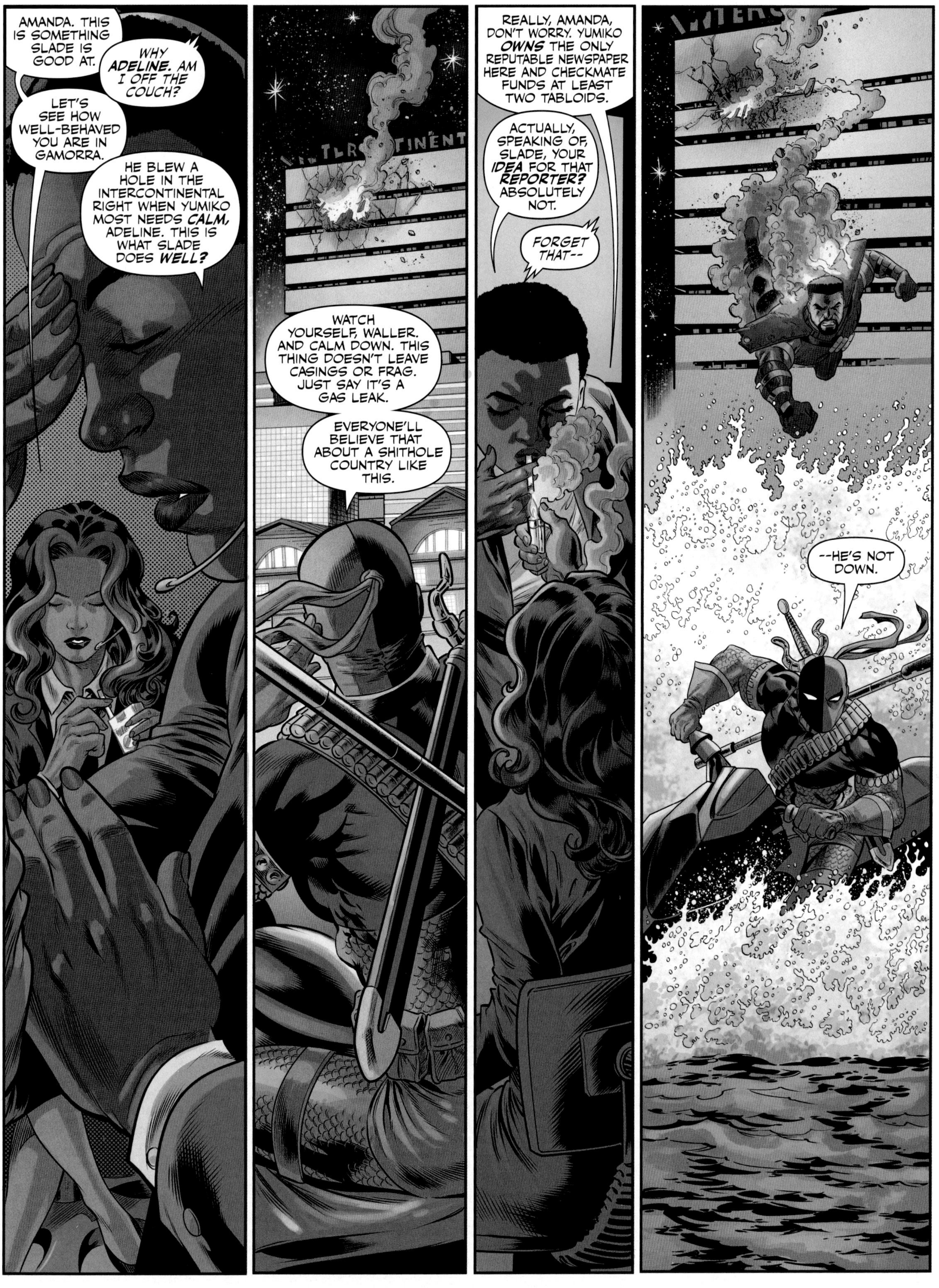
AMANDA. THIS IS SOMETHING SLADE IS GOOD AT.
WHY ADELINE. AM I OFF THE COUCH?
LET'S SEE HOW WELL-BEHAVED YOU ARE IN GAMORRA.
HE BLEW A HOLE IN THE INTERCONTINENTAL RIGHT WHEN YUMIKO MOST NEEDS CALM, ADELINE. THIS IS WHAT SLADE DOES WELL?
WATCH YOURSELF, WALLER. AND CALM DOWN. THIS THING DOESN'T LEAVE CASINGS OR FRAG. JUST SAY IT'S A GAS LEAK.
EVERYONE'LL BELIEVE THAT ABOUT A SHITHOLE COUNTRY LIKE THIS.
REALLY, AMANDA, DON'T WORRY. YUMIKO OWNS THE ONLY REPUTABLE NEWSPAPER HERE AND CHECKMATE FUNDS AT LEAST TWO TABLOIDS.
ACTUALLY, SPEAKING OF, SLADE, YOUR IDEA FOR THAT REPORTER? ABSOLUTELY NOT.
FORGET THAT--
--HE'S NOT DOWN.

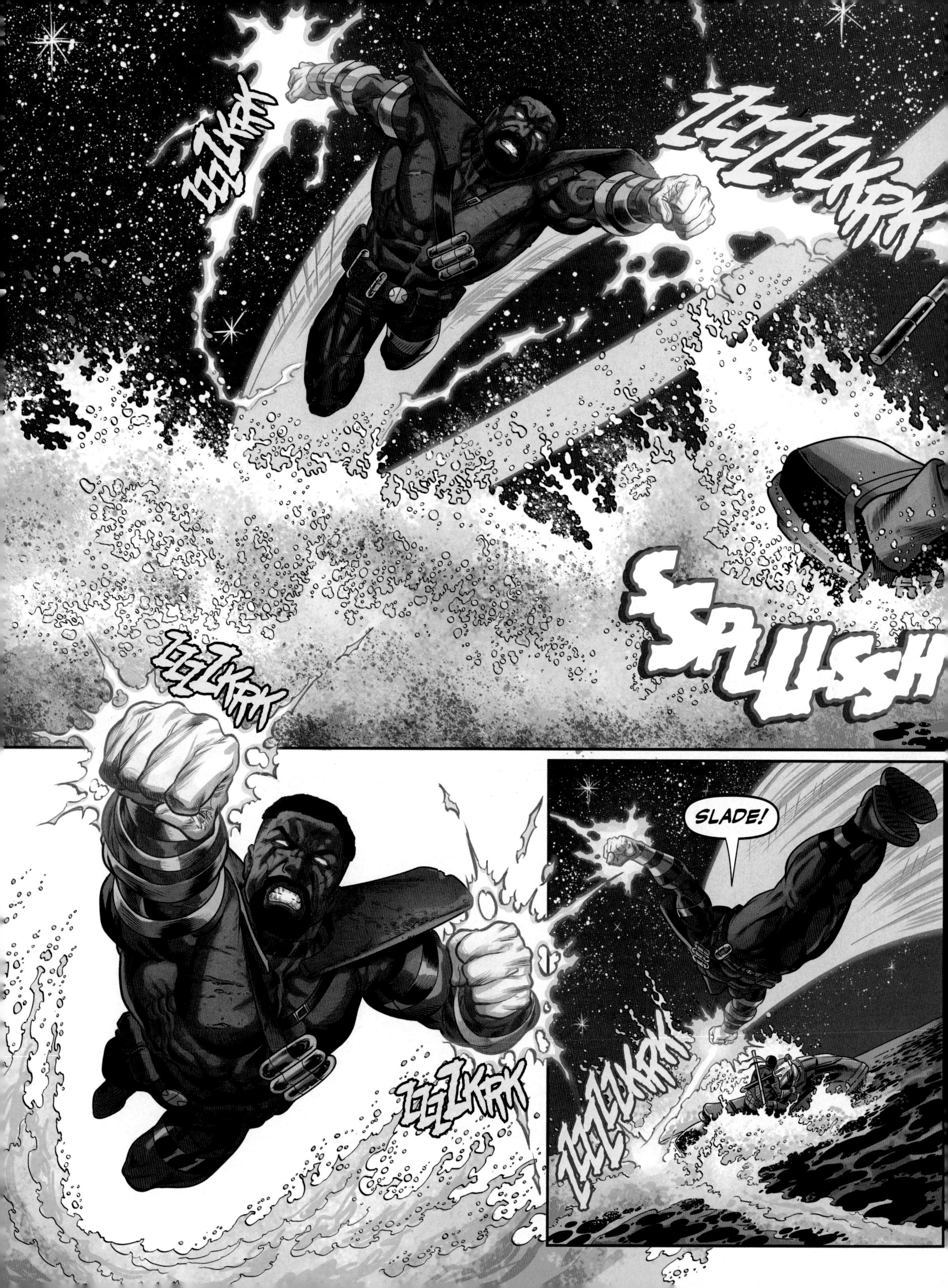
ZZZKRK
ZZZZZKRK
SPLUSH
ZZZKRK
ZZZKRK
SLADE!
ZZZZKRK

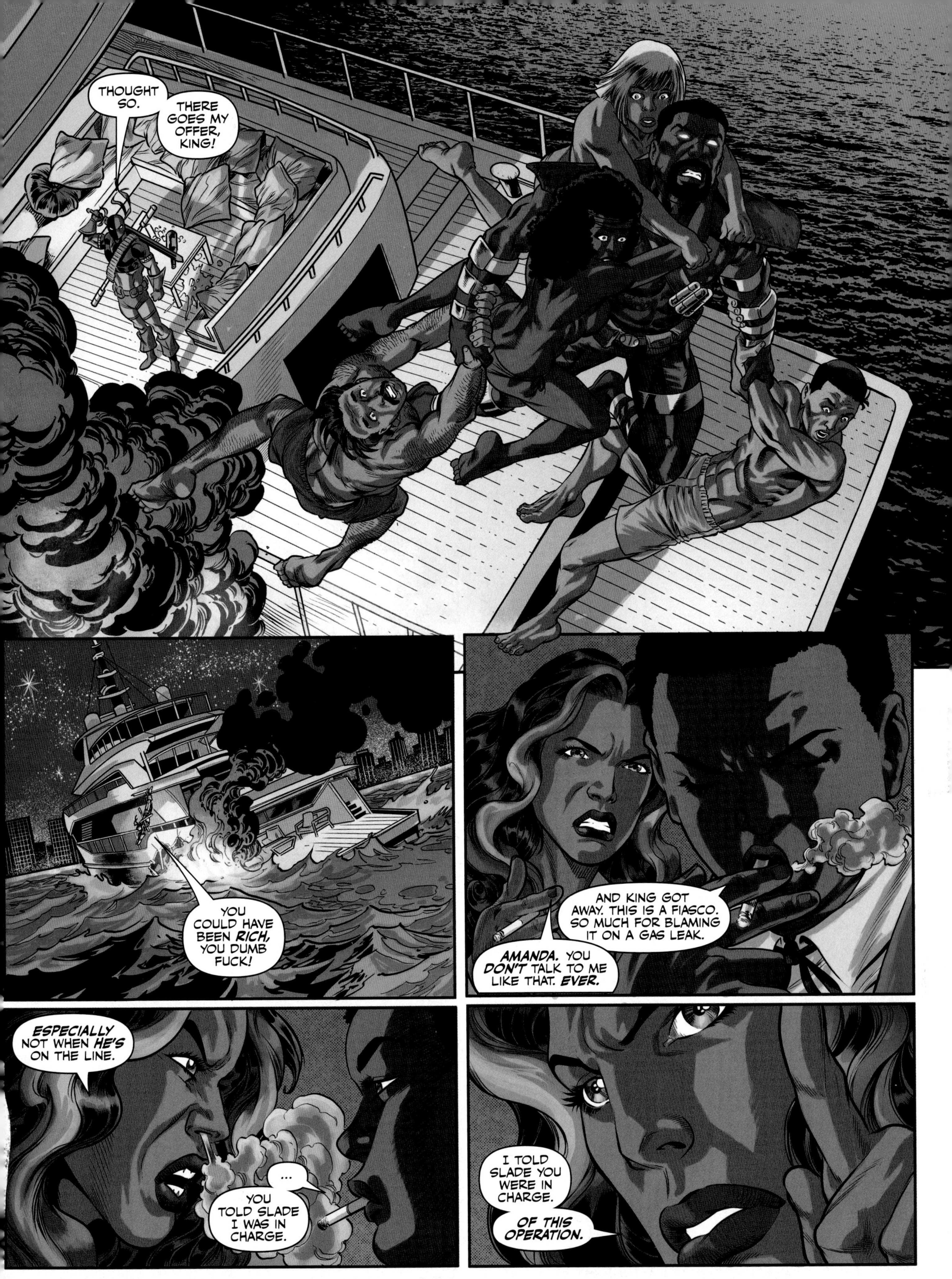
THOUGHT SO.
THERE GOES MY OFFER, KING!
YOU COULD HAVE BEEN RICH, YOU DUMB FUCK!
AND KING GOT AWAY. THIS IS A FIASCO. SO MUCH FOR BLAMING IT ON A GAS LEAK.
AMANDA. YOU DON'T TALK TO ME LIKE THAT. EVER.
ESPECIALLY NOT WHEN HE'S ON THE LINE.
...
YOU TOLD SLADE I WAS IN CHARGE.
I TOLD SLADE YOU WERE IN CHARGE.
OF THIS OPERATION.

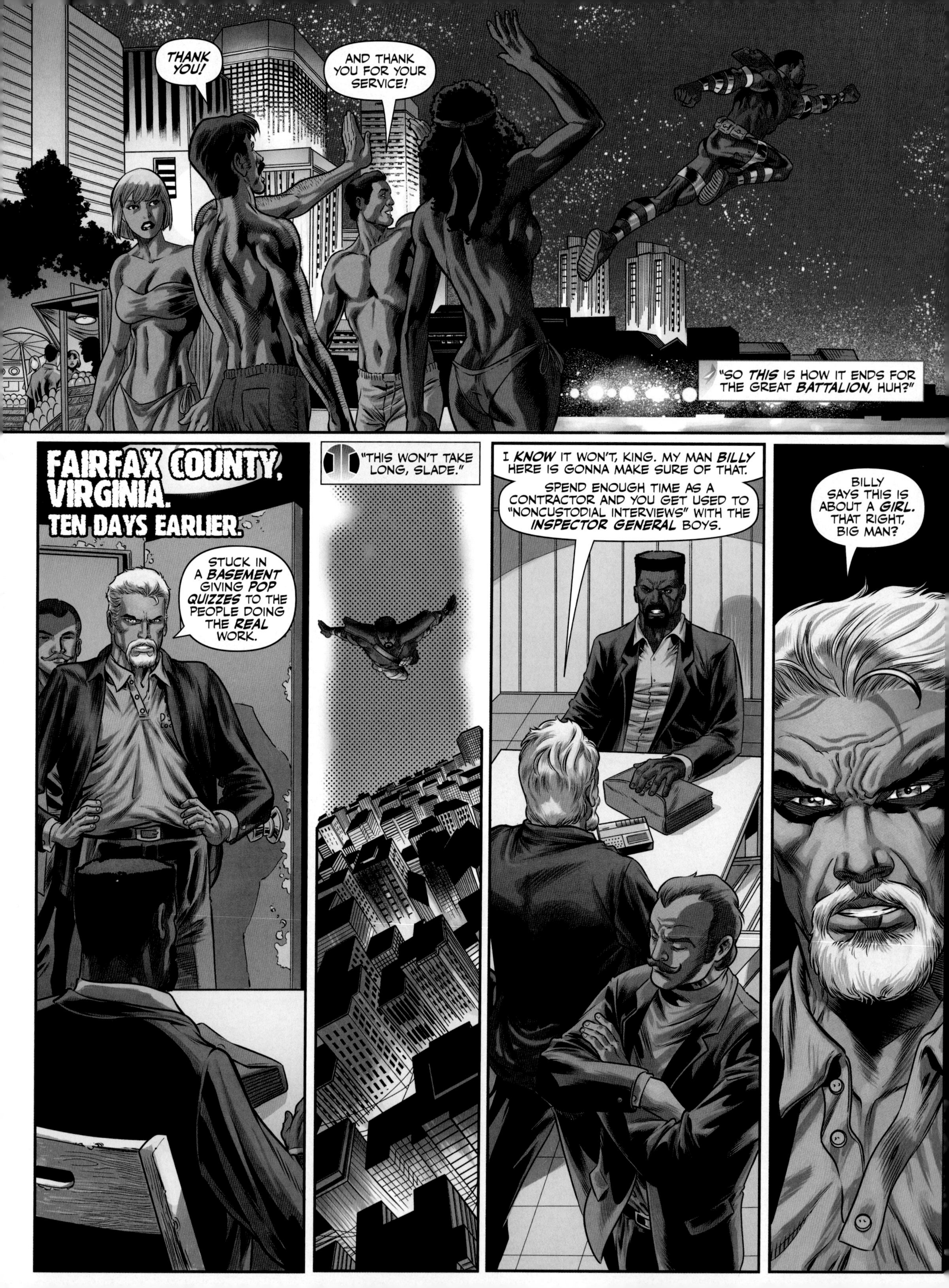
THANK YOU!
AND THANK YOU FOR YOUR SERVICE!
"SO THIS IS HOW IT ENDS FOR THE GREAT BATTALION, HUH?"
FAIRFAX COUNTY, VIRGINIA. TEN DAYS EARLIER.
STUCK IN A BASEMENT GIVING POP QUIZZES TO THE PEOPLE DOING THE REAL WORK.
"THIS WON'T TAKE LONG, SLADE."
I KNOW IT WON'T, KING. MY MAN BILLY HERE IS GONNA MAKE SURE OF THAT.
SPEND ENOUGH TIME AS A CONTRACTOR AND YOU GET USED TO "NONCUSTODIAL INTERVIEWS" WITH THE INSPECTOR GENERAL BOYS.
BILLY SAYS THIS IS ABOUT A GIRL. THAT RIGHT, BIG MAN?

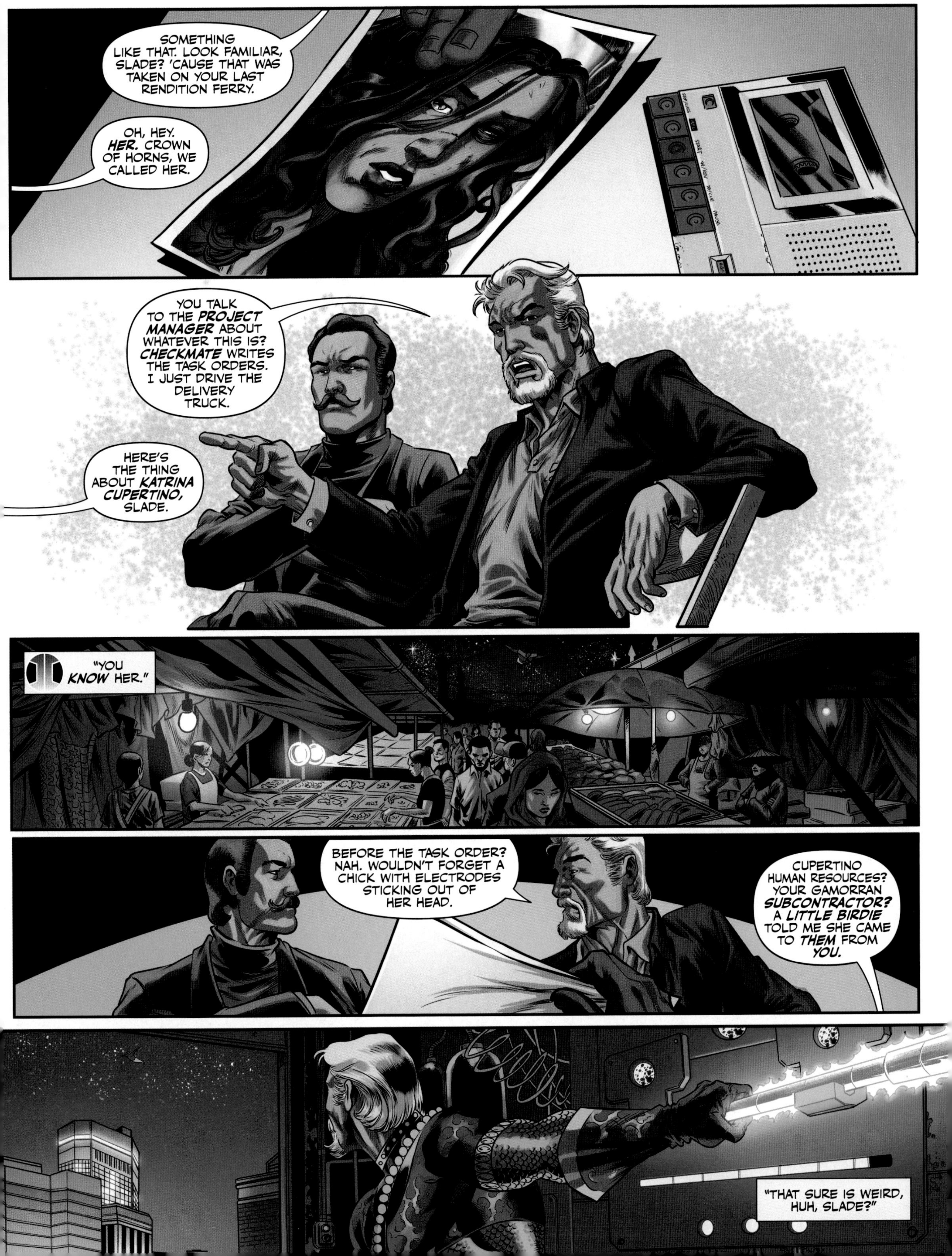
SOMETHING LIKE THAT. LOOK FAMILIAR, SLADE? 'CAUSE THAT WAS TAKEN ON YOUR LAST RENDITION FERRY.
OH, HEY. HER. CROWN OF HORNS, WE CALLED HER.
YOU TALK TO THE PROJECT MANAGER ABOUT WHATEVER THIS IS? CHECKMATE WRITES THE TASK ORDERS. I JUST DRIVE THE DELIVERY TRUCK.
HERE'S THE THING ABOUT KATRINA CUPERTINO, SLADE.
"YOU KNOW HER."
BEFORE THE TASK ORDER? NAH. WOULDN'T FORGET A CHICK WITH ELECTRODES STICKING OUT OF HER HEAD.
CUPERTINO HUMAN RESOURCES? YOUR GAMORRAN SUBCONTRACTOR? A LITTLE BIRDIE TOLD ME SHE CAME TO THEM FROM YOU.
"THAT SURE IS WEIRD, HUH, SLADE?"

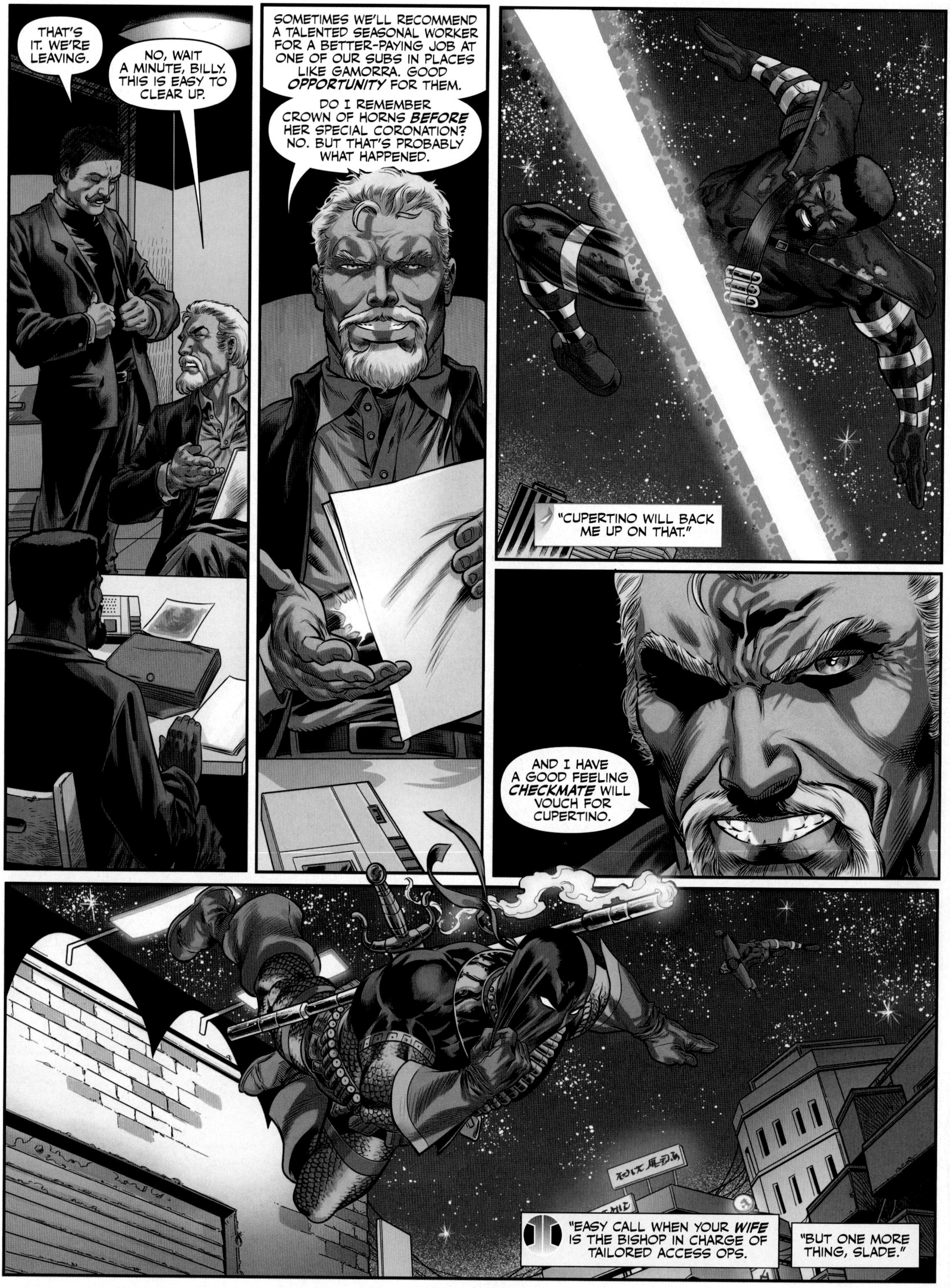
THAT'S IT. WE'RE LEAVING.
NO, WAIT A MINUTE, BILLY. THIS IS EASY TO CLEAR UP.
SOMETIMES WE'LL RECOMMEND A TALENTED SEASONAL WORKER FOR A BETTER-PAYING JOB AT ONE OF OUR SUBS IN PLACES LIKE GAMORRA. GOOD *OPPORTUNITY* FOR THEM.
DO I REMEMBER CROWN OF HORNS *BEFORE* HER SPECIAL CORONATION? NO. BUT THAT'S PROBABLY WHAT HAPPENED.
"CUPERTINO WILL BACK ME UP ON THAT."
AND I HAVE A GOOD FEELING ***CHECKMATE*** WILL VOUCH FOR CUPERTINO.
"EASY CALL WHEN YOUR *WIFE* IS THE BISHOP IN CHARGE OF TAILORED ACCESS OPS.
"BUT ONE MORE THING, SLADE."

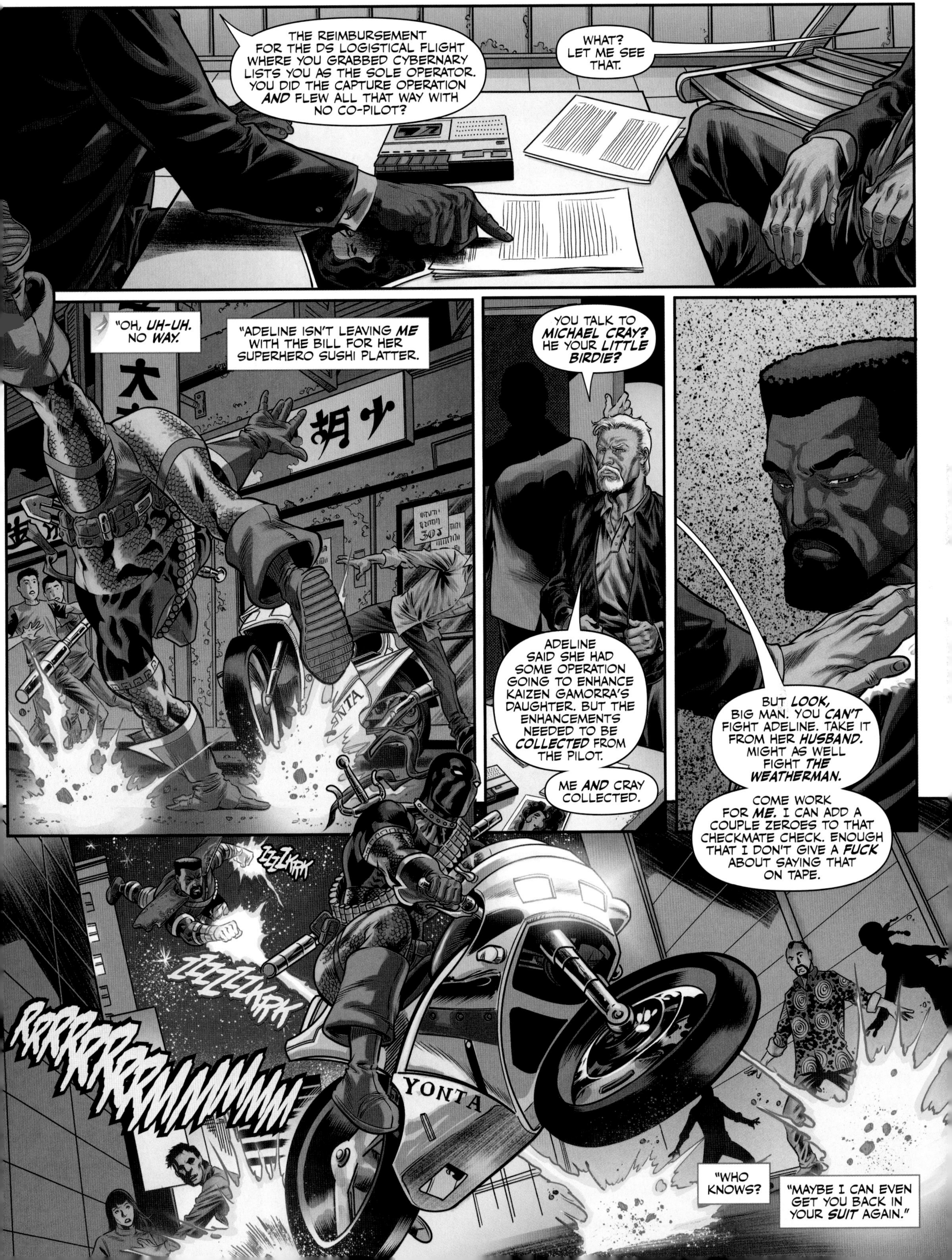
THE REIMBURSEMENT FOR THE DS LOGISTICAL FLIGHT WHERE YOU GRABBED CYBERNARY LISTS YOU AS THE SOLE OPERATOR. YOU DID THE CAPTURE OPERATION *AND* FLEW ALL THAT WAY WITH NO CO-PILOT?
WHAT? LET ME SEE THAT.
"OH, *UH-UH.* NO *WAY.*
"ADELINE ISN'T LEAVING *ME* WITH THE BILL FOR HER SUPERHERO SUSHI PLATTER.
YOU TALK TO *MICHAEL CRAY?* HE YOUR *LITTLE BIRDIE?*
ADELINE SAID SHE HAD SOME OPERATION GOING TO ENHANCE KAIZEN GAMORRA'S DAUGHTER. BUT THE ENHANCEMENTS NEEDED TO BE *COLLECTED* FROM THE PILOT.
ME *AND* CRAY COLLECTED.
BUT *LOOK,* BIG MAN. YOU *CAN'T* FIGHT ADELINE. TAKE IT FROM HER *HUSBAND.* MIGHT AS WELL FIGHT *THE WEATHERMAN.*
COME WORK FOR *ME.* I CAN ADD A COUPLE ZEROES TO THAT CHECKMATE CHECK. ENOUGH THAT I DON'T GIVE A *FUCK* ABOUT SAYING THAT ON TAPE.
ZZZZKRK
ZZZZZZZKRK
RRRRRRRRMMMMMM
YONTA
"WHO KNOWS?
"MAYBE I CAN EVEN GET YOU BACK IN YOUR *SUIT* AGAIN."

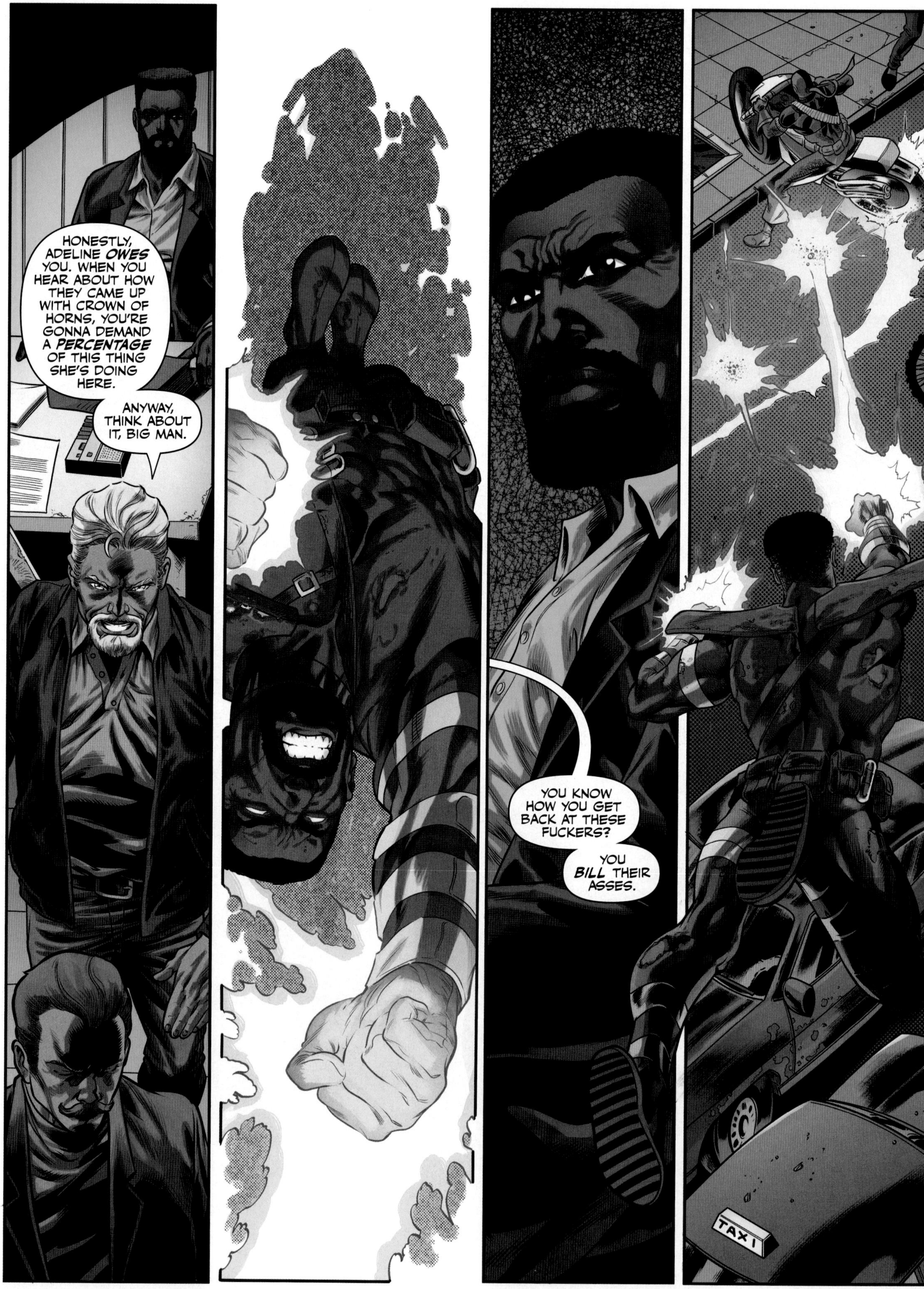
HONESTLY, ADELINE OWES YOU. WHEN YOU HEAR ABOUT HOW THEY CAME UP WITH CROWN OF HORNS, YOU'RE GONNA DEMAND A PERCENTAGE OF THIS THING SHE'S DOING HERE.
ANYWAY, THINK ABOUT IT, BIG MAN.
YOU KNOW HOW YOU GET BACK AT THESE FUCKERS?
YOU BILL THEIR ASSES.
TAXI

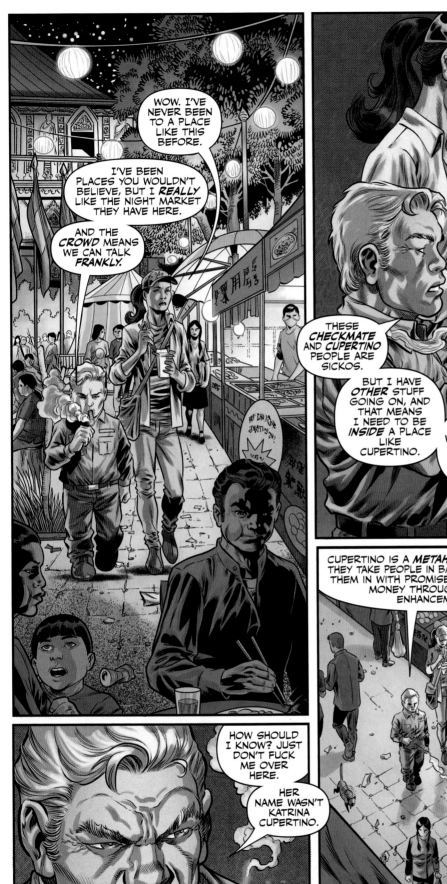

WOW. I'VE NEVER BEEN TO A PLACE LIKE THIS BEFORE.

I'VE BEEN PLACES YOU WOULDN'T BELIEVE, BUT I *REALLY* LIKE THE NIGHT MARKET THEY HAVE HERE.

AND THE *CROWD* MEANS WE CAN TALK *FRANKLY.*

HOW SHOULD I KNOW? JUST DON'T FUCK ME OVER HERE.

HER NAME WASN'T KATRINA CUPERTINO.

THESE *CHECKMATE* AND *CUPERTINO* PEOPLE ARE SICKOS.

BUT I HAVE *OTHER* STUFF GOING ON, AND THAT MEANS I NEED TO BE *INSIDE* A PLACE LIKE CUPERTINO.

AND THAT MEANS *YOU* CAN'T WRITE YOUR *STORY* IN A WAY THAT SUGGESTS YOU HAVE A GUY ON THE INSIDE.

THIS IS THE GREATEST THING I'VE EVER TASTED. OH MY GOD.

THAT'S NO PROBLEM, MR. MARLOWE. WE USUALLY PUT IT LIKE, "ACCORDING TO A SOURCE FAMILIAR." DOES THAT WORK?

CUPERTINO IS A *METAHUMAN CHOP SHOP.* THEY TAKE PEOPLE IN BAD SITUATIONS. LURE THEM IN WITH PROMISES OF MAKING FAST MONEY THROUGH GETTING ENHANCEMENTS.

CUPERTINO'S ALSO A PROVING GROUND FOR *HUMAN WEAPONS.*

THEY CATALOGUE DIFFERENT POWER SETS ALPHABETICALLY AND *MARKET* THEM TO VARIOUS *UNSAVORY* CHARACTERS.

THE WOMAN IN YOUR PICTURE IS NAMED *IVANA BAIUL.*

KATRINA CUPERTINO IS A *CATEGORY.* A *PROPRIETARY TECHNOLOGY.*

THE *CYBERNARY* ENHANCEMENT.

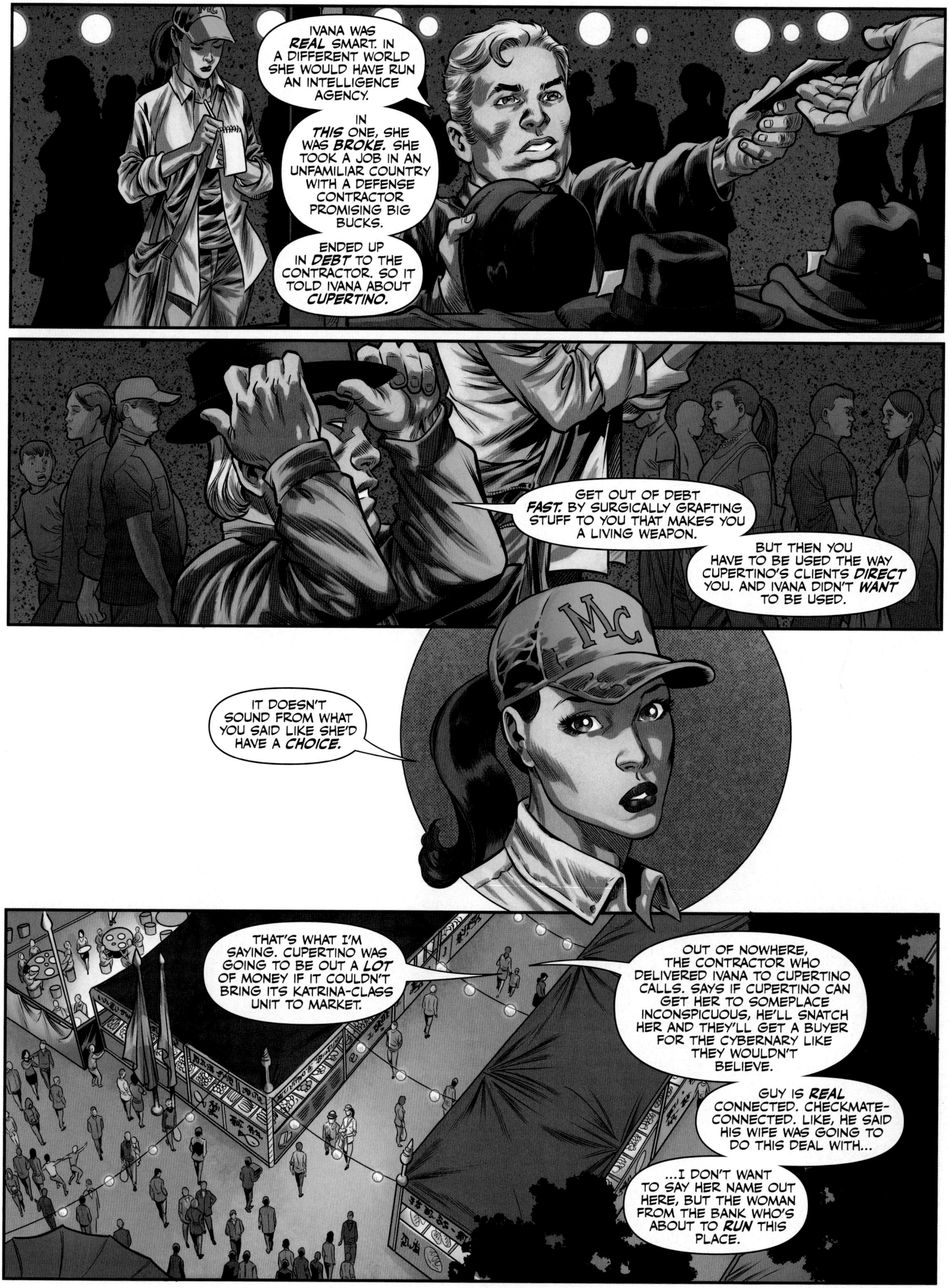
IVANA WAS REAL SMART. IN A DIFFERENT WORLD SHE WOULD HAVE RUN AN INTELLIGENCE AGENCY.
IN THIS ONE, SHE WAS BROKE. SHE TOOK A JOB IN AN UNFAMILIAR COUNTRY WITH A DEFENSE CONTRACTOR PROMISING BIG BUCKS.
ENDED UP IN DEBT TO THE CONTRACTOR. SO IT TOLD IVANA ABOUT CUPERTINO.
GET OUT OF DEBT FAST. BY SURGICALLY GRAFTING STUFF TO YOU THAT MAKES YOU A LIVING WEAPON.
BUT THEN YOU HAVE TO BE USED THE WAY CUPERTINO'S CLIENTS DIRECT YOU. AND IVANA DIDN'T WANT TO BE USED.
IT DOESN'T SOUND FROM WHAT YOU SAID LIKE SHE'D HAVE A CHOICE.
THAT'S WHAT I'M SAYING. CUPERTINO WAS GOING TO BE OUT A LOT OF MONEY IF IT COULDN'T BRING ITS KATRINA-CLASS UNIT TO MARKET.
OUT OF NOWHERE, THE CONTRACTOR WHO DELIVERED IVANA TO CUPERTINO CALLS. SAYS IF CUPERTINO CAN GET HER TO SOMEPLACE INCONSPICUOUS, HE'LL SNATCH HER AND THEY'LL GET A BUYER FOR THE CYBERNARY LIKE THEY WOULDN'T BELIEVE.
GUY IS REAL CONNECTED. CHECKMATE-CONNECTED. LIKE, HE SAID HIS WIFE WAS GOING TO DO THIS DEAL WITH...
...I DON'T WANT TO SAY HER NAME OUT HERE, BUT THE WOMAN FROM THE BANK WHO'S ABOUT TO RUN THIS PLACE.

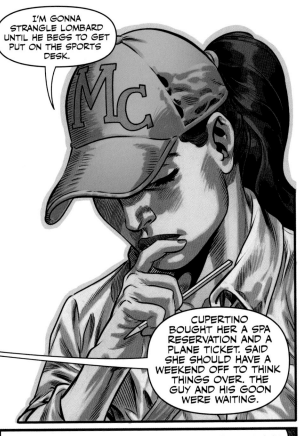

I'M GONNA STRANGLE LOMBARD UNTIL HE BEGS TO GET PUT ON THE SPORTS DESK.

CUPERTINO BOUGHT HER A SPA RESERVATION AND A PLANE TICKET. SAID SHE SHOULD HAVE A WEEKEND OFF TO THINK THINGS OVER. THE GUY AND HIS GOON WERE WAITING.

THAT'S ALL I KNOW.

IT'S A *TON*, AND THANK YOU SO MUCH. BUT I HAVE TO ASK HOW YOU *KNOW* ALL THIS. YOU'RE A *JANITOR*?

LIKE I SAID, I HAVE MY OWN THING GOING. IT MEANS I HAVE TO KEEP AN EYE ON WHAT'S SHAPING UP TO BE A METAHUMAN ARMS TRADE. *QUIETLY.*

YOU PAY MUCH ATTENTION TO THE GUY WHO EMPTIES *YOUR* TRASH AT THE *DAILY PLANET,* MS. LANE?

NO, LOOK, THAT'S FAIR. THIS IS...ASTONISHINGLY SPECIFIC. SO I *HAVE* TO ASK YOU HOW YOU'D KNOW ALL THIS.

BEFORE I GO, HERE'S SOMETHING *ELSE* YOU MIGHT NOT THINK A JANITOR WOULD KNOW.

THIS WHOLE SCHEME IS THE KIND OF SHIT THAT GETS YOU MADE *WEATHERMAN.* IF YOU CAN PULL IT OFF.

DON'T PUT MY NAME IN THE PAPER, LOIS.

RRRRRRRMMMMM

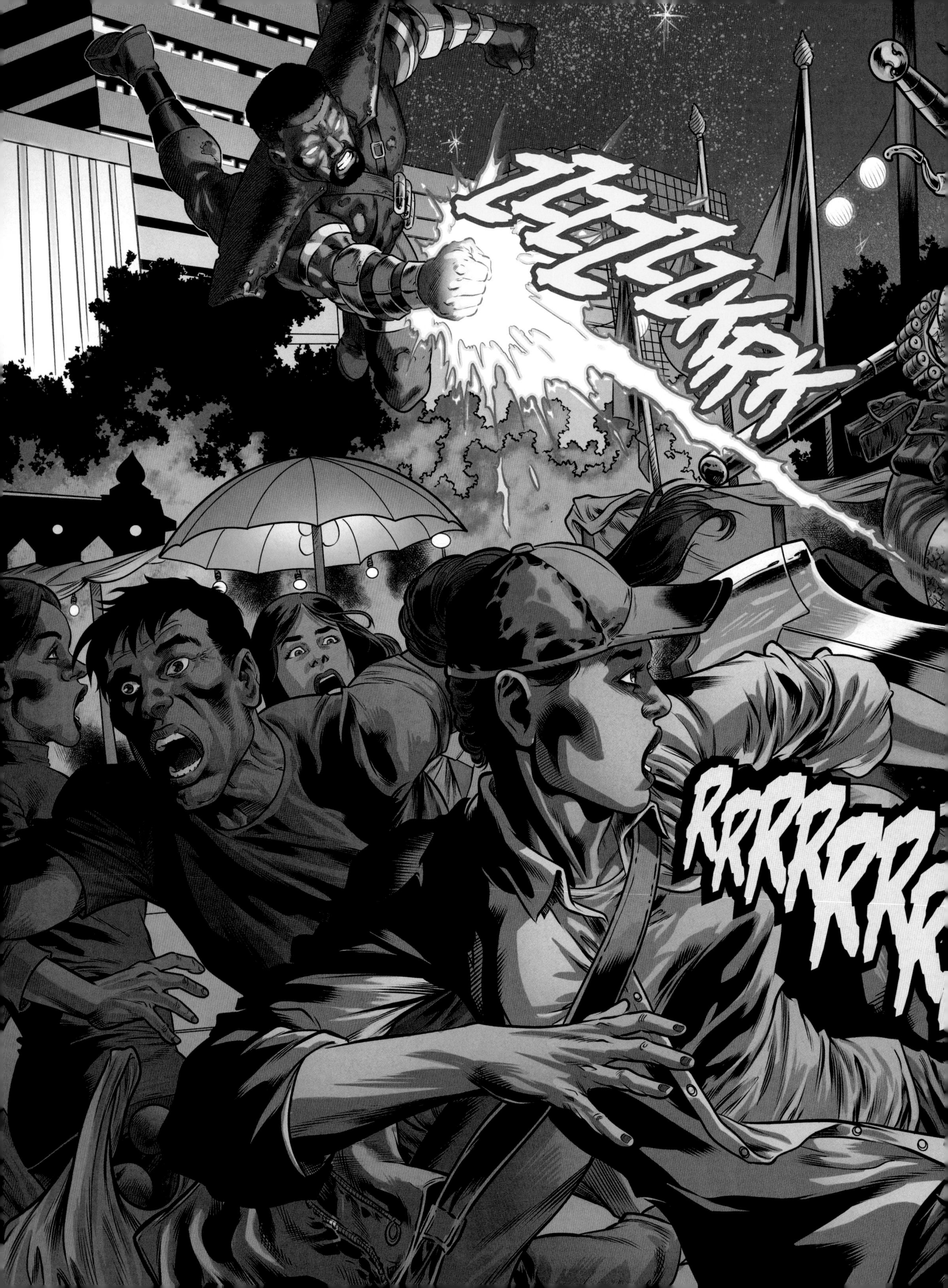

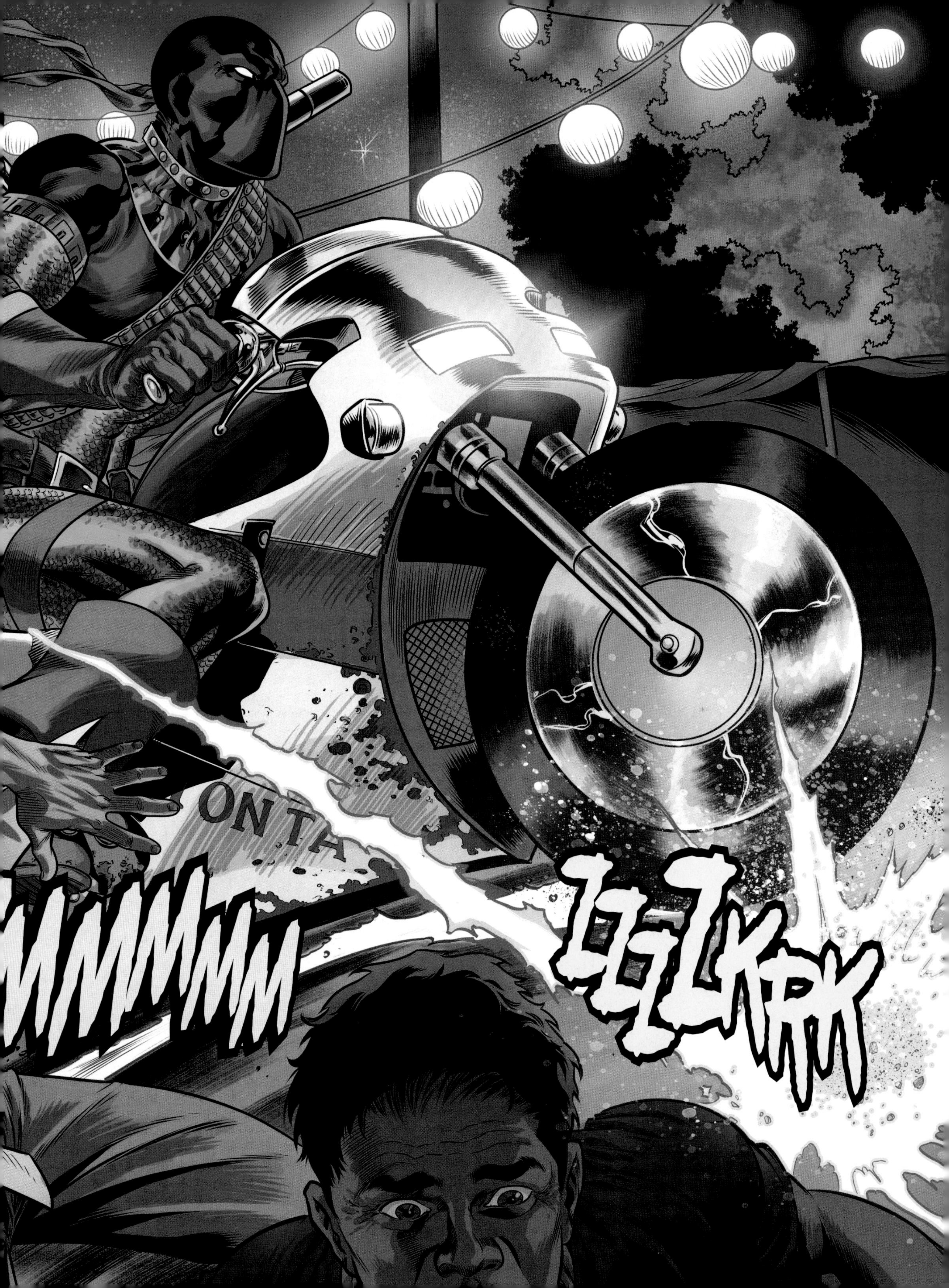
ON TA
MMMMMMM
ZZZKRRK

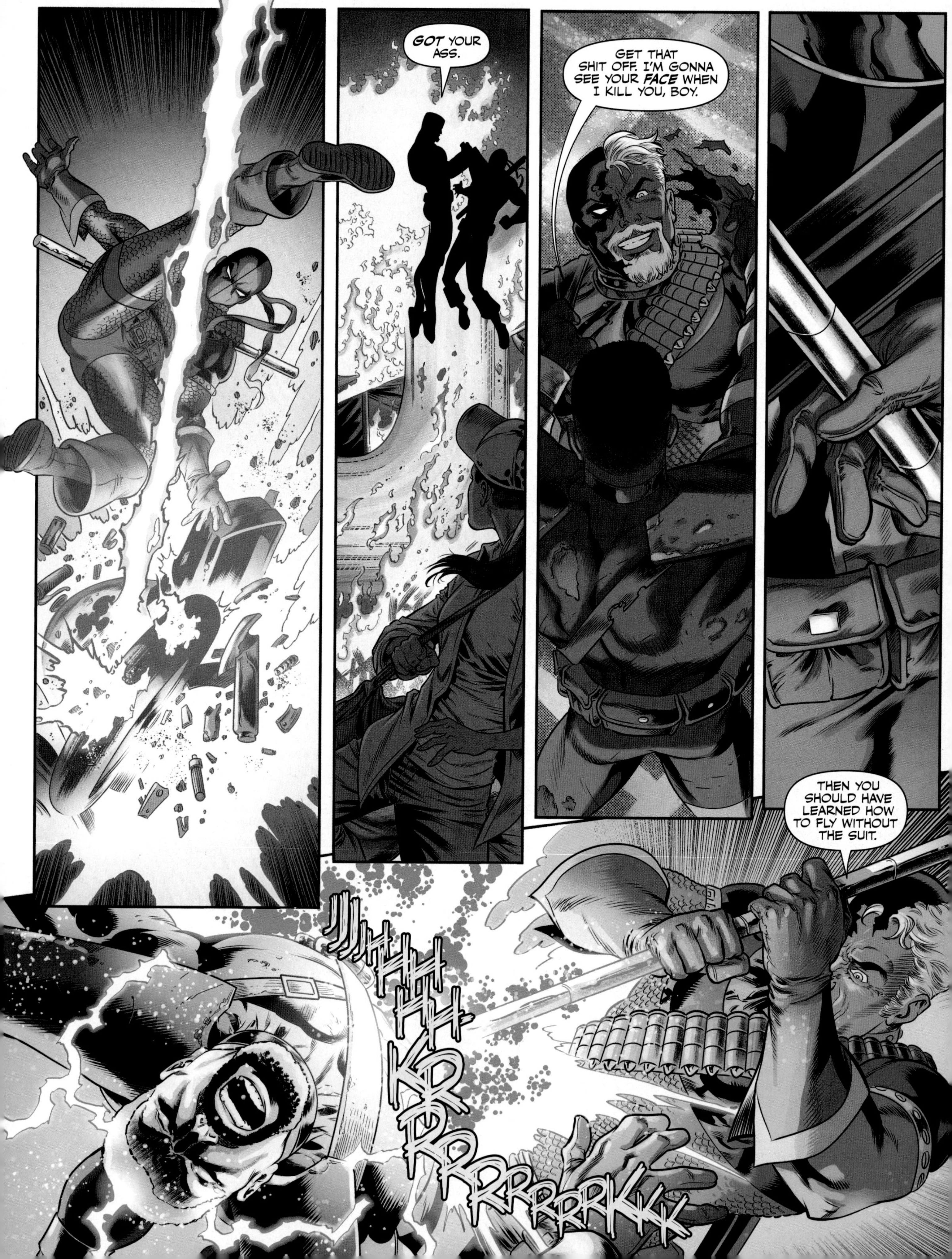
GOT YOUR ASS.
GET THAT SHIT OFF. I'M GONNA SEE YOUR FACE WHEN I KILL YOU, BOY.
THEN YOU SHOULD HAVE LEARNED HOW TO FLY WITHOUT THE SUIT.
JJHHHHHHKRKRKRRRRRRKKK

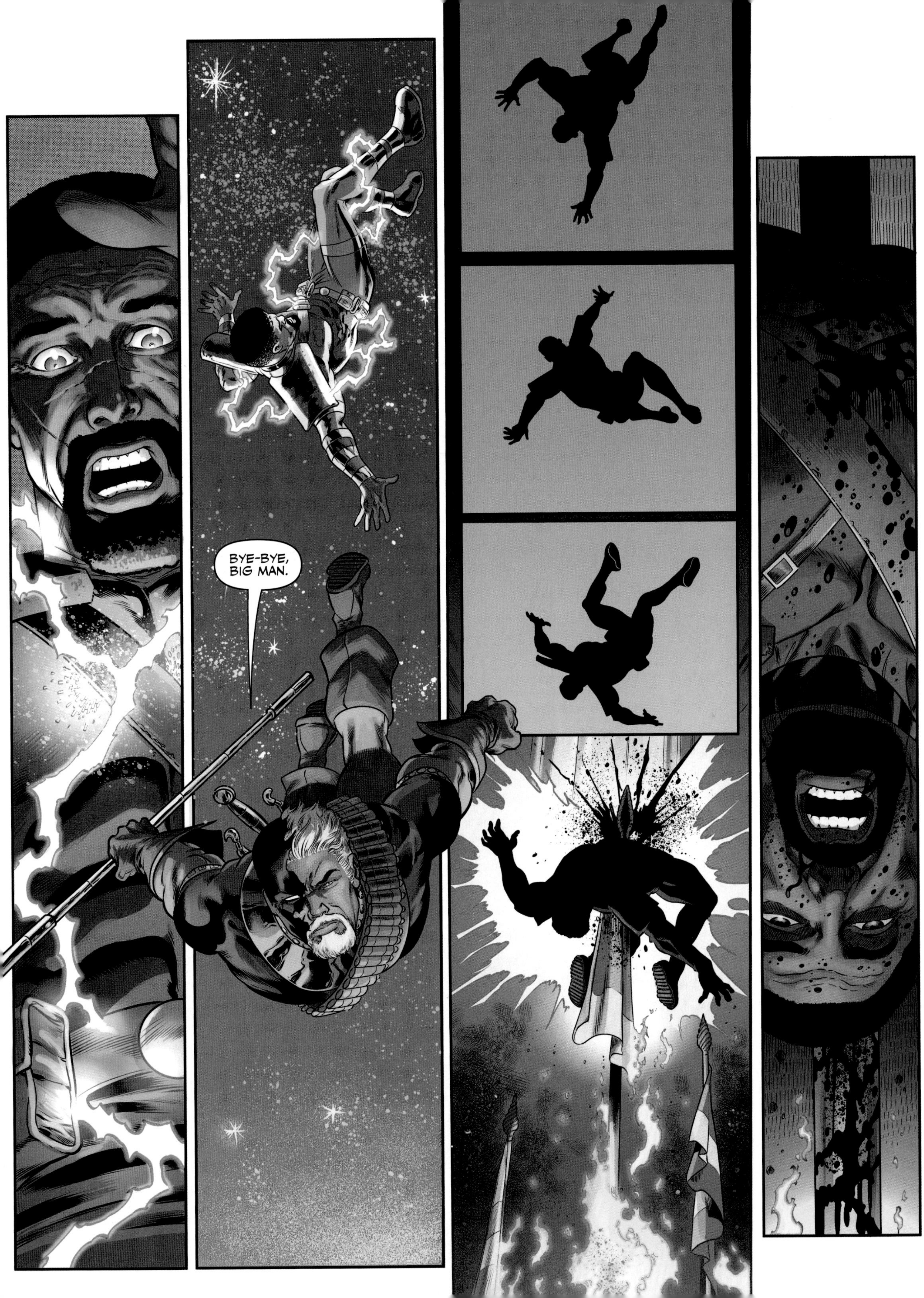
BYE-BYE, BIG MAN.

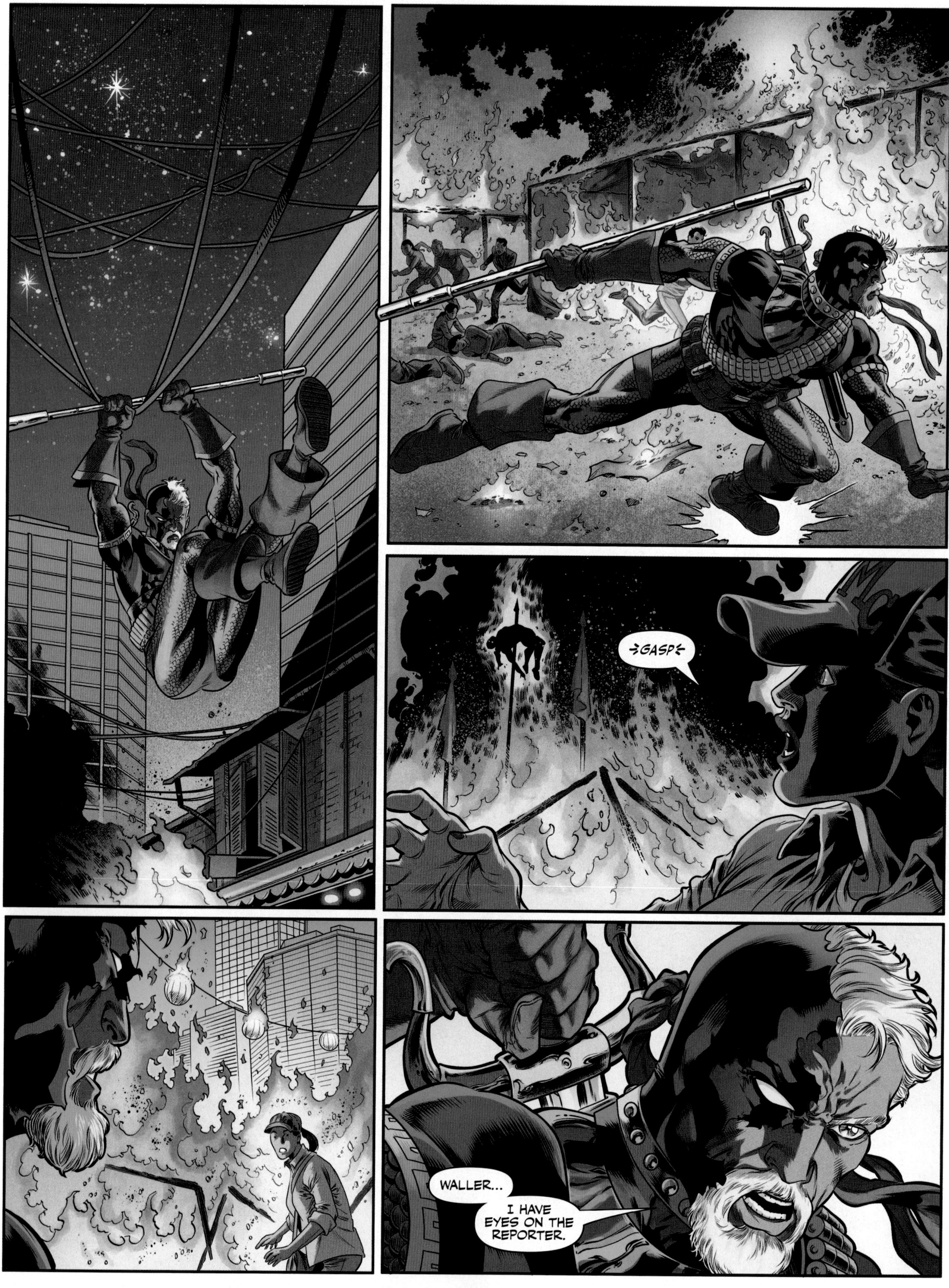
GASP
WALLER...
I HAVE EYES ON THE REPORTER.

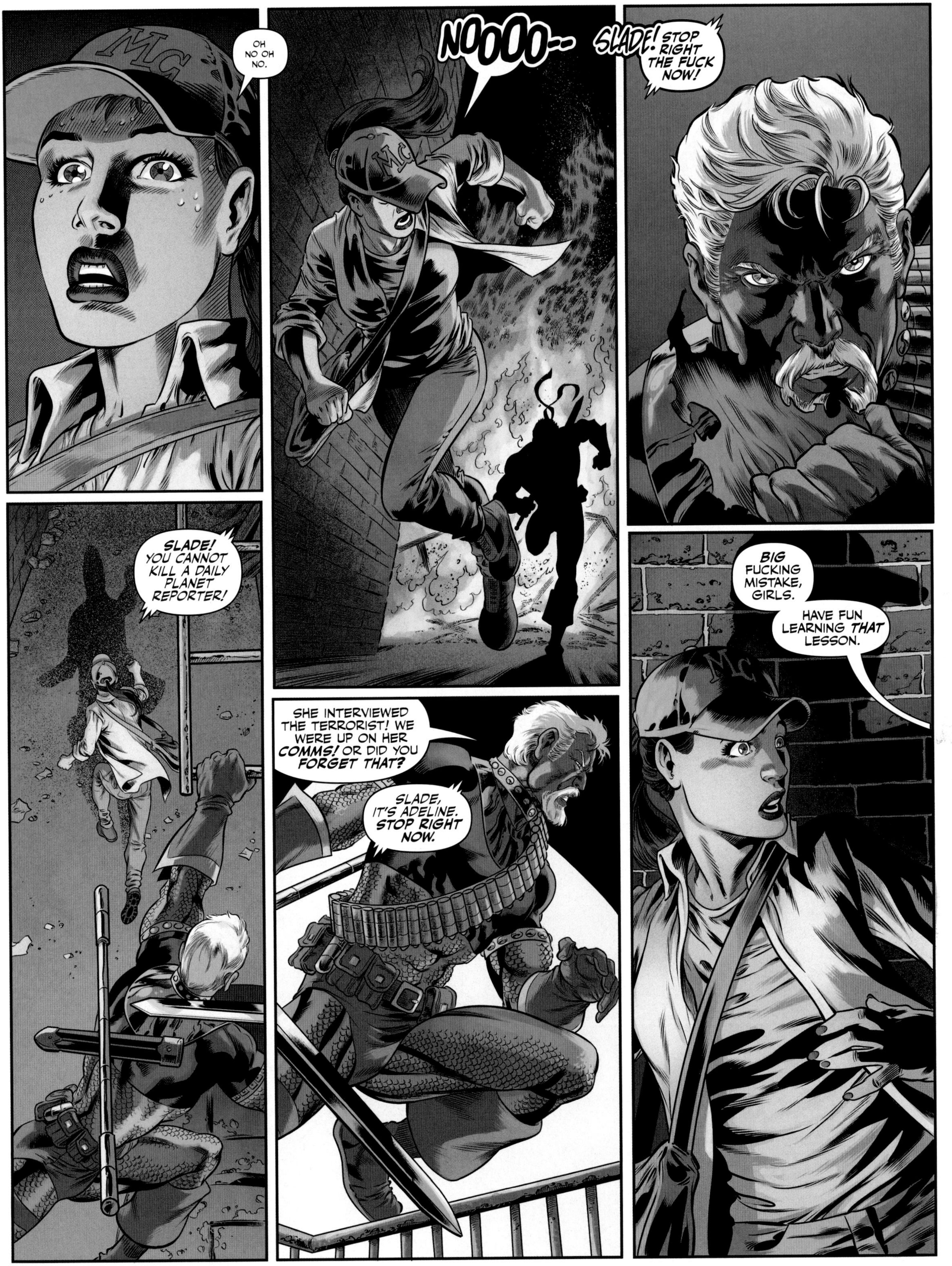
OH NO OH NO.
NOOOO--
SLADE! STOP RIGHT THE FUCK NOW!
SLADE! YOU CANNOT KILL A DAILY PLANET REPORTER!
SHE INTERVIEWED THE TERRORIST! WE WERE UP ON HER COMMS! OR DID YOU FORGET THAT?
SLADE, IT'S ADELINE. STOP RIGHT NOW.
BIG FUCKING MISTAKE, GIRLS.
HAVE FUN LEARNING THAT LESSON.

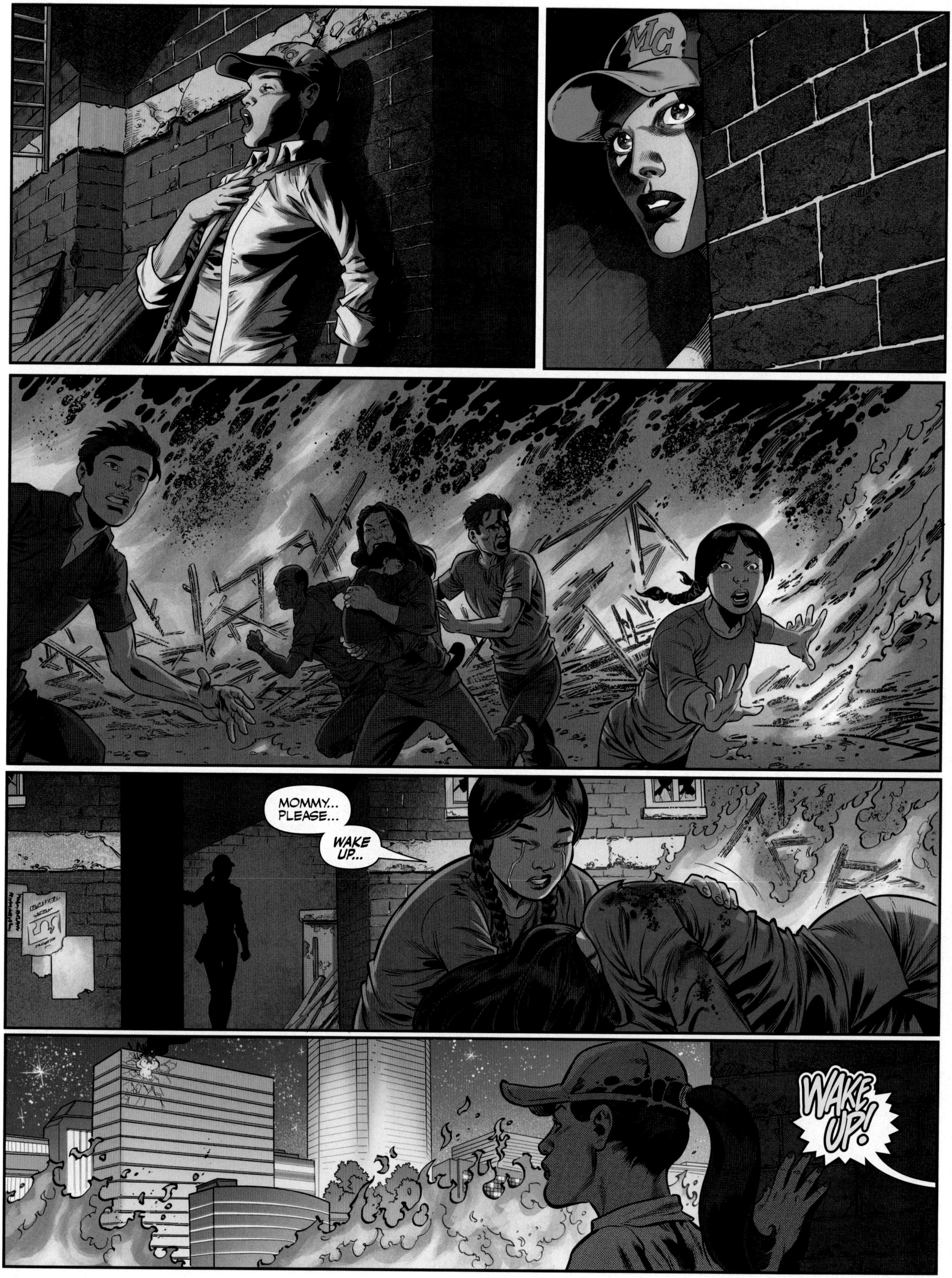

MOMMY... PLEASE...
WAKE UP...
WAKE UP!

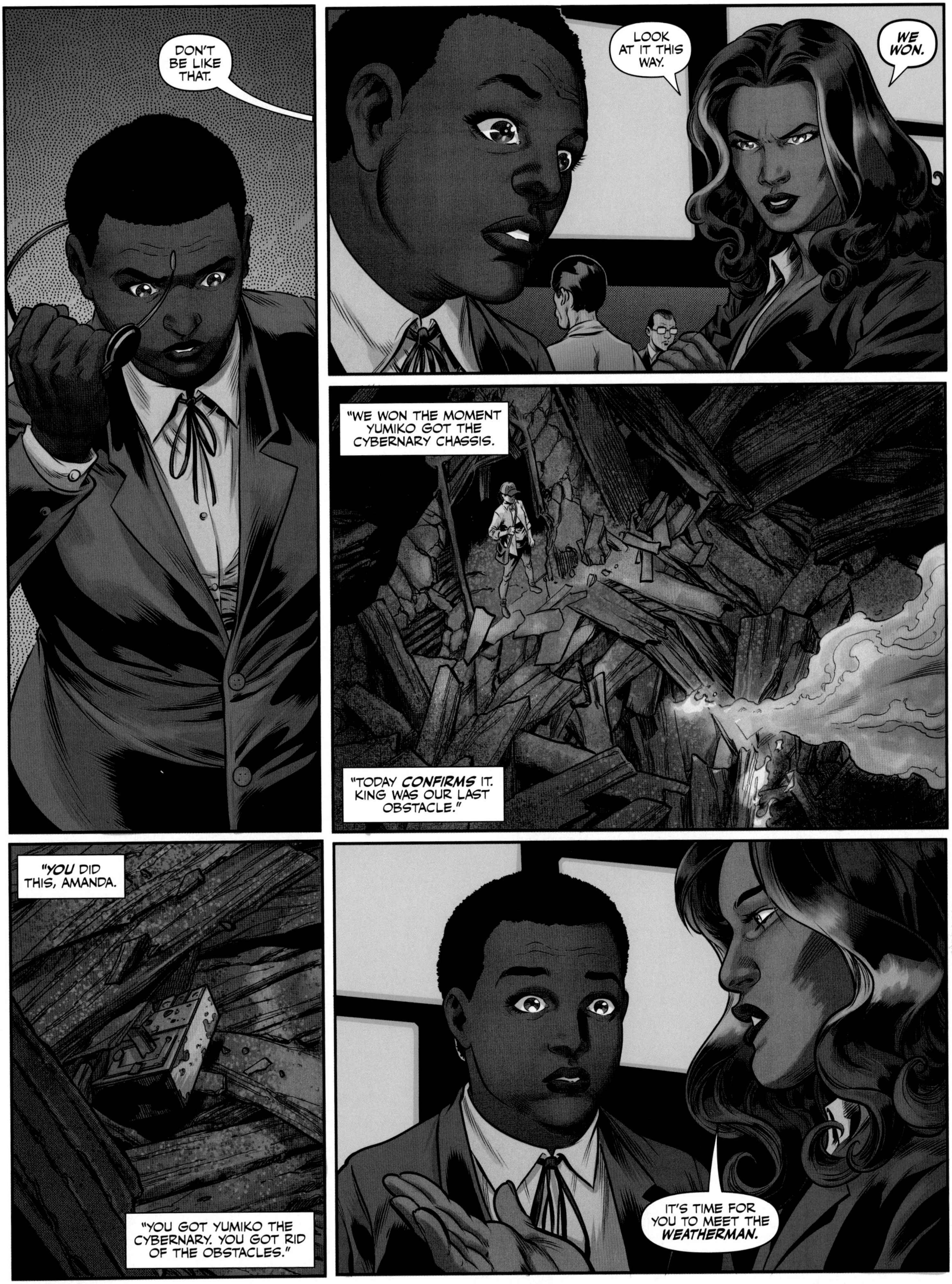
DON'T BE LIKE THAT.
LOOK AT IT THIS WAY.
WE WON.
"WE WON THE MOMENT YUMIKO GOT THE CYBERNARY CHASSIS.
"TODAY CONFIRMS IT. KING WAS OUR LAST OBSTACLE."
"YOU DID THIS, AMANDA.
"YOU GOT YUMIKO THE CYBERNARY. YOU GOT RID OF THE OBSTACLES."
IT'S TIME FOR YOU TO MEET THE WEATHERMAN.

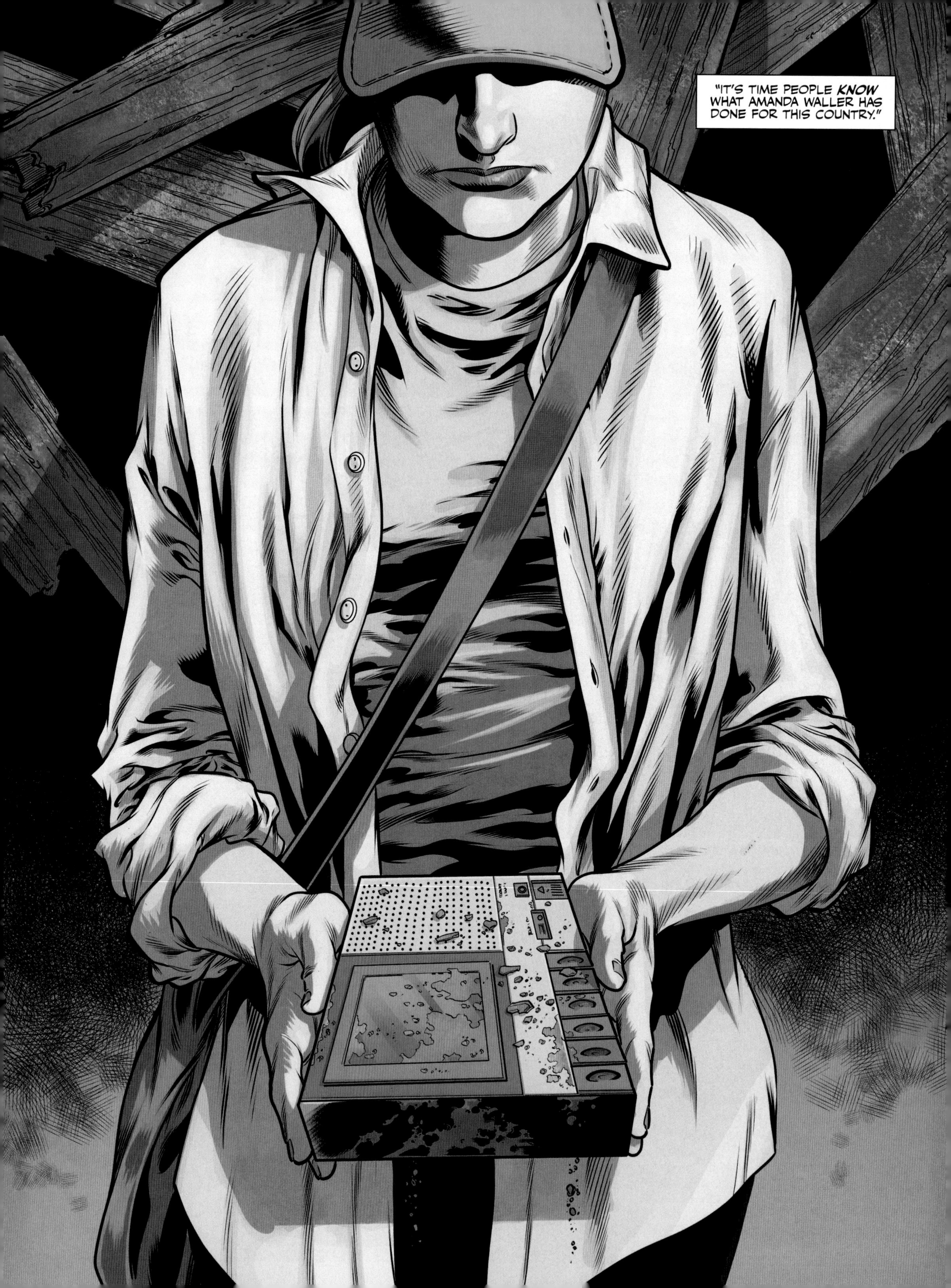
"IT'S TIME PEOPLE KNOW WHAT AMANDA WALLER HAS DONE FOR THIS COUNTRY."

FINAL EXPLOSIVE ISSUE

"Chilling and plausible." —METAHUMAN POLICY REVIEW

Waller vs. Wildstorm

Book Four

★ ★ ★ ★ ★

ACKERMAN - NARCISSE - MERINO - CIFUENTES - ATIYEH

"...Gamorra was MY operation."

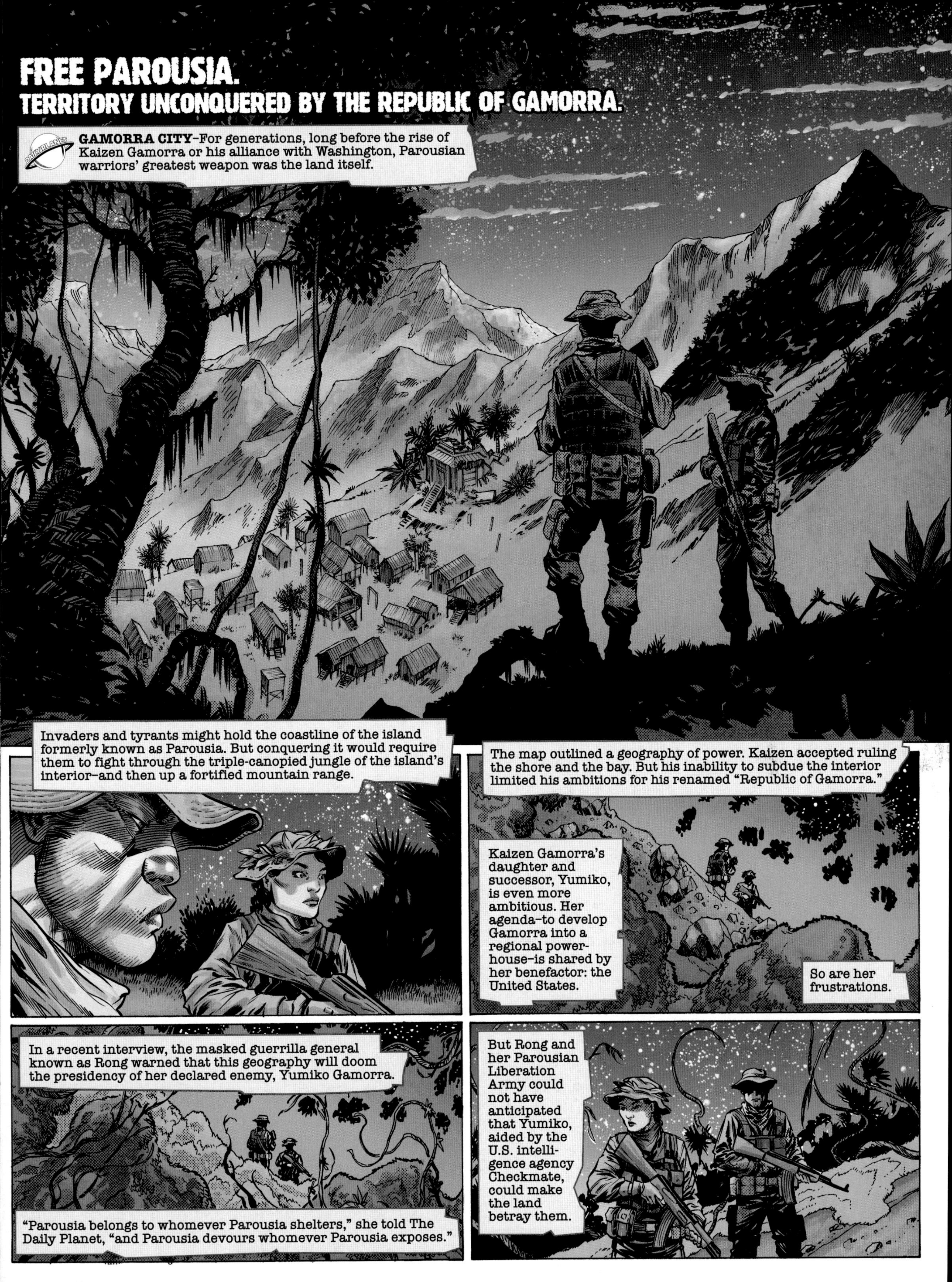
FREE PAROUSIA.
TERRITORY UNCONQUERED BY THE REPUBLIC OF GAMORRA.
DAILY PLANET
GAMORRA CITY–For generations, long before the rise of Kaizen Gamorra or his alliance with Washington, Parousian warriors' greatest weapon was the land itself.
Invaders and tyrants might hold the coastline of the island formerly known as Parousia. But conquering it would require them to fight through the triple-canopied jungle of the island's interior–and then up a fortified mountain range.
The map outlined a geography of power. Kaizen accepted ruling the shore and the bay. But his inability to subdue the interior limited his ambitions for his renamed "Republic of Gamorra."
Kaizen Gamorra's daughter and successor, Yumiko, is even more ambitious. Her agenda–to develop Gamorra into a regional power-house–is shared by her benefactor: the United States.
So are her frustrations.
In a recent interview, the masked guerrilla general known as Rong warned that this geography will doom the presidency of her declared enemy, Yumiko Gamorra.
"Parousia belongs to whomever Parousia shelters," she told The Daily Planet, "and Parousia devours whomever Parousia exposes."
But Rong and her Parousian Liberation Army could not have anticipated that Yumiko, aided by the U.S. intelli-gence agency Checkmate, could make the land betray them.

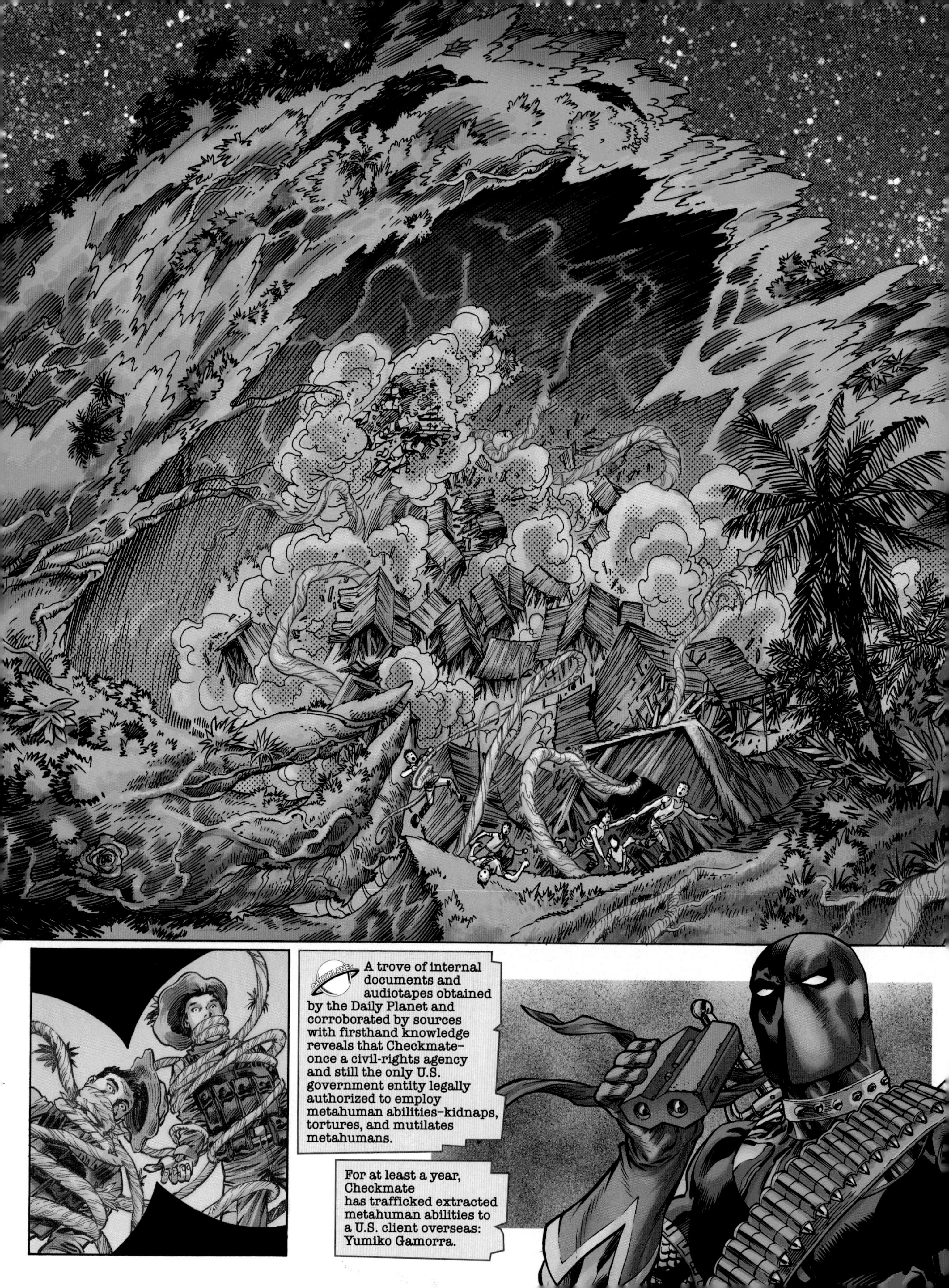
A trove of internal documents and audiotapes obtained by the Daily Planet and corroborated by sources with firsthand knowledge reveals that Checkmate–once a civil-rights agency and still the only U.S. government entity legally authorized to employ metahuman abilities–kidnaps, tortures, and mutilates metahumans.
For at least a year, Checkmate has trafficked extracted metahuman abilities to a U.S. client overseas: Yumiko Gamorra.

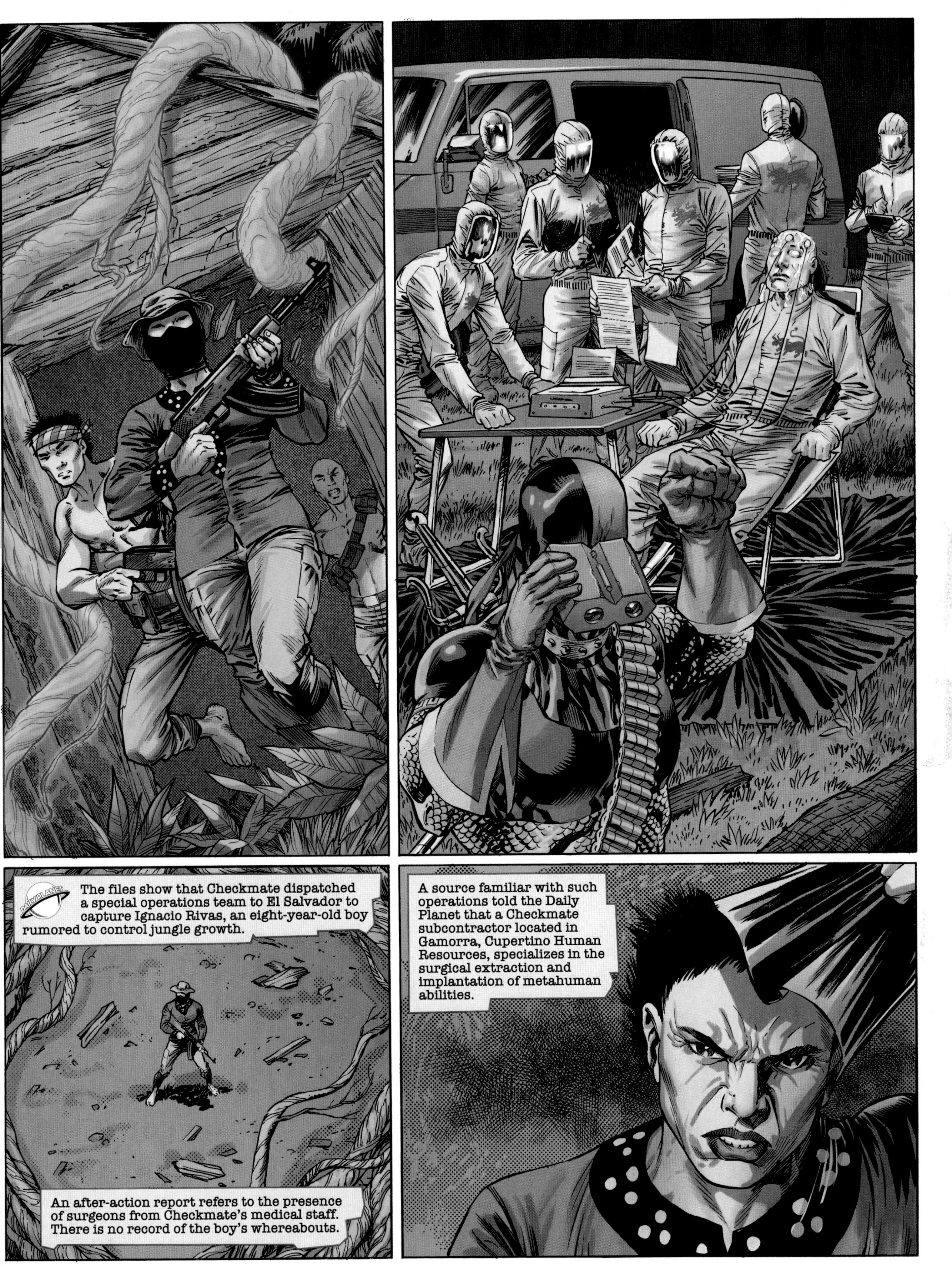
The files show that Checkmate dispatched a special operations team to El Salvador to capture Ignacio Rivas, an eight-year-old boy rumored to control jungle growth.
An after-action report refers to the presence of surgeons from Checkmate's medical staff. There is no record of the boy's whereabouts.
A source familiar with such operations told the Daily Planet that a Checkmate subcontractor located in Gamorra, Cupertino Human Resources, specializes in the surgical extraction and implantation of metahuman abilities.

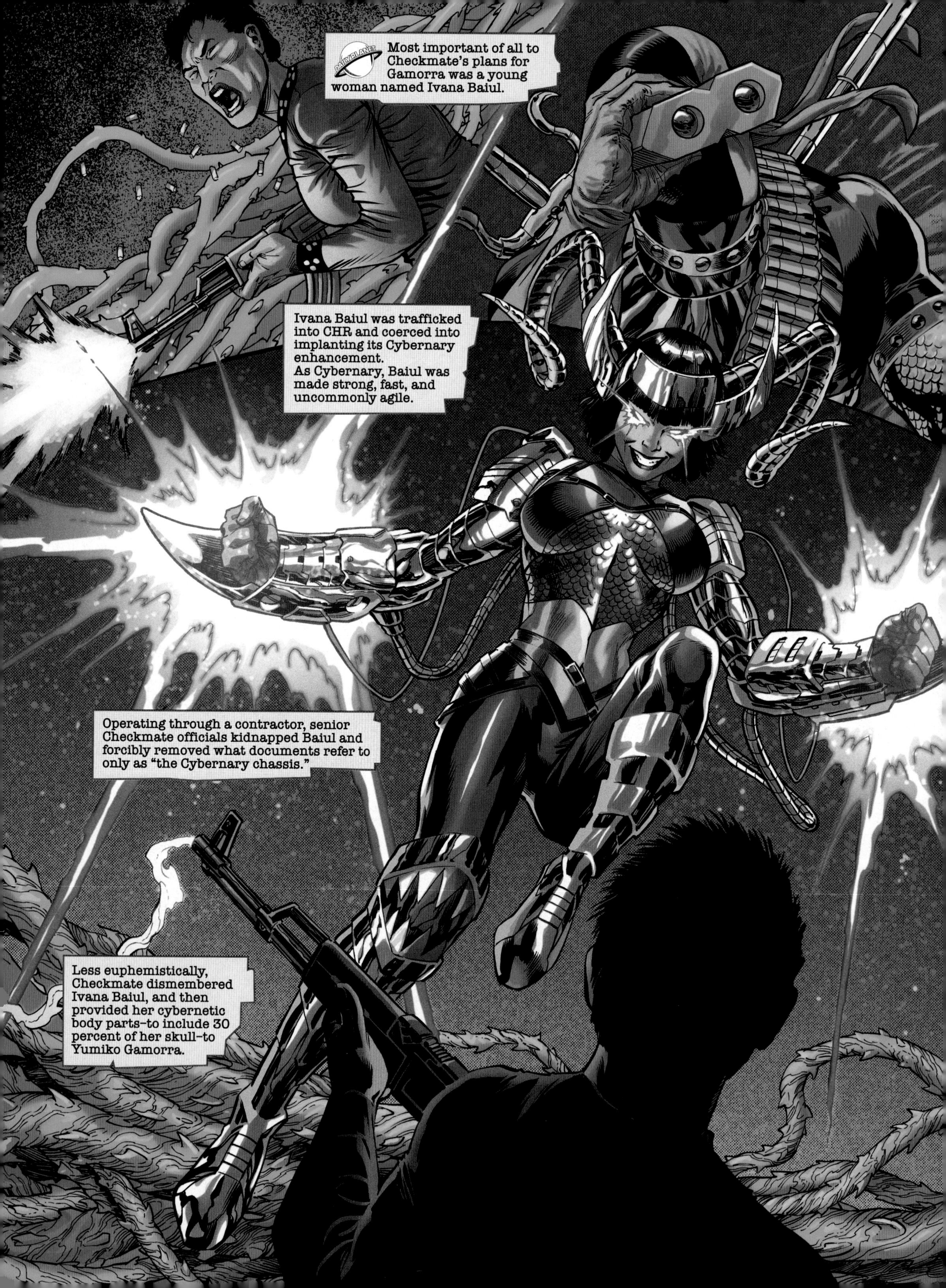
Most important of all to Checkmate's plans for Gamorra was a young woman named Ivana Baiul.
Ivana Baiul was trafficked into CHR and coerced into implanting its Cybernary enhancement.
As Cybernary, Baiul was made strong, fast, and uncommonly agile.
Operating through a contractor, senior Checkmate officials kidnapped Baiul and forcibly removed what documents refer to only as "the Cybernary chassis."
Less euphemistically, Checkmate dismembered Ivana Baiul, and then provided her cybernetic body parts–to include 30 percent of her skull–to Yumiko Gamorra.

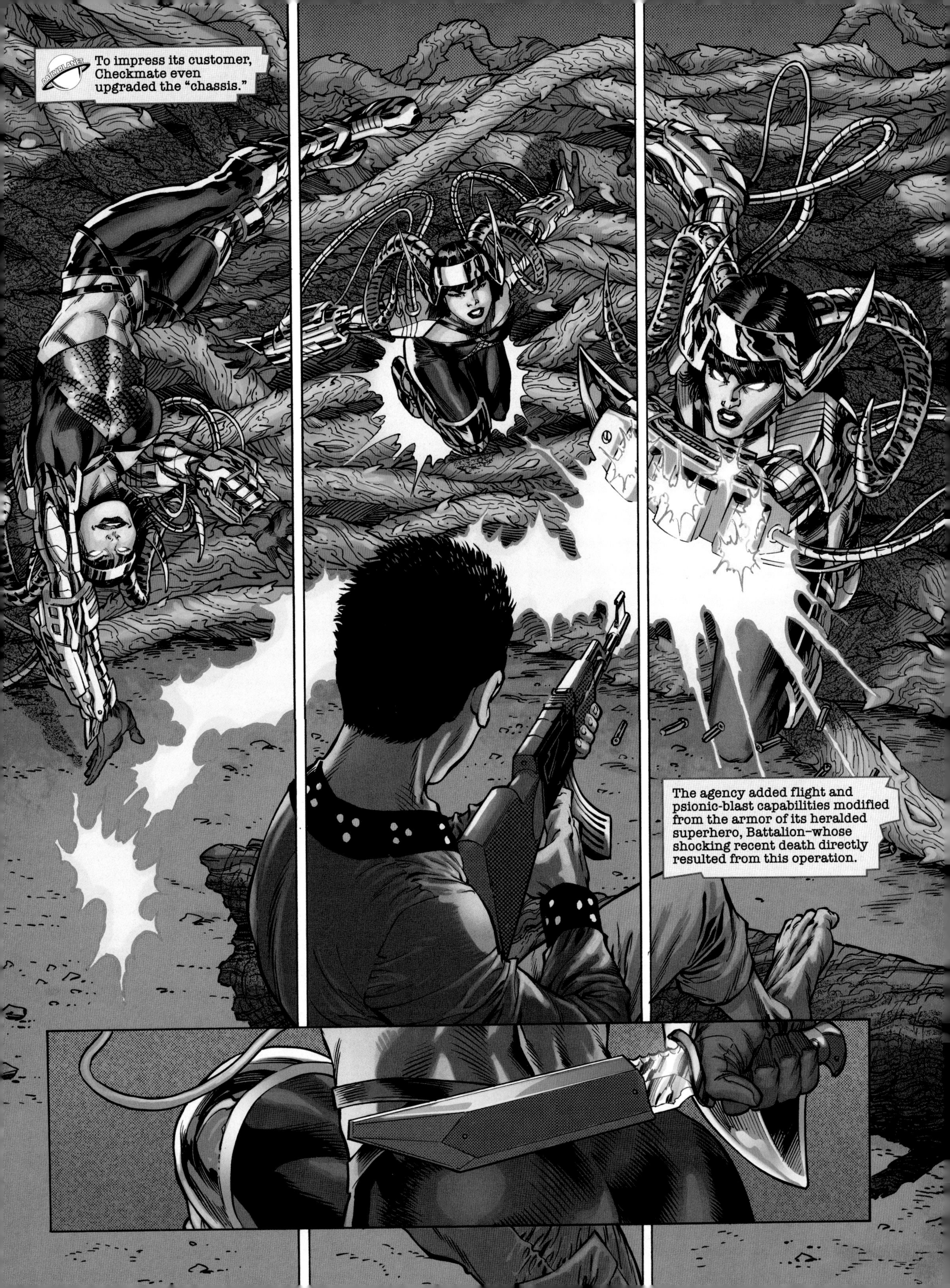
To impress its customer, Checkmate even upgraded the "chassis."
The agency added flight and psionic-blast capabilities modified from the armor of its heralded superhero, Battalion–whose shocking recent death directly resulted from this operation.

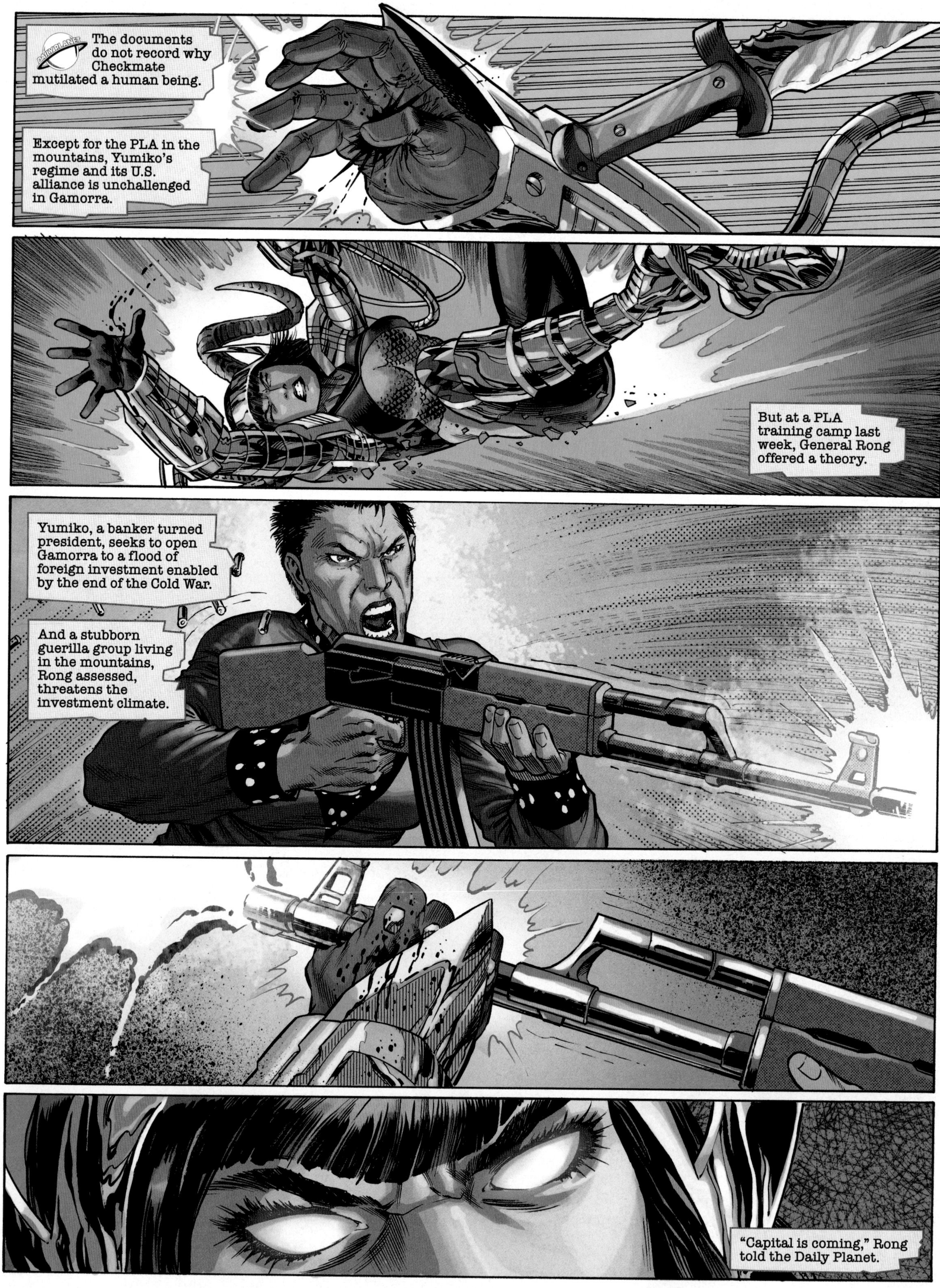
DAILY PLANET
The documents do not record why Checkmate mutilated a human being.
Except for the PLA in the mountains, Yumiko's regime and its U.S. alliance is unchallenged in Gamorra.
But at a PLA training camp last week, General Rong offered a theory.
Yumiko, a banker turned president, seeks to open Gamorra to a flood of foreign investment enabled by the end of the Cold War.
And a stubborn guerilla group living in the mountains, Rong assessed, threatens the investment climate.
"Capital is coming," Rong told the Daily Planet.

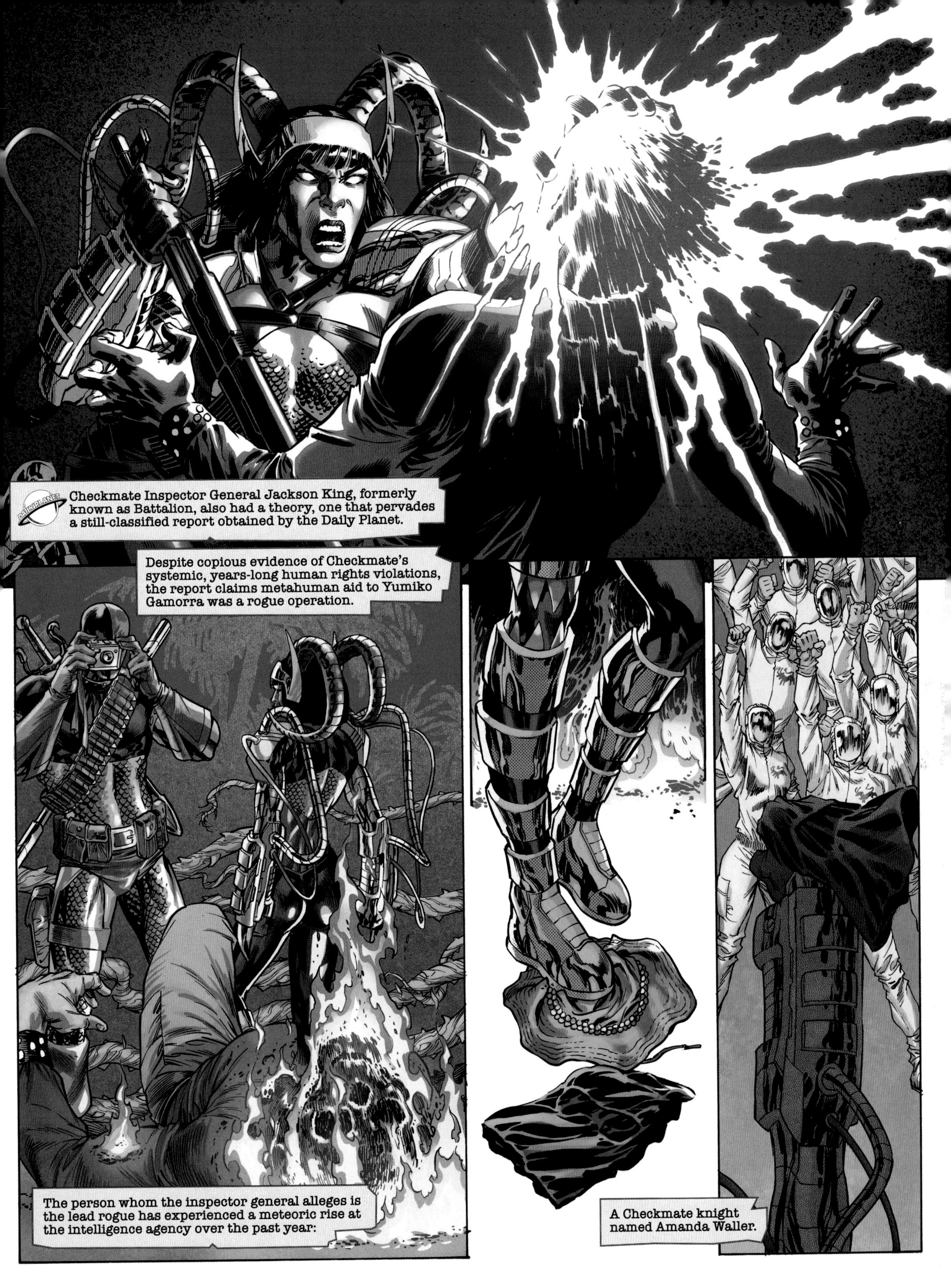
DAILY PLANET
Checkmate Inspector General Jackson King, formerly known as Battalion, also had a theory, one that pervades a still-classified report obtained by the Daily Planet.
Despite copious evidence of Checkmate's systemic, years-long human rights violations, the report claims metahuman aid to Yumiko Gamorra was a rogue operation.
The person whom the inspector general alleges is the lead rogue has experienced a meteoric rise at the intelligence agency over the past year:
A Checkmate knight named Amanda Waller.

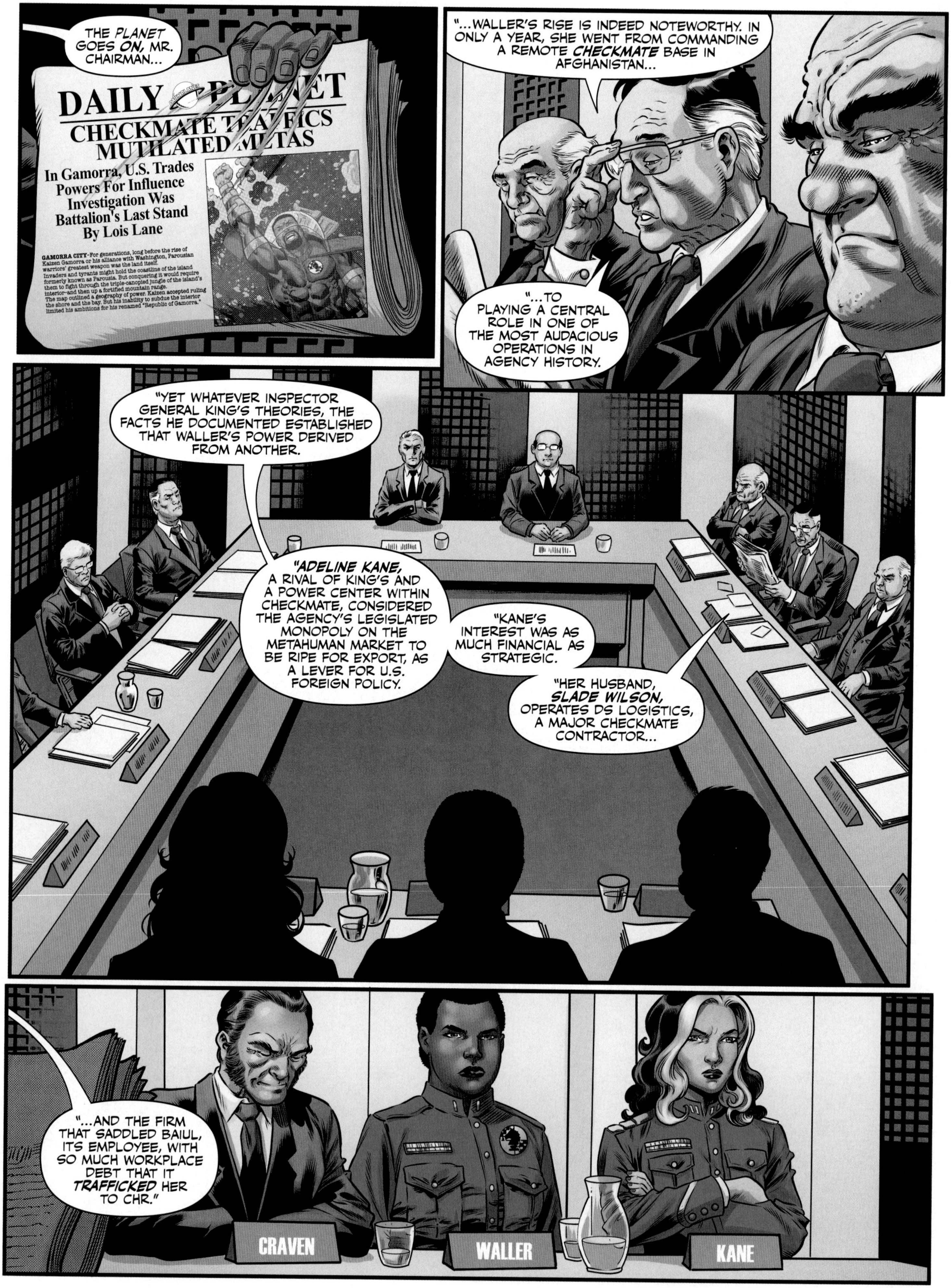
THE *PLANET* GOES *ON,* MR. CHAIRMAN...
DAILY P NET
CHECKMATE T AFFICS
MUTILATED METAS
In Gamorra, U.S. Trades Powers For Influence
Investigation Was Battalion's Last Stand
By Lois Lane
GAMORRA CITY–For generations, long before the rise of Kaizen Gamorra or his alliance with Washington, Parousian warriors' greatest weapon was the land itself. Invaders and tyrants might hold the coastline of the island formerly known as Parousia. But conquering it would require them to fight through the triple-canopied jungle of the island's interior–and then up a fortified mountain range. The map outlined a geography of power. Kaizen accepted ruling the shore and the bay. But his inability to subdue the interior limited his ambitions for his renamed "Republic of Gamorra."
"...WALLER'S RISE IS INDEED NOTEWORTHY. IN ONLY A YEAR, SHE WENT FROM COMMANDING A REMOTE *CHECKMATE* BASE IN AFGHANISTAN...
"...TO PLAYING A CENTRAL ROLE IN ONE OF THE MOST AUDACIOUS OPERATIONS IN AGENCY HISTORY.
"YET WHATEVER INSPECTOR GENERAL KING'S THEORIES, THE FACTS HE DOCUMENTED ESTABLISHED THAT WALLER'S POWER DERIVED FROM ANOTHER.
"***ADELINE KANE,*** A RIVAL OF KING'S AND A POWER CENTER WITHIN CHECKMATE, CONSIDERED THE AGENCY'S LEGISLATED MONOPOLY ON THE METAHUMAN MARKET TO BE RIPE FOR EXPORT, AS A LEVER FOR U.S. FOREIGN POLICY.
"KANE'S INTEREST WAS AS MUCH FINANCIAL AS STRATEGIC.
"HER HUSBAND, ***SLADE WILSON,*** OPERATES DS LOGISTICS, A MAJOR CHECKMATE CONTRACTOR...
"...AND THE FIRM THAT SADDLED BAIUL, ITS EMPLOYEE, WITH SO MUCH WORKPLACE DEBT THAT IT *TRAFFICKED* HER TO CHR."
CRAVEN
WALLER
KANE

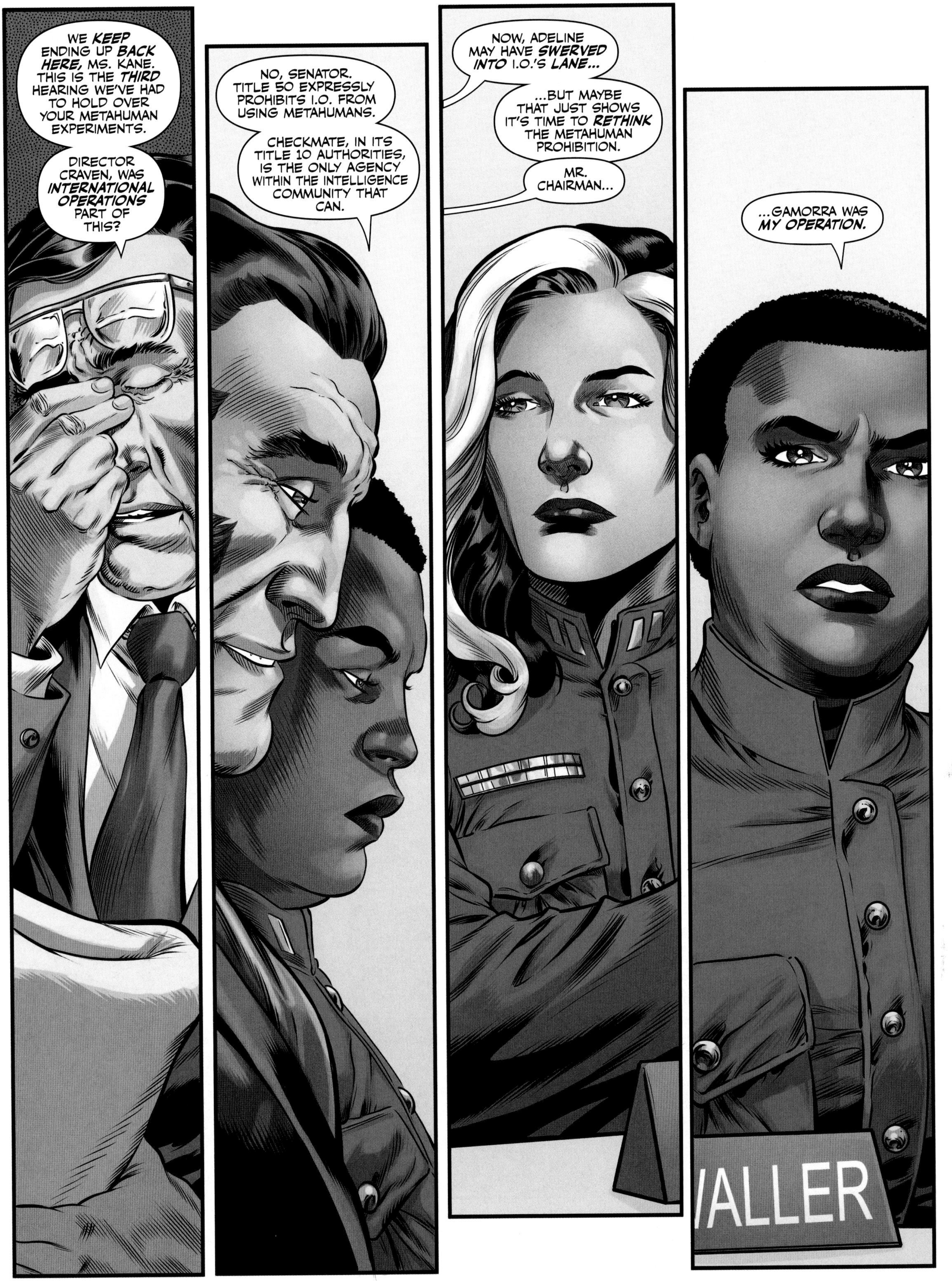
WE KEEP ENDING UP BACK HERE, MS. KANE. THIS IS THE THIRD HEARING WE'VE HAD TO HOLD OVER YOUR METAHUMAN EXPERIMENTS.
DIRECTOR CRAVEN, WAS INTERNATIONAL OPERATIONS PART OF THIS?
NO, SENATOR. TITLE 50 EXPRESSLY PROHIBITS I.O. FROM USING METAHUMANS.
CHECKMATE, IN ITS TITLE 10 AUTHORITIES, IS THE ONLY AGENCY WITHIN THE INTELLIGENCE COMMUNITY THAT CAN.
NOW, ADELINE MAY HAVE SWERVED INTO I.O.'S LANE...
...BUT MAYBE THAT JUST SHOWS IT'S TIME TO RETHINK THE METAHUMAN PROHIBITION.
MR. CHAIRMAN...
...GAMORRA WAS MY OPERATION.
WALLER

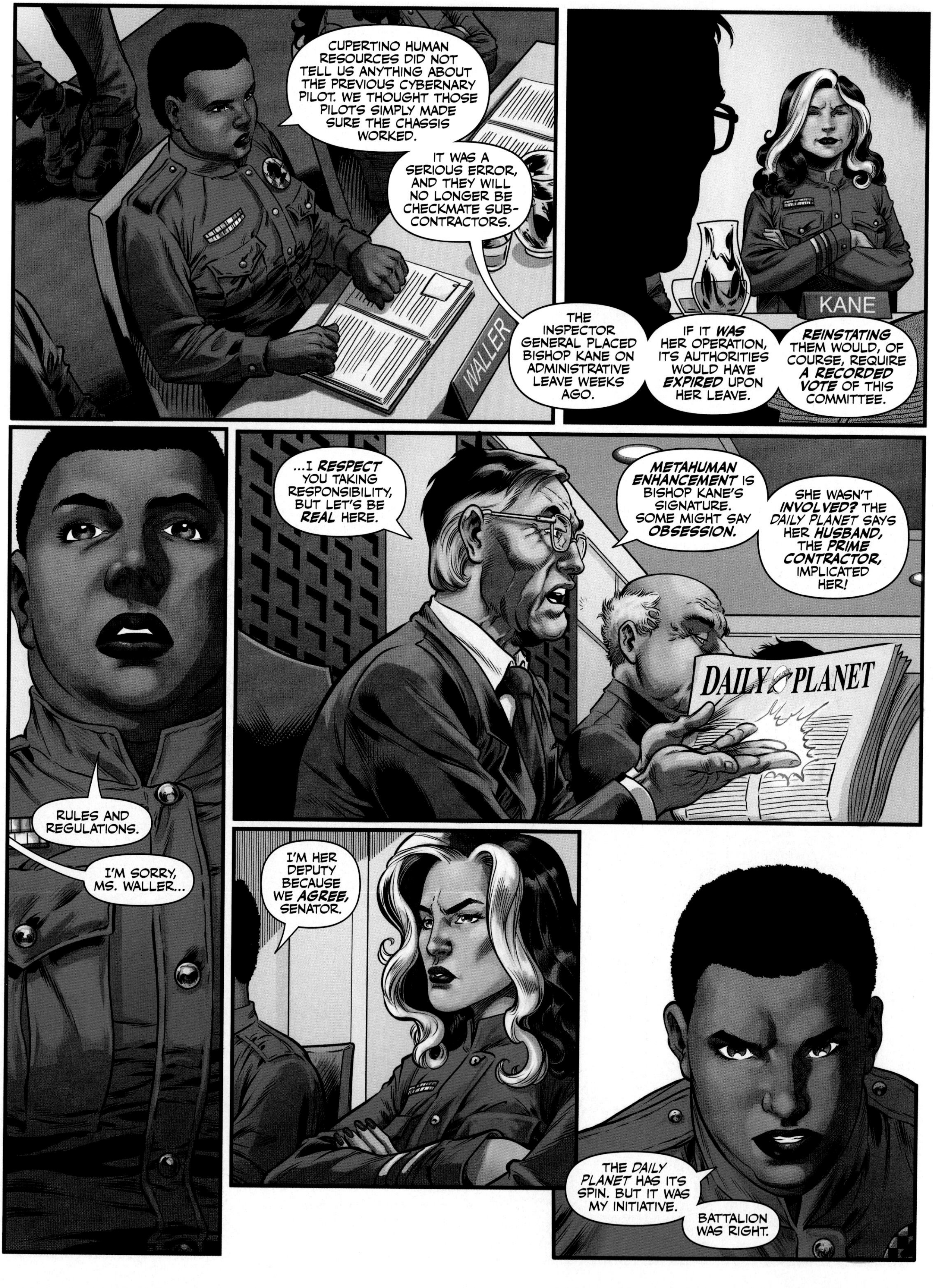
CUPERTINO HUMAN RESOURCES DID NOT TELL US ANYTHING ABOUT THE PREVIOUS CYBERNARY PILOT. WE THOUGHT THOSE PILOTS SIMPLY MADE SURE THE CHASSIS WORKED.
IT WAS A SERIOUS ERROR, AND THEY WILL NO LONGER BE CHECKMATE SUB-CONTRACTORS.
WALLER
KANE
THE INSPECTOR GENERAL PLACED BISHOP KANE ON ADMINISTRATIVE LEAVE WEEKS AGO.
IF IT WAS HER OPERATION, ITS AUTHORITIES WOULD HAVE EXPIRED UPON HER LEAVE.
REINSTATING THEM WOULD, OF COURSE, REQUIRE A RECORDED VOTE OF THIS COMMITTEE.
RULES AND REGULATIONS.
I'M SORRY, MS. WALLER...
...I RESPECT YOU TAKING RESPONSIBILITY, BUT LET'S BE REAL HERE.
METAHUMAN ENHANCEMENT IS BISHOP KANE'S SIGNATURE. SOME MIGHT SAY OBSESSION.
SHE WASN'T INVOLVED? THE DAILY PLANET SAYS HER HUSBAND, THE PRIME CONTRACTOR, IMPLICATED HER!
DAILY PLANET
I'M HER DEPUTY BECAUSE WE AGREE, SENATOR.
THE DAILY PLANET HAS ITS SPIN. BUT IT WAS MY INITIATIVE.
BATTALION WAS RIGHT.

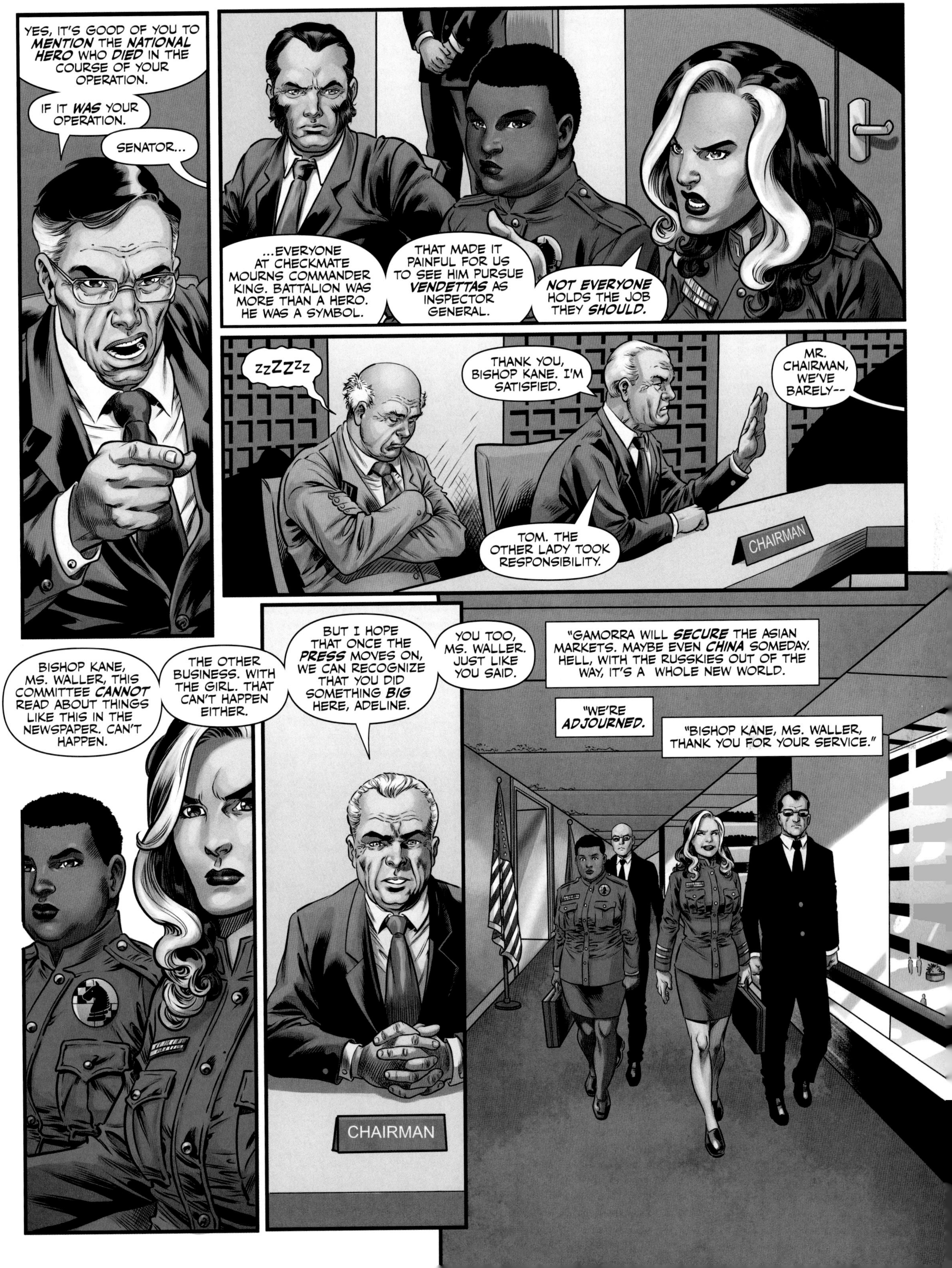
YES, IT'S GOOD OF YOU TO MENTION THE NATIONAL HERO WHO DIED IN THE COURSE OF YOUR OPERATION.
IF IT WAS YOUR OPERATION.
SENATOR...
...EVERYONE AT CHECKMATE MOURNS COMMANDER KING. BATTALION WAS MORE THAN A HERO. HE WAS A SYMBOL.
THAT MADE IT PAINFUL FOR US TO SEE HIM PURSUE VENDETTAS AS INSPECTOR GENERAL.
NOT EVERYONE HOLDS THE JOB THEY SHOULD.
zzZZzz
THANK YOU, BISHOP KANE. I'M SATISFIED.
MR. CHAIRMAN, WE'VE BARELY--
TOM. THE OTHER LADY TOOK RESPONSIBILITY.
CHAIRMAN
BISHOP KANE, MS. WALLER, THIS COMMITTEE CANNOT READ ABOUT THINGS LIKE THIS IN THE NEWSPAPER. CAN'T HAPPEN.
THE OTHER BUSINESS. WITH THE GIRL. THAT CAN'T HAPPEN EITHER.
BUT I HOPE THAT ONCE THE PRESS MOVES ON, WE CAN RECOGNIZE THAT YOU DID SOMETHING BIG HERE, ADELINE.
YOU TOO, MS. WALLER. JUST LIKE YOU SAID.
CHAIRMAN
"GAMORRA WILL SECURE THE ASIAN MARKETS. MAYBE EVEN CHINA SOMEDAY. HELL, WITH THE RUSSKIES OUT OF THE WAY, IT'S A WHOLE NEW WORLD.
"WE'RE ADJOURNED.
"BISHOP KANE, MS. WALLER, THANK YOU FOR YOUR SERVICE."

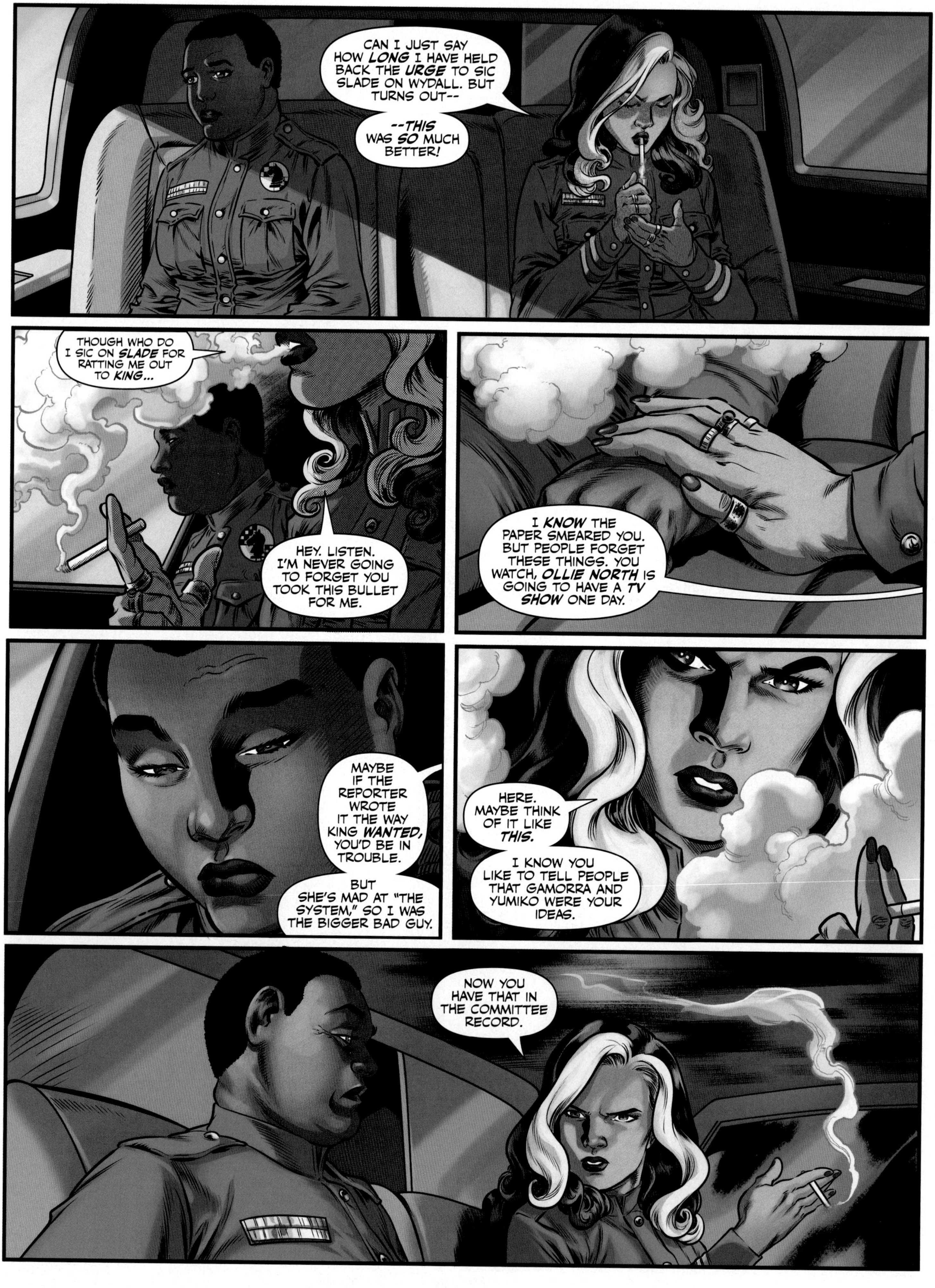
CAN I JUST SAY HOW LONG I HAVE HELD BACK THE URGE TO SIC SLADE ON WYDALL. BUT TURNS OUT--
--THIS WAS SO MUCH BETTER!
THOUGH WHO DO I SIC ON SLADE FOR RATTING ME OUT TO KING...
HEY. LISTEN. I'M NEVER GOING TO FORGET YOU TOOK THIS BULLET FOR ME.
I KNOW THE PAPER SMEARED YOU. BUT PEOPLE FORGET THESE THINGS. YOU WATCH, OLLIE NORTH IS GOING TO HAVE A TV SHOW ONE DAY.
MAYBE IF THE REPORTER WROTE IT THE WAY KING WANTED, YOU'D BE IN TROUBLE.
BUT SHE'S MAD AT "THE SYSTEM," SO I WAS THE BIGGER BAD GUY.
HERE. MAYBE THINK OF IT LIKE THIS.
I KNOW YOU LIKE TO TELL PEOPLE THAT GAMORRA AND YUMIKO WERE YOUR IDEAS.
NOW YOU HAVE THAT IN THE COMMITTEE RECORD.

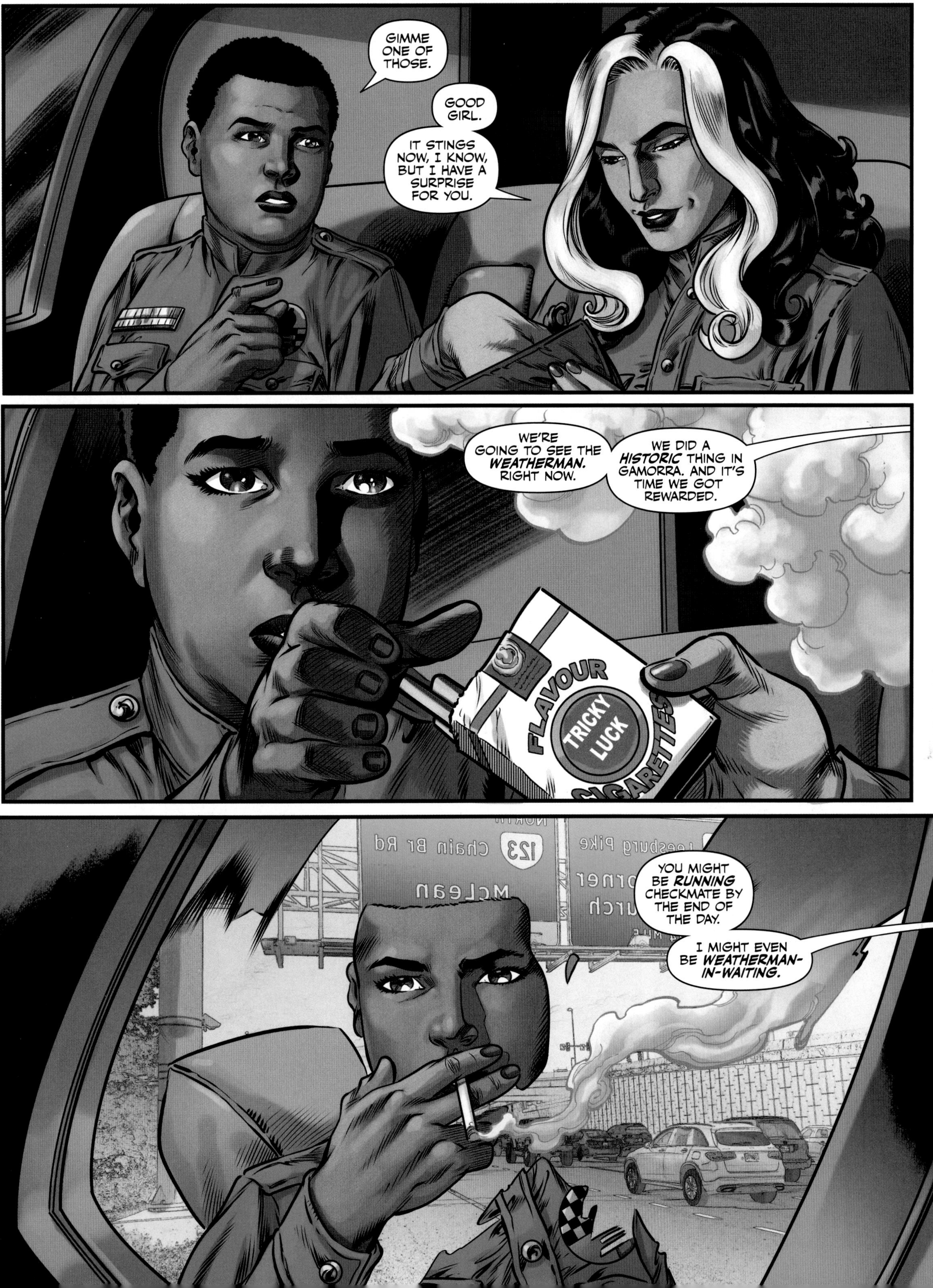
GIMME ONE OF THOSE.
GOOD GIRL.
IT STINGS NOW, I KNOW, BUT I HAVE A SURPRISE FOR YOU.
WE'RE GOING TO SEE THE *WEATHERMAN.* RIGHT NOW.
WE DID A *HISTORIC* THING IN GAMORRA. AND IT'S TIME WE GOT REWARDED.
FLAVOUR
TRICKY LUCK
CIGARETTES
YOU MIGHT BE *RUNNING* CHECKMATE BY THE END OF THE DAY.
I MIGHT EVEN BE *WEATHERMAN-IN-WAITING.*

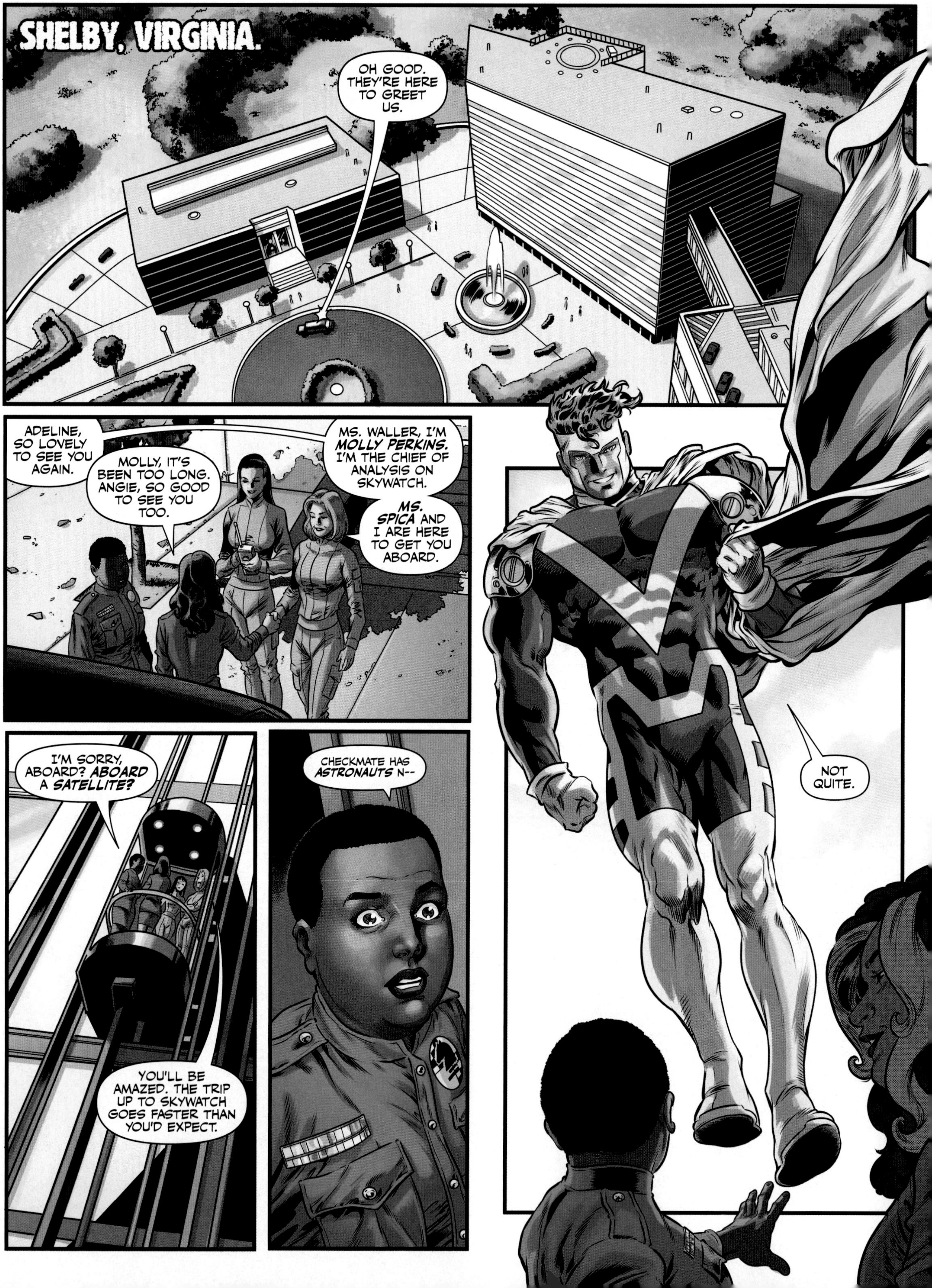
SHELBY, VIRGINIA.
OH GOOD. THEY'RE HERE TO GREET US.
ADELINE, SO LOVELY TO SEE YOU AGAIN.
MOLLY, IT'S BEEN TOO LONG. ANGIE, SO GOOD TO SEE YOU TOO.
MS. WALLER, I'M MOLLY PERKINS. I'M THE CHIEF OF ANALYSIS ON SKYWATCH.
MS. SPICA AND I ARE HERE TO GET YOU ABOARD.
I'M SORRY, ABOARD? ABOARD A SATELLITE?
YOU'LL BE AMAZED. THE TRIP UP TO SKYWATCH GOES FASTER THAN YOU'D EXPECT.
CHECKMATE HAS ASTRONAUTS N--
NOT QUITE.

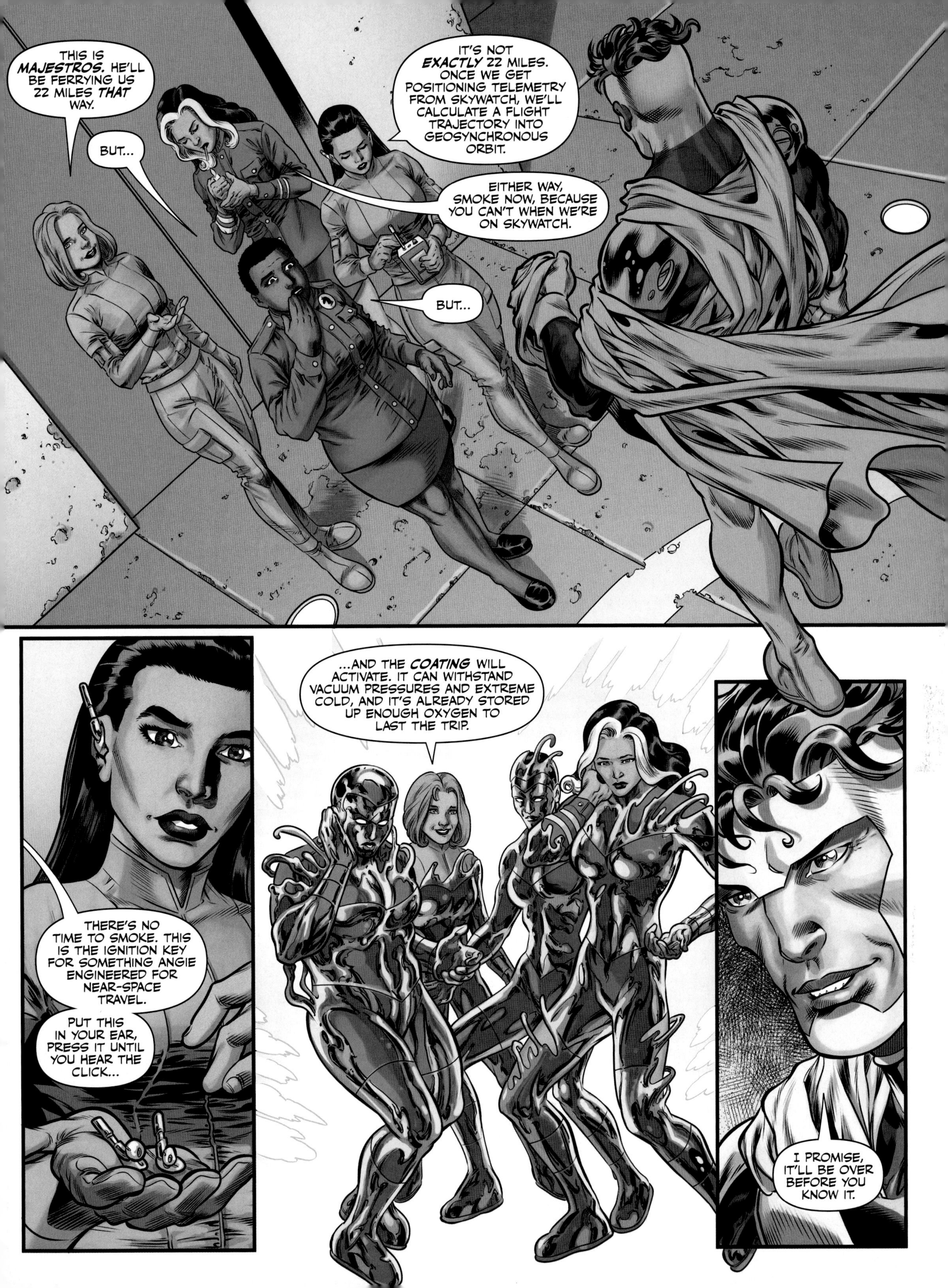

THIS IS MAJESTROS. HE'LL BE FERRYING US 22 MILES THAT WAY.
BUT...
IT'S NOT EXACTLY 22 MILES. ONCE WE GET POSITIONING TELEMETRY FROM SKYWATCH, WE'LL CALCULATE A FLIGHT TRAJECTORY INTO GEOSYNCHRONOUS ORBIT.
EITHER WAY, SMOKE NOW, BECAUSE YOU CAN'T WHEN WE'RE ON SKYWATCH.
BUT...
THERE'S NO TIME TO SMOKE. THIS IS THE IGNITION KEY FOR SOMETHING ANGIE ENGINEERED FOR NEAR-SPACE TRAVEL.
PUT THIS IN YOUR EAR, PRESS IT UNTIL YOU HEAR THE CLICK...
...AND THE COATING WILL ACTIVATE. IT CAN WITHSTAND VACUUM PRESSURES AND EXTREME COLD, AND IT'S ALREADY STORED UP ENOUGH OXYGEN TO LAST THE TRIP.
I PROMISE, IT'LL BE OVER BEFORE YOU KNOW IT.

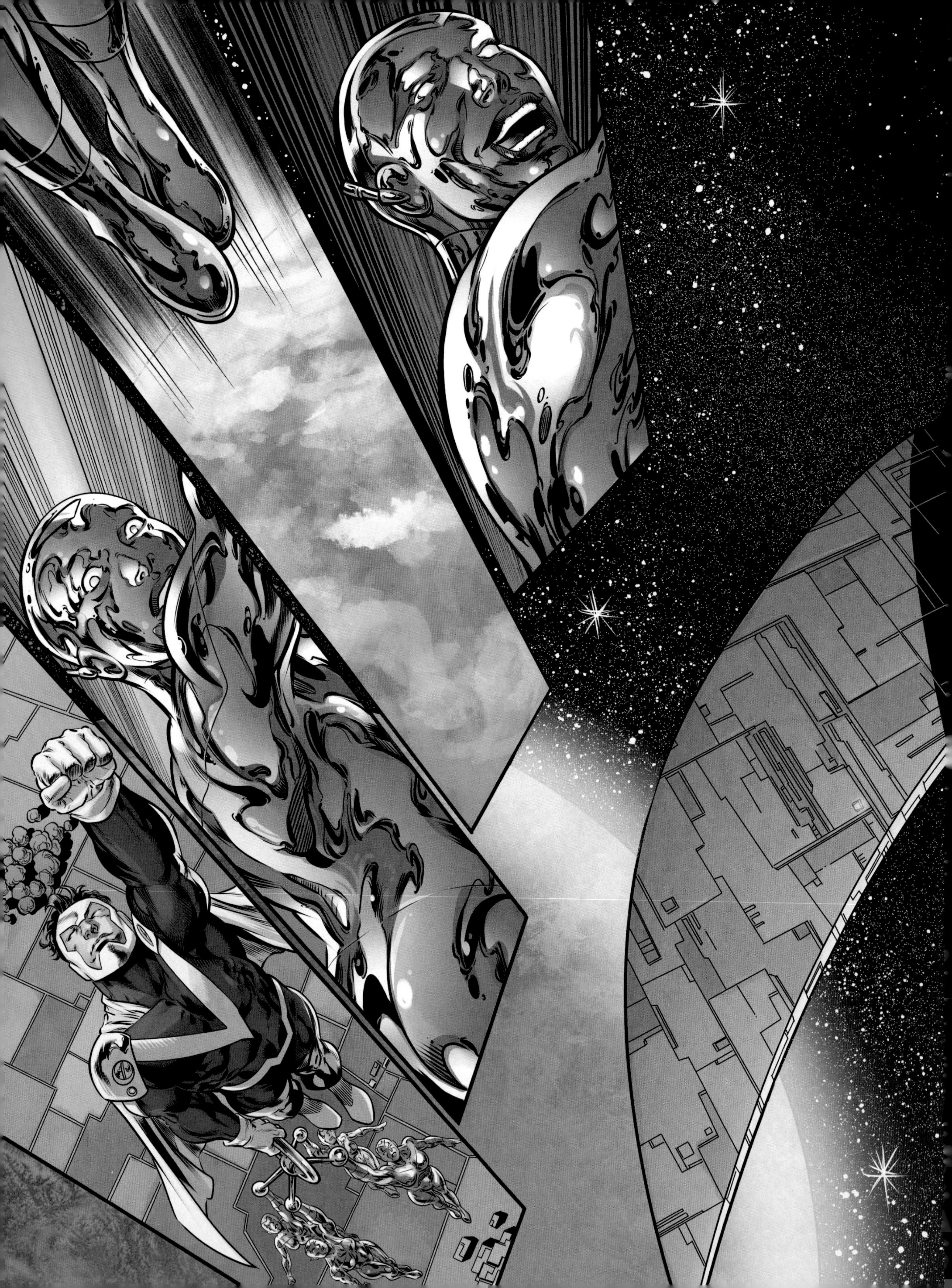

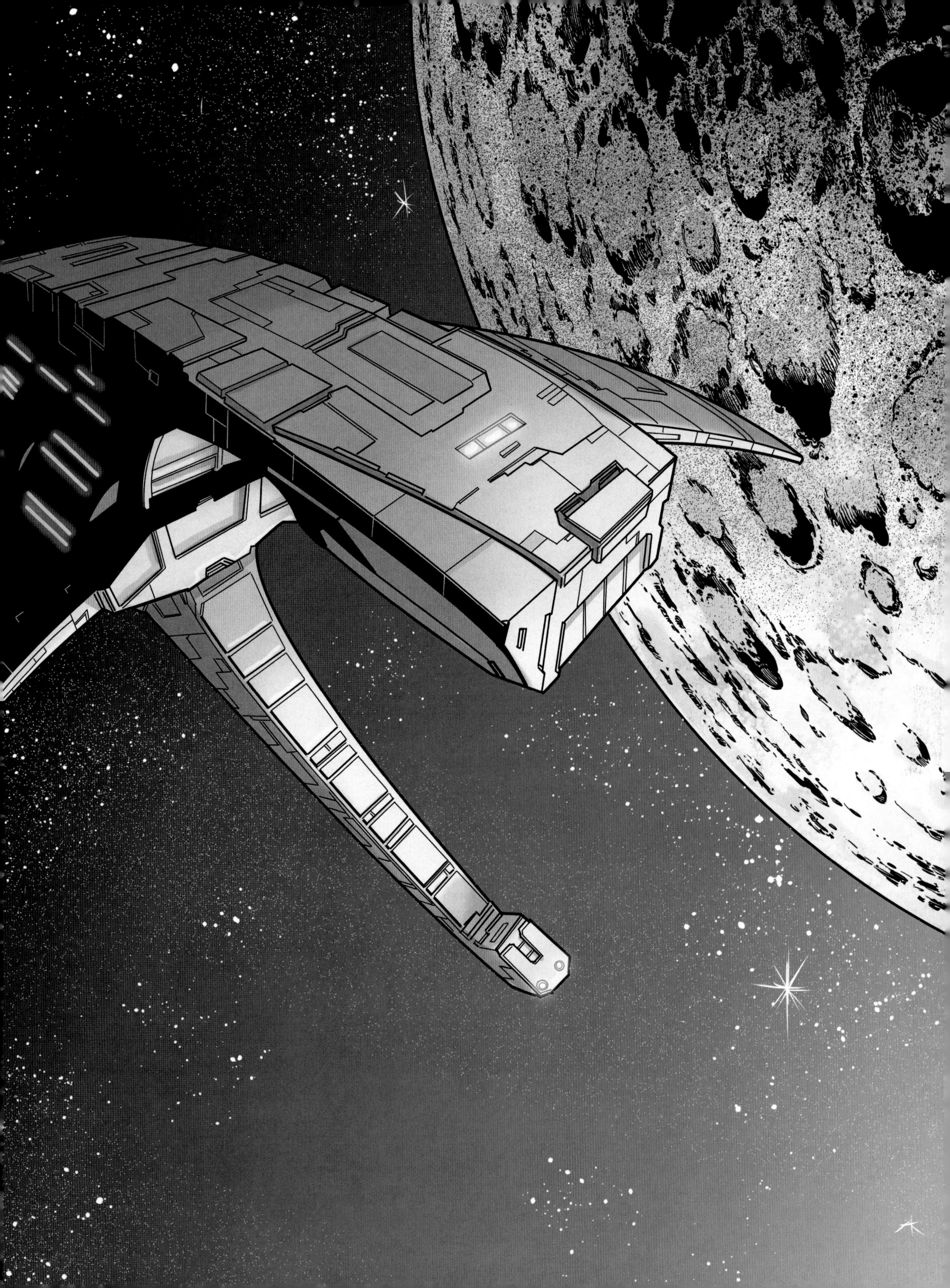

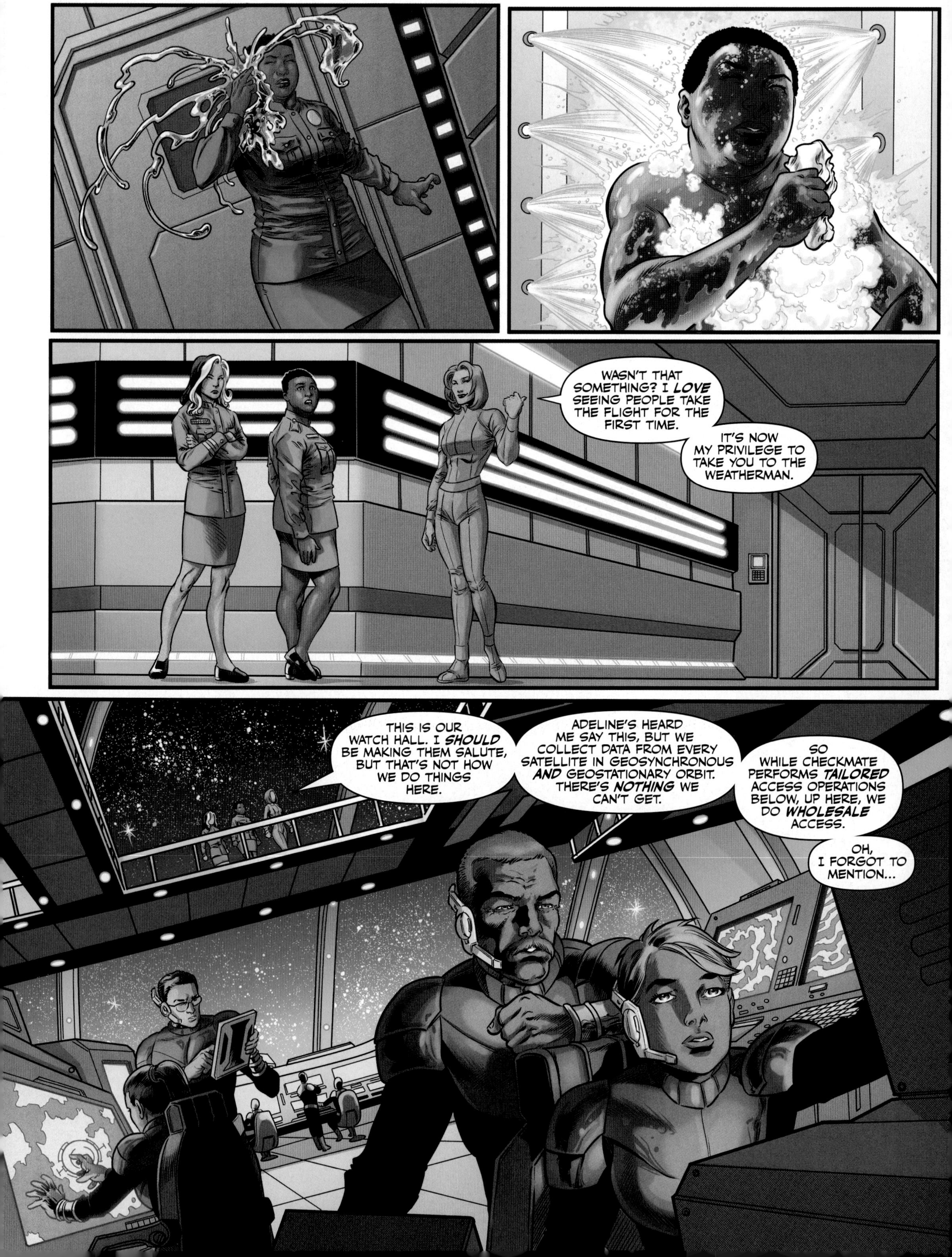
WASN'T THAT SOMETHING? I LOVE SEEING PEOPLE TAKE THE FLIGHT FOR THE FIRST TIME.
IT'S NOW MY PRIVILEGE TO TAKE YOU TO THE WEATHERMAN.
THIS IS OUR WATCH HALL. I SHOULD BE MAKING THEM SALUTE, BUT THAT'S NOT HOW WE DO THINGS HERE.
ADELINE'S HEARD ME SAY THIS, BUT WE COLLECT DATA FROM EVERY SATELLITE IN GEOSYNCHRONOUS AND GEOSTATIONARY ORBIT. THERE'S NOTHING WE CAN'T GET.
SO WHILE CHECKMATE PERFORMS TAILORED ACCESS OPERATIONS BELOW, UP HERE, WE DO WHOLESALE ACCESS.
OH, I FORGOT TO MENTION...

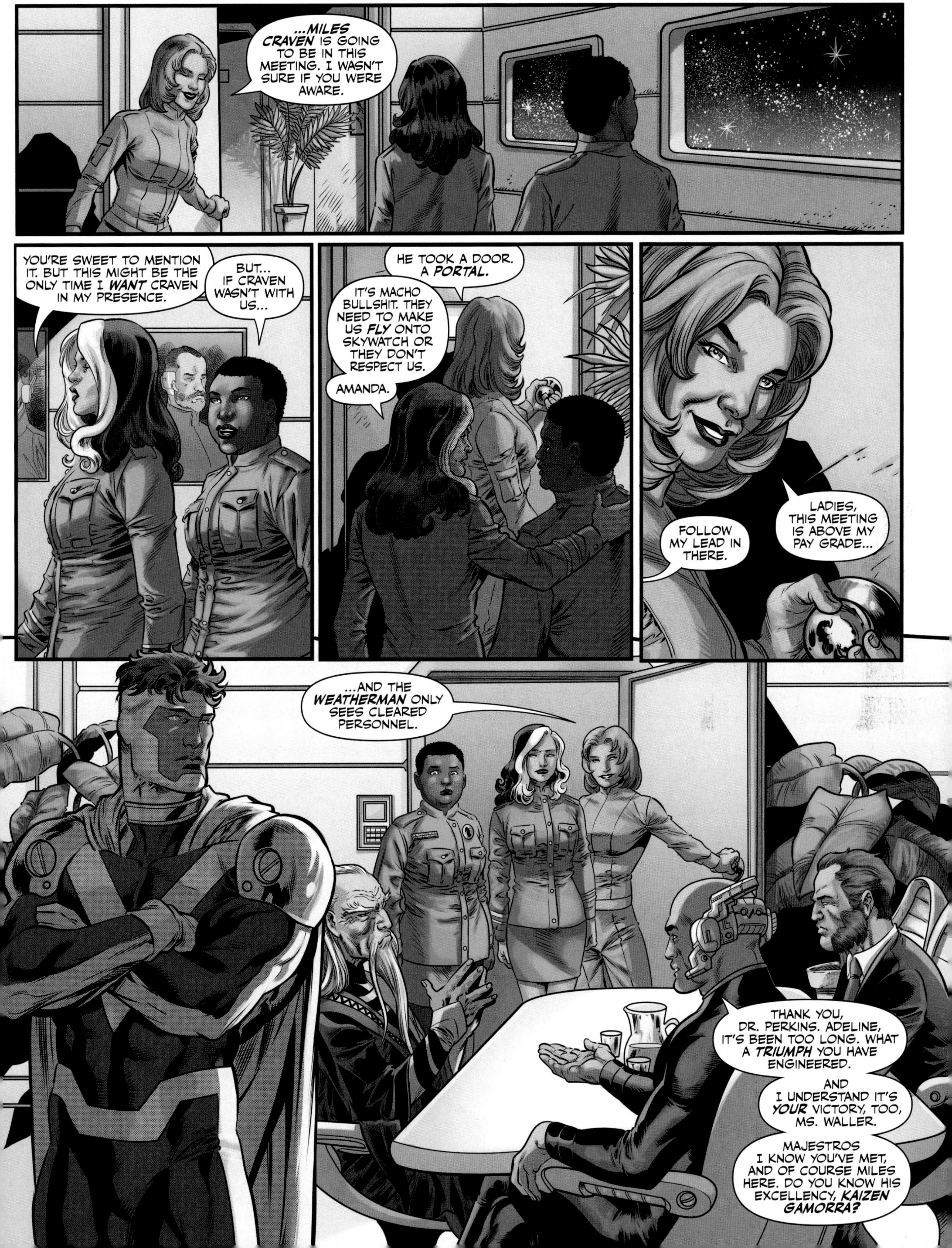
...MILES CRAVEN IS GOING TO BE IN THIS MEETING. I WASN'T SURE IF YOU WERE AWARE.
YOU'RE SWEET TO MENTION IT. BUT THIS MIGHT BE THE ONLY TIME I WANT CRAVEN IN MY PRESENCE.
BUT... IF CRAVEN WASN'T WITH US...
HE TOOK A DOOR. A PORTAL.
IT'S MACHO BULLSHIT. THEY NEED TO MAKE US FLY ONTO SKYWATCH OR THEY DON'T RESPECT US.
AMANDA.
LADIES, THIS MEETING IS ABOVE MY PAY GRADE...
FOLLOW MY LEAD IN THERE.
...AND THE WEATHERMAN ONLY SEES CLEARED PERSONNEL.
THANK YOU, DR. PERKINS. ADELINE, IT'S BEEN TOO LONG. WHAT A TRIUMPH YOU HAVE ENGINEERED.
AND I UNDERSTAND IT'S YOUR VICTORY, TOO, MS. WALLER.
MAJESTROS I KNOW YOU'VE MET, AND OF COURSE MILES HERE. DO YOU KNOW HIS EXCELLENCY, KAIZEN GAMORRA?

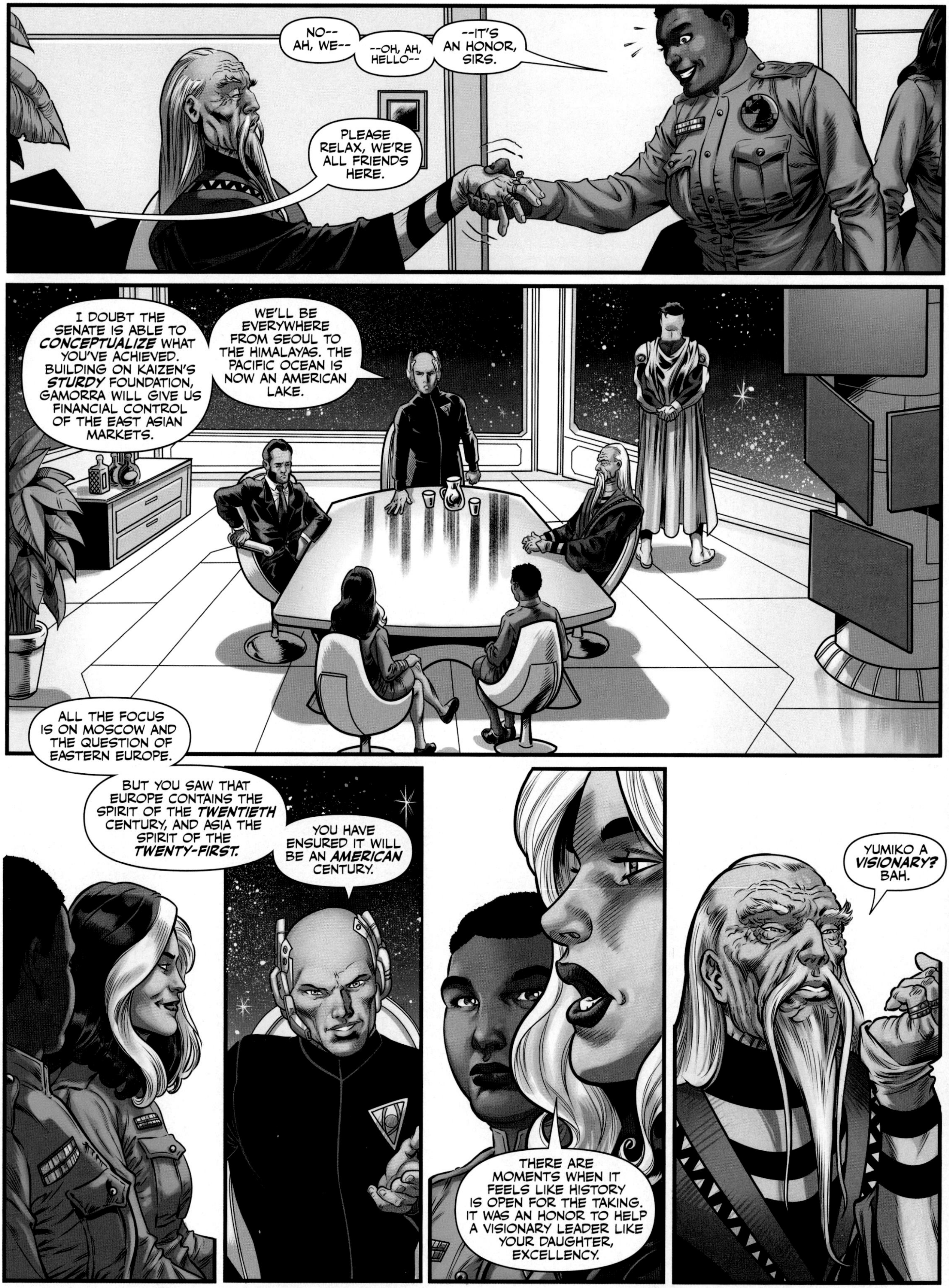
NO-- AH, WE--
--OH, AH, HELLO--
--IT'S AN HONOR, SIRS.
PLEASE RELAX, WE'RE ALL FRIENDS HERE.
I DOUBT THE SENATE IS ABLE TO *CONCEPTUALIZE* WHAT YOU'VE ACHIEVED. BUILDING ON KAIZEN'S *STURDY* FOUNDATION, GAMORRA WILL GIVE US FINANCIAL CONTROL OF THE EAST ASIAN MARKETS.
WE'LL BE EVERYWHERE FROM SEOUL TO THE HIMALAYAS. THE PACIFIC OCEAN IS NOW AN AMERICAN LAKE.
ALL THE FOCUS IS ON MOSCOW AND THE QUESTION OF EASTERN EUROPE.
BUT YOU SAW THAT EUROPE CONTAINS THE SPIRIT OF THE *TWENTIETH* CENTURY, AND ASIA THE SPIRIT OF THE *TWENTY-FIRST.*
YOU HAVE ENSURED IT WILL BE AN *AMERICAN* CENTURY.
THERE ARE MOMENTS WHEN IT FEELS LIKE HISTORY IS OPEN FOR THE TAKING. IT WAS AN HONOR TO HELP A VISIONARY LEADER LIKE YOUR DAUGHTER, EXCELLENCY.
YUMIKO A *VISIONARY?* BAH.

INTERESTING! YOU DON'T THINK SO?

MY DAUGHTER RESPECTS NEITHER THE MOUNTAINS OF GAMORRA NOR THE PEOPLE SHELTERED BY THEM.

SHE CAN CONQUER THEM, BUT THEY WILL NEVER STAY CONQUERED. NOW SHE IS YOKED TO SUBDUING THEM FOREVER.

PLEASE DO NOT MISUNDERSTAND ME. CHECKMATE'S PLAN IS FLAWLESS. YOU SHOULD ENJOY YOUR VICTORY.

YUMIKO DOES NOT SEE THAT SHE HAS MADE HERSELF DEPENDENT UPON CHECKMATE. THE PEOPLE, GIVEN TIME, WILL FIND THE FLAWS IN HER ENHANCEMENTS.

WHAT ELSE CAN SHE DO BUT COME TO CHECKMATE FOR MORE?

YOU WERE WISE TO EXPLOIT HER.

SHE BELIEVES HERSELF UNBOUND BY HER HISTORY. SHE IS LIKE YOU IN THAT RESPECT.

THOUGH SHE HAS LEFT YOU WITH A PROBLEM, I UNDERSTAND...

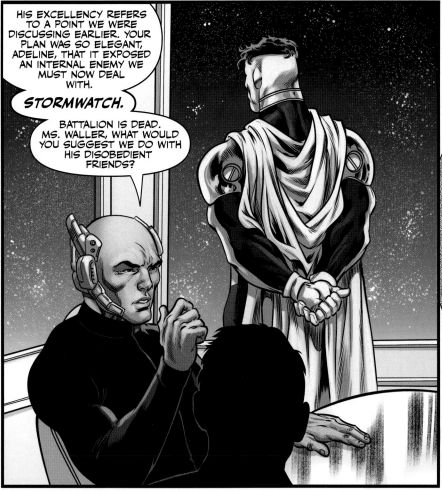

HIS EXCELLENCY REFERS TO A POINT WE WERE DISCUSSING EARLIER. YOUR PLAN WAS SO ELEGANT, ADELINE, THAT IT EXPOSED AN INTERNAL ENEMY WE MUST NOW DEAL WITH.

STORMWATCH.

BATTALION IS DEAD. MS. WALLER, WHAT WOULD YOU SUGGEST WE DO WITH HIS DISOBEDIENT FRIENDS?

...

I WOULD GIVE STORMWATCH TO THE UNITED NATIONS.

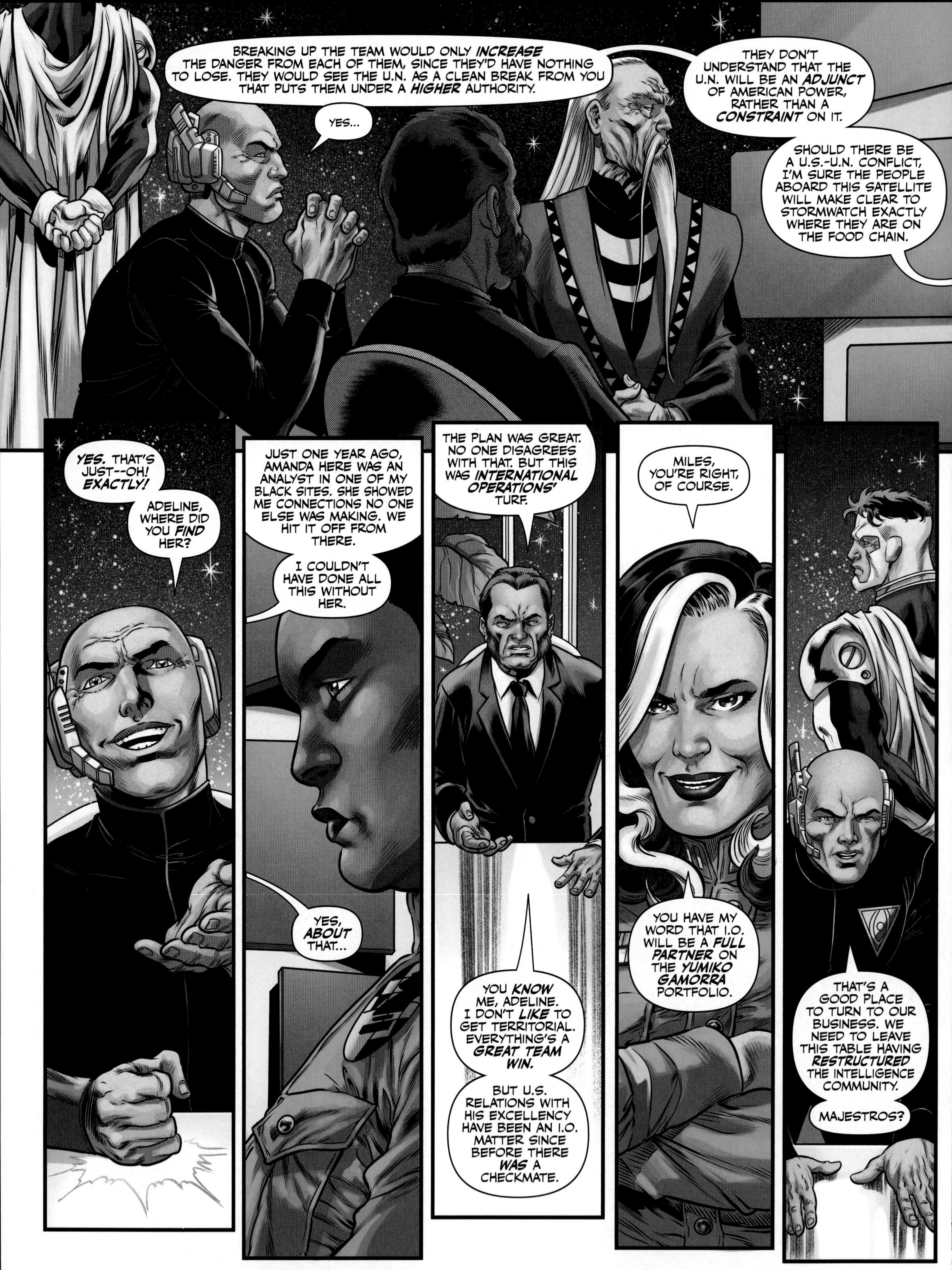
BREAKING UP THE TEAM WOULD ONLY *INCREASE* THE DANGER FROM EACH OF THEM, SINCE THEY'D HAVE NOTHING TO LOSE. THEY WOULD SEE THE U.N. AS A CLEAN BREAK FROM YOU THAT PUTS THEM UNDER A *HIGHER* AUTHORITY.
YES...
THEY DON'T UNDERSTAND THAT THE U.N. WILL BE AN *ADJUNCT* OF AMERICAN POWER, RATHER THAN A *CONSTRAINT* ON IT.
SHOULD THERE BE A U.S.-U.N. CONFLICT, I'M SURE THE PEOPLE ABOARD THIS SATELLITE WILL MAKE CLEAR TO STORMWATCH EXACTLY WHERE THEY ARE ON THE FOOD CHAIN.
YES. THAT'S JUST--OH! *EXACTLY!*
ADELINE, WHERE DID YOU *FIND* HER?
JUST ONE YEAR AGO, AMANDA HERE WAS AN ANALYST IN ONE OF MY BLACK SITES. SHE SHOWED ME CONNECTIONS NO ONE ELSE WAS MAKING. WE HIT IT OFF FROM THERE.
I COULDN'T HAVE DONE ALL THIS WITHOUT HER.
YES, *ABOUT* THAT...
THE PLAN WAS GREAT. NO ONE DISAGREES WITH THAT. BUT THIS WAS *INTERNATIONAL OPERATIONS'* TURF.
YOU *KNOW* ME, ADELINE. I DON'T *LIKE* TO GET TERRITORIAL. EVERYTHING'S A *GREAT TEAM WIN.*
BUT U.S. RELATIONS WITH HIS EXCELLENCY HAVE BEEN AN I.O. MATTER SINCE BEFORE THERE *WAS* A CHECKMATE.
MILES, YOU'RE RIGHT, OF COURSE.
YOU HAVE MY WORD THAT I.O. WILL BE A *FULL PARTNER* ON THE *YUMIKO GAMORRA* PORTFOLIO.
THAT'S A GOOD PLACE TO TURN TO OUR BUSINESS. WE NEED TO LEAVE THIS TABLE HAVING *RESTRUCTURED* THE INTELLIGENCE COMMUNITY.
MAJESTROS?

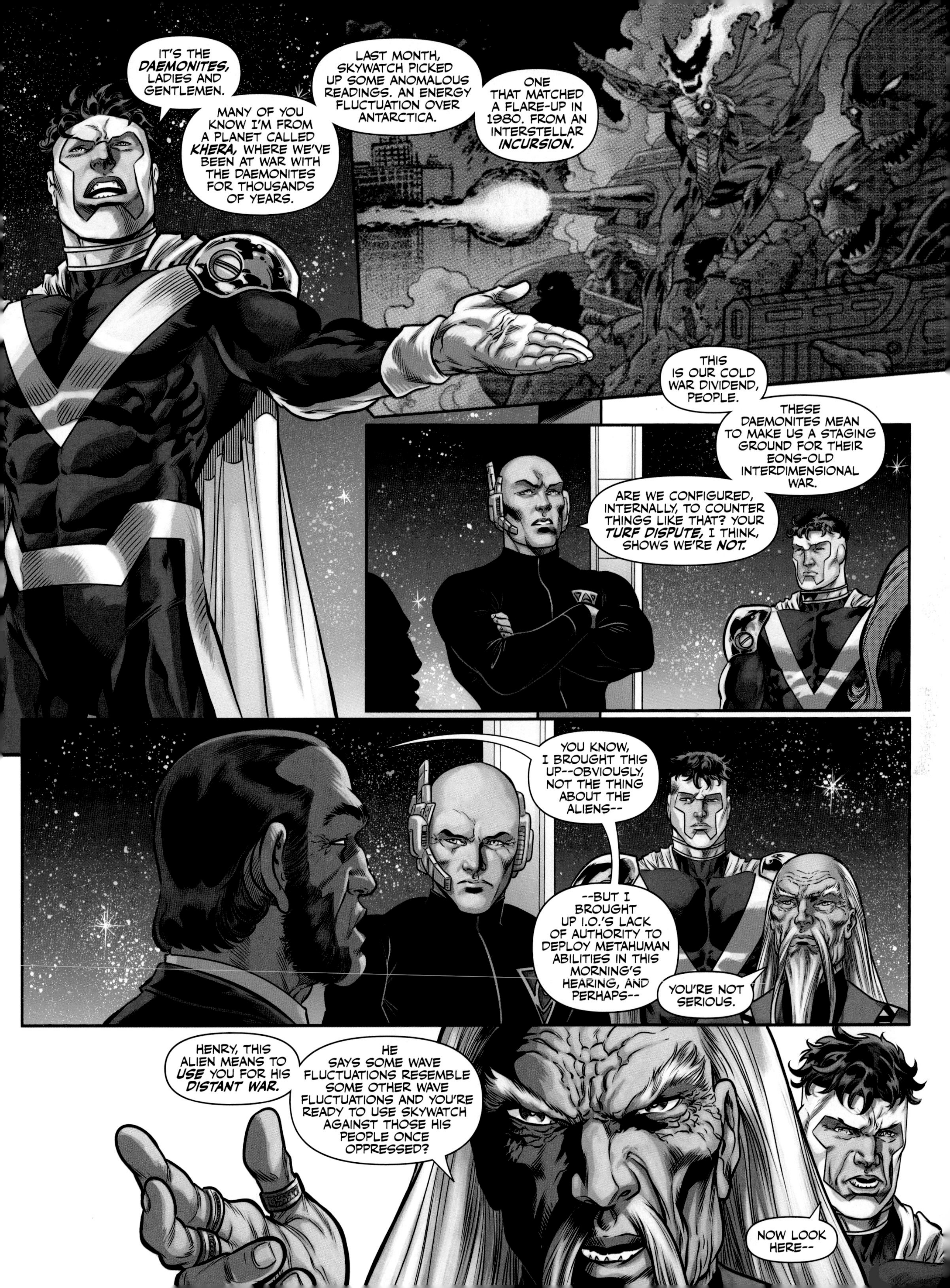
IT'S THE DAEMONITES, LADIES AND GENTLEMEN.
MANY OF YOU KNOW I'M FROM A PLANET CALLED KHERA, WHERE WE'VE BEEN AT WAR WITH THE DAEMONITES FOR THOUSANDS OF YEARS.
LAST MONTH, SKYWATCH PICKED UP SOME ANOMALOUS READINGS. AN ENERGY FLUCTUATION OVER ANTARCTICA.
ONE THAT MATCHED A FLARE-UP IN 1980. FROM AN INTERSTELLAR INCURSION.
THIS IS OUR COLD WAR DIVIDEND, PEOPLE.
THESE DAEMONITES MEAN TO MAKE US A STAGING GROUND FOR THEIR EONS-OLD INTERDIMENSIONAL WAR.
ARE WE CONFIGURED, INTERNALLY, TO COUNTER THINGS LIKE THAT? YOUR TURF DISPUTE, I THINK, SHOWS WE'RE NOT.
YOU KNOW, I BROUGHT THIS UP--OBVIOUSLY, NOT THE THING ABOUT THE ALIENS--
--BUT I BROUGHT UP I.O.'S LACK OF AUTHORITY TO DEPLOY METAHUMAN ABILITIES IN THIS MORNING'S HEARING, AND PERHAPS--
YOU'RE NOT SERIOUS.
HENRY, THIS ALIEN MEANS TO USE YOU FOR HIS DISTANT WAR.
HE SAYS SOME WAVE FLUCTUATIONS RESEMBLE SOME OTHER WAVE FLUCTUATIONS AND YOU'RE READY TO USE SKYWATCH AGAINST THOSE HIS PEOPLE ONCE OPPRESSED?
NOW LOOK HERE--

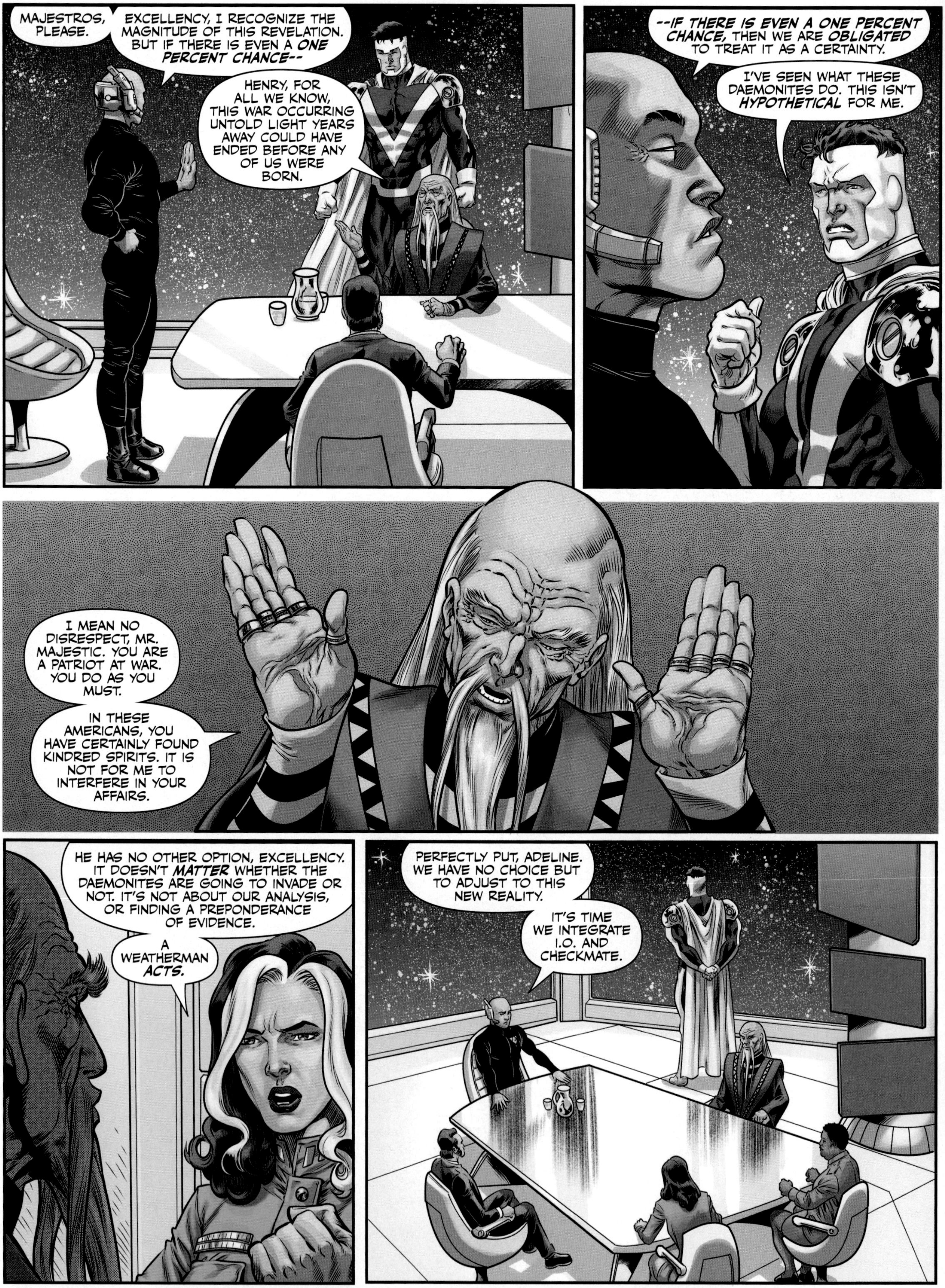
MAJESTROS, PLEASE.
EXCELLENCY, I RECOGNIZE THE MAGNITUDE OF THIS REVELATION. BUT IF THERE IS EVEN A ONE PERCENT CHANCE--
HENRY, FOR ALL WE KNOW, THIS WAR OCCURRING UNTOLD LIGHT YEARS AWAY COULD HAVE ENDED BEFORE ANY OF US WERE BORN.
--IF THERE IS EVEN A ONE PERCENT CHANCE, THEN WE ARE OBLIGATED TO TREAT IT AS A CERTAINTY.
I'VE SEEN WHAT THESE DAEMONITES DO. THIS ISN'T HYPOTHETICAL FOR ME.
I MEAN NO DISRESPECT, MR. MAJESTIC. YOU ARE A PATRIOT AT WAR. YOU DO AS YOU MUST.
IN THESE AMERICANS, YOU HAVE CERTAINLY FOUND KINDRED SPIRITS. IT IS NOT FOR ME TO INTERFERE IN YOUR AFFAIRS.
HE HAS NO OTHER OPTION, EXCELLENCY. IT DOESN'T MATTER WHETHER THE DAEMONITES ARE GOING TO INVADE OR NOT. IT'S NOT ABOUT OUR ANALYSIS, OR FINDING A PREPONDERANCE OF EVIDENCE.
A WEATHERMAN ACTS.
PERFECTLY PUT, ADELINE. WE HAVE NO CHOICE BUT TO ADJUST TO THIS NEW REALITY.
IT'S TIME WE INTEGRATE I.O. AND CHECKMATE.

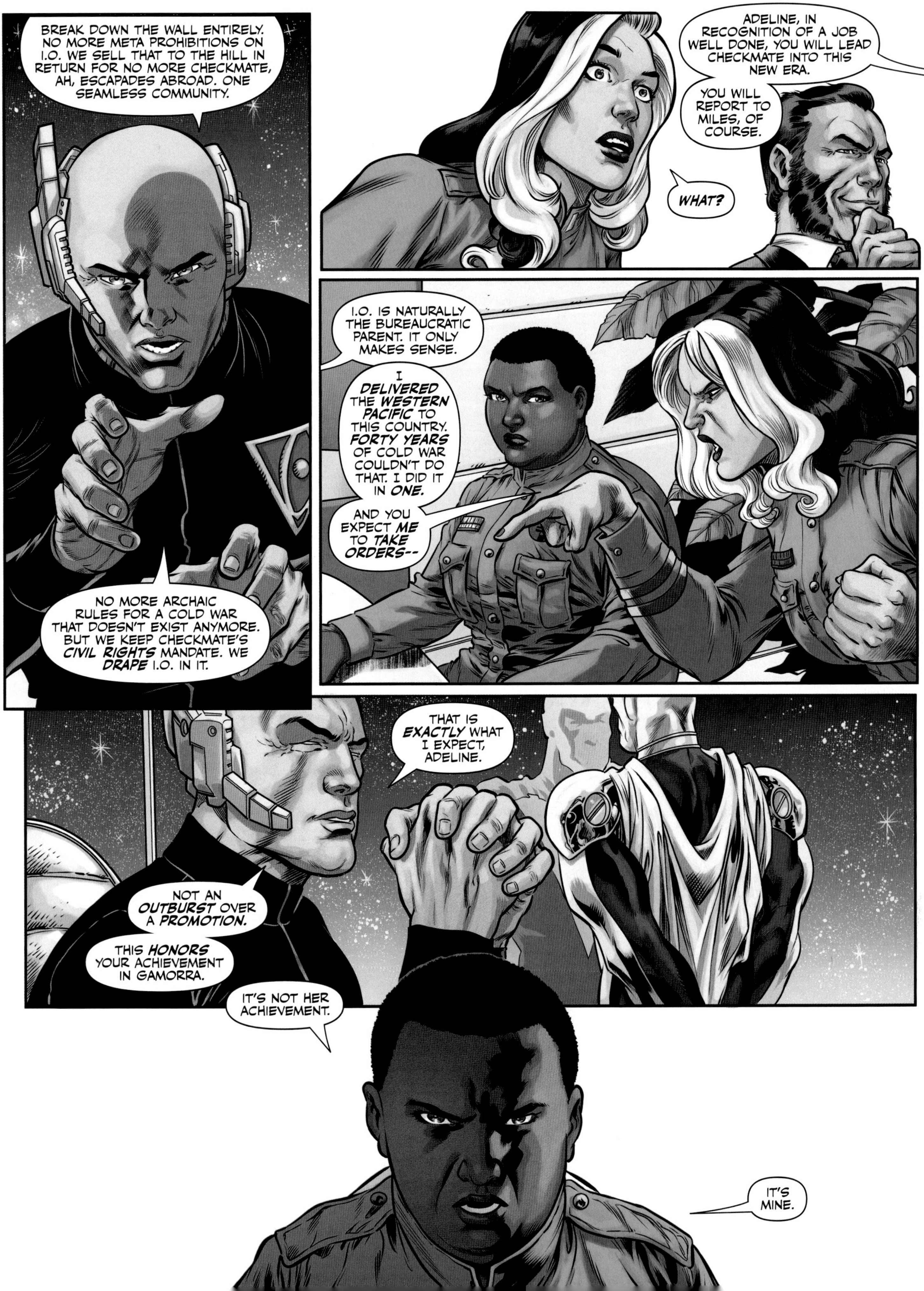
BREAK DOWN THE WALL ENTIRELY. NO MORE META PROHIBITIONS ON I.O. WE SELL THAT TO THE HILL IN RETURN FOR NO MORE CHECKMATE, AH, ESCAPADES ABROAD. ONE SEAMLESS COMMUNITY.
NO MORE ARCHAIC RULES FOR A COLD WAR THAT DOESN'T EXIST ANYMORE. BUT WE KEEP CHECKMATE'S CIVIL RIGHTS MANDATE. WE DRAPE I.O. IN IT.
ADELINE, IN RECOGNITION OF A JOB WELL DONE, YOU WILL LEAD CHECKMATE INTO THIS NEW ERA.
YOU WILL REPORT TO MILES, OF COURSE.
WHAT?
I.O. IS NATURALLY THE BUREAUCRATIC PARENT. IT ONLY MAKES SENSE.
I DELIVERED THE WESTERN PACIFIC TO THIS COUNTRY. FORTY YEARS OF COLD WAR COULDN'T DO THAT. I DID IT IN ONE.
AND YOU EXPECT ME TO TAKE ORDERS--
THAT IS EXACTLY WHAT I EXPECT, ADELINE.
NOT AN OUTBURST OVER A PROMOTION.
THIS HONORS YOUR ACHIEVEMENT IN GAMORRA.
IT'S NOT HER ACHIEVEMENT.
IT'S MINE.

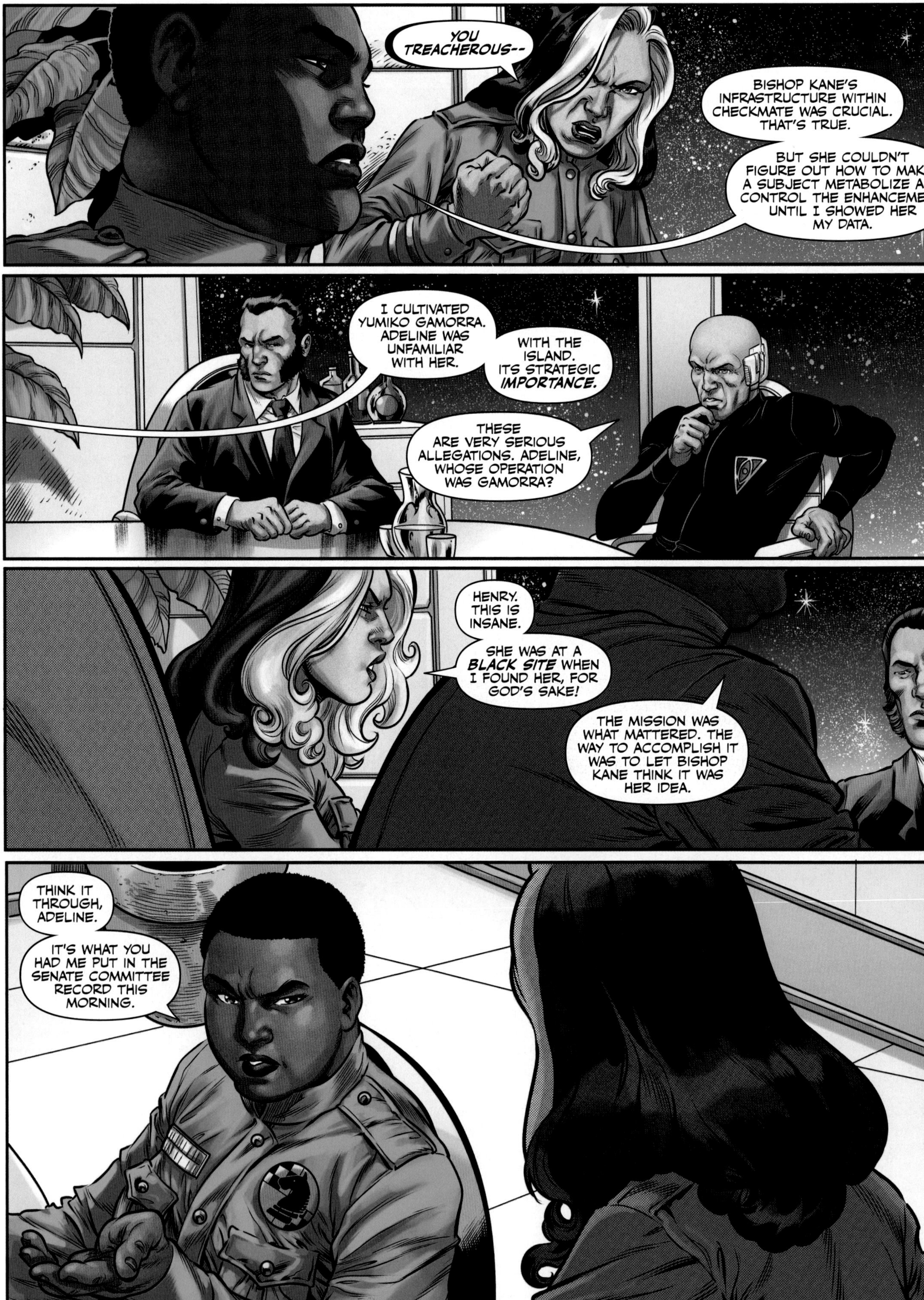
YOU TREACHEROUS--
BISHOP KANE'S INFRASTRUCTURE WITHIN CHECKMATE WAS CRUCIAL. THAT'S TRUE.
BUT SHE COULDN'T FIGURE OUT HOW TO MAKE A SUBJECT METABOLIZE AND CONTROL THE ENHANCEMENT. UNTIL I SHOWED HER MY DATA.
I CULTIVATED YUMIKO GAMORRA. ADELINE WAS UNFAMILIAR WITH HER.
WITH THE ISLAND. ITS STRATEGIC *IMPORTANCE.*
THESE ARE VERY SERIOUS ALLEGATIONS. ADELINE, WHOSE OPERATION WAS GAMORRA?
HENRY. THIS IS INSANE.
SHE WAS AT A *BLACK SITE* WHEN I FOUND HER, FOR GOD'S SAKE!
THE MISSION WAS WHAT MATTERED. THE WAY TO ACCOMPLISH IT WAS TO LET BISHOP KANE THINK IT WAS HER IDEA.
THINK IT THROUGH, ADELINE.
IT'S WHAT YOU HAD ME PUT IN THE SENATE COMMITTEE RECORD THIS MORNING.

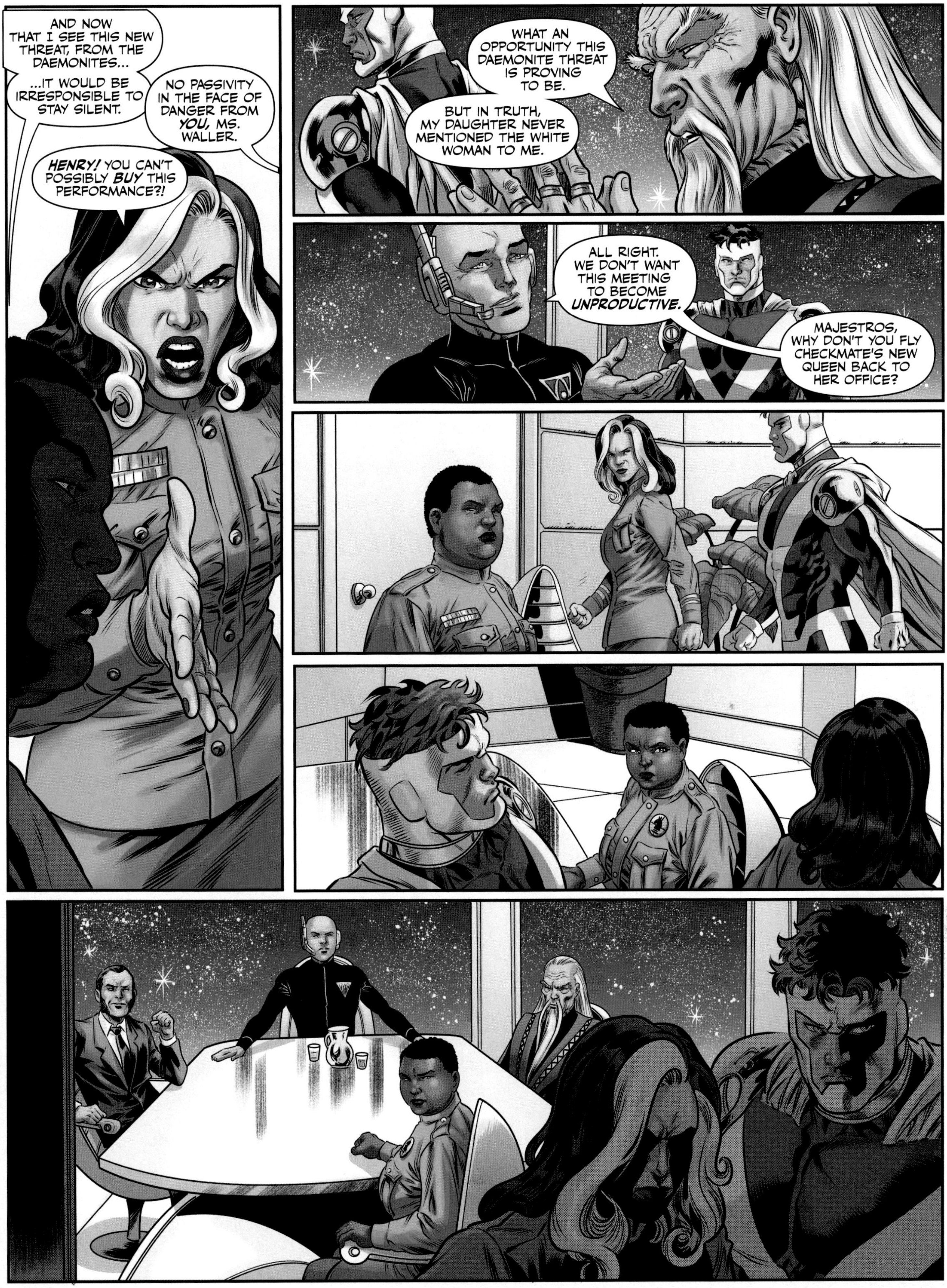
AND NOW THAT I SEE THIS NEW THREAT, FROM THE DAEMONITES...
...IT WOULD BE IRRESPONSIBLE TO STAY SILENT.
NO PASSIVITY IN THE FACE OF DANGER FROM YOU, MS. WALLER.
HENRY! YOU CAN'T POSSIBLY BUY THIS PERFORMANCE?!
WHAT AN OPPORTUNITY THIS DAEMONITE THREAT IS PROVING TO BE.
BUT IN TRUTH, MY DAUGHTER NEVER MENTIONED THE WHITE WOMAN TO ME.
ALL RIGHT. WE DON'T WANT THIS MEETING TO BECOME UNPRODUCTIVE.
MAJESTROS, WHY DON'T YOU FLY CHECKMATE'S NEW QUEEN BACK TO HER OFFICE?

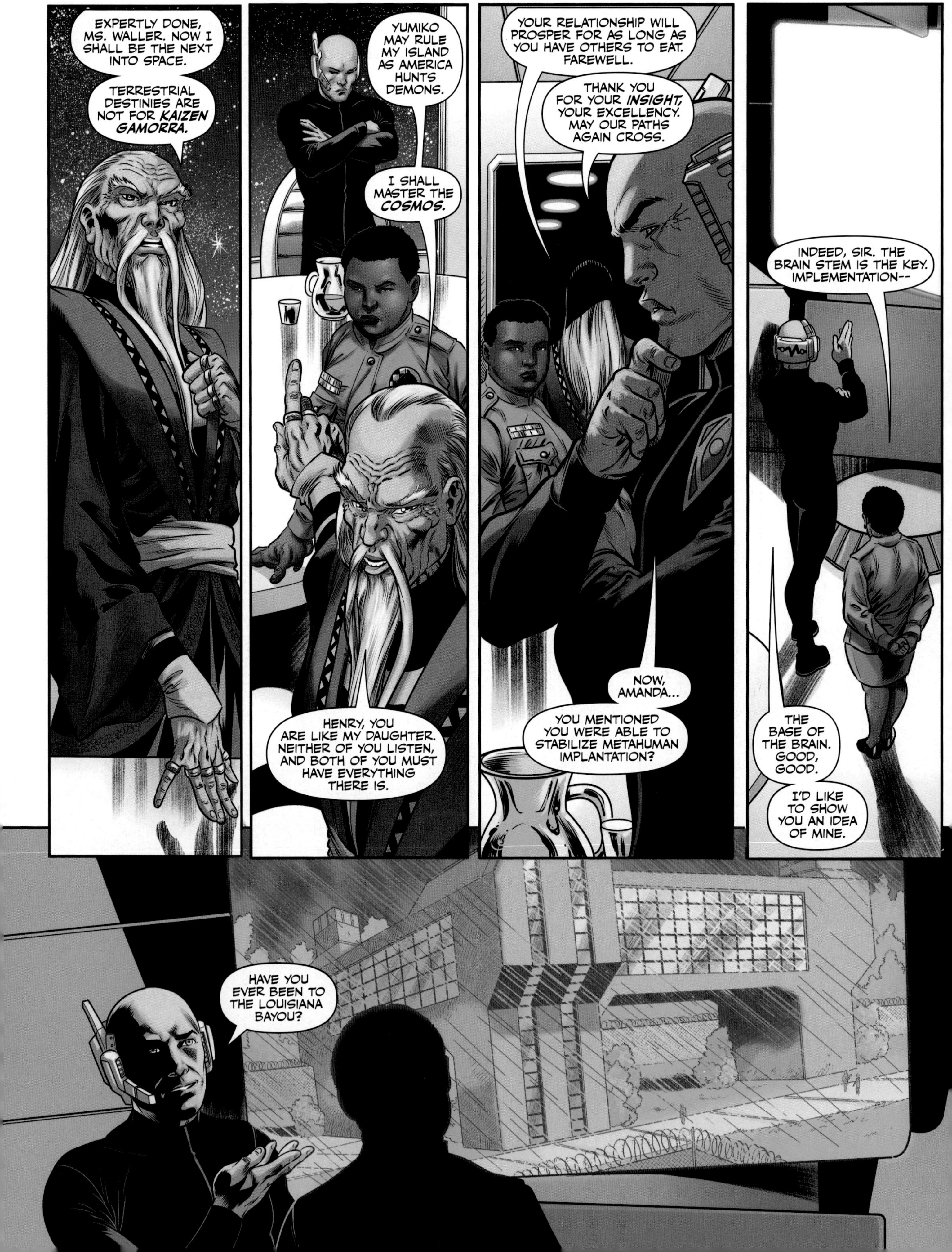
EXPERTLY DONE, MS. WALLER. NOW I SHALL BE THE NEXT INTO SPACE.
TERRESTRIAL DESTINIES ARE NOT FOR KAIZEN GAMORRA.
YUMIKO MAY RULE MY ISLAND AS AMERICA HUNTS DEMONS.
I SHALL MASTER THE COSMOS.
HENRY, YOU ARE LIKE MY DAUGHTER. NEITHER OF YOU LISTEN, AND BOTH OF YOU MUST HAVE EVERYTHING THERE IS.
YOUR RELATIONSHIP WILL PROSPER FOR AS LONG AS YOU HAVE OTHERS TO EAT. FAREWELL.
THANK YOU FOR YOUR INSIGHT, YOUR EXCELLENCY. MAY OUR PATHS AGAIN CROSS.
NOW, AMANDA...
YOU MENTIONED YOU WERE ABLE TO STABILIZE METAHUMAN IMPLANTATION?
INDEED, SIR. THE BRAIN STEM IS THE KEY. IMPLEMENTATION--
THE BASE OF THE BRAIN. GOOD, GOOD.
I'D LIKE TO SHOW YOU AN IDEA OF MINE.
HAVE YOU EVER BEEN TO THE LOUISIANA BAYOU?

...A PRISON.

WELL, ADELINE *SAID* YOU RAN A BLACK SITE, CORRECT?

QUITE THE BRUTALIST BUILDING, I KNOW. BUT THE BAYOU ITSELF IS LOVELY. BELLE REVE IS BUILT ON ONE OF TERREBONE PARRISH'S GRANDEST, UH, ESTATES.

THAT'S-- *THAT'S* WHAT Y'ALL CALLING THEM NOW? A *GRAND ESTATE* WITH A *PRISON* ON IT?

THIS IS A PLACE TO *STOCKPILE* THESE METAS. USING *YOUR* CONTROL PROCESS, WE CAN GENERATE *ASSETS.*

WHAT'S THAT SUPPOSED TO DO AGAINST THE DAEMONITES? HAHAHAHAHA--

HENRY--*HENRY!* DOES SHE THINK YOU WERE GOING TO MAKE HER *WEATHERMAN?* HAHAHAHAHA--

BUT--BUT *THE WESTERN PACIFIC!* I *DELIVERED* THAT TO THE UNITED STATES!

MILES, THAT'S UNCALLED FOR.

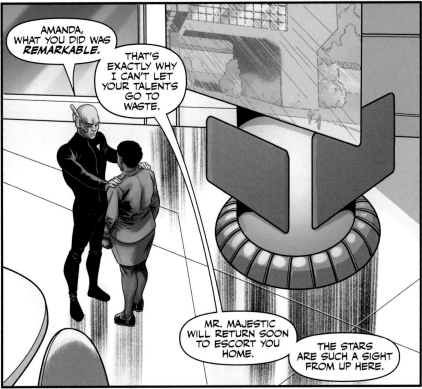

AMANDA, WHAT YOU DID WAS *REMARKABLE.*

THAT'S EXACTLY WHY I CAN'T LET YOUR TALENTS GO TO WASTE.

MR. MAJESTIC WILL RETURN SOON TO ESCORT YOU HOME.

THE STARS ARE SUCH A SIGHT FROM UP HERE.

YOU SHOULD SEE THEM WHILE YOU CAN. THE TRIP BACK DOWN GOES FASTER THAN YOU'D EXPECT.

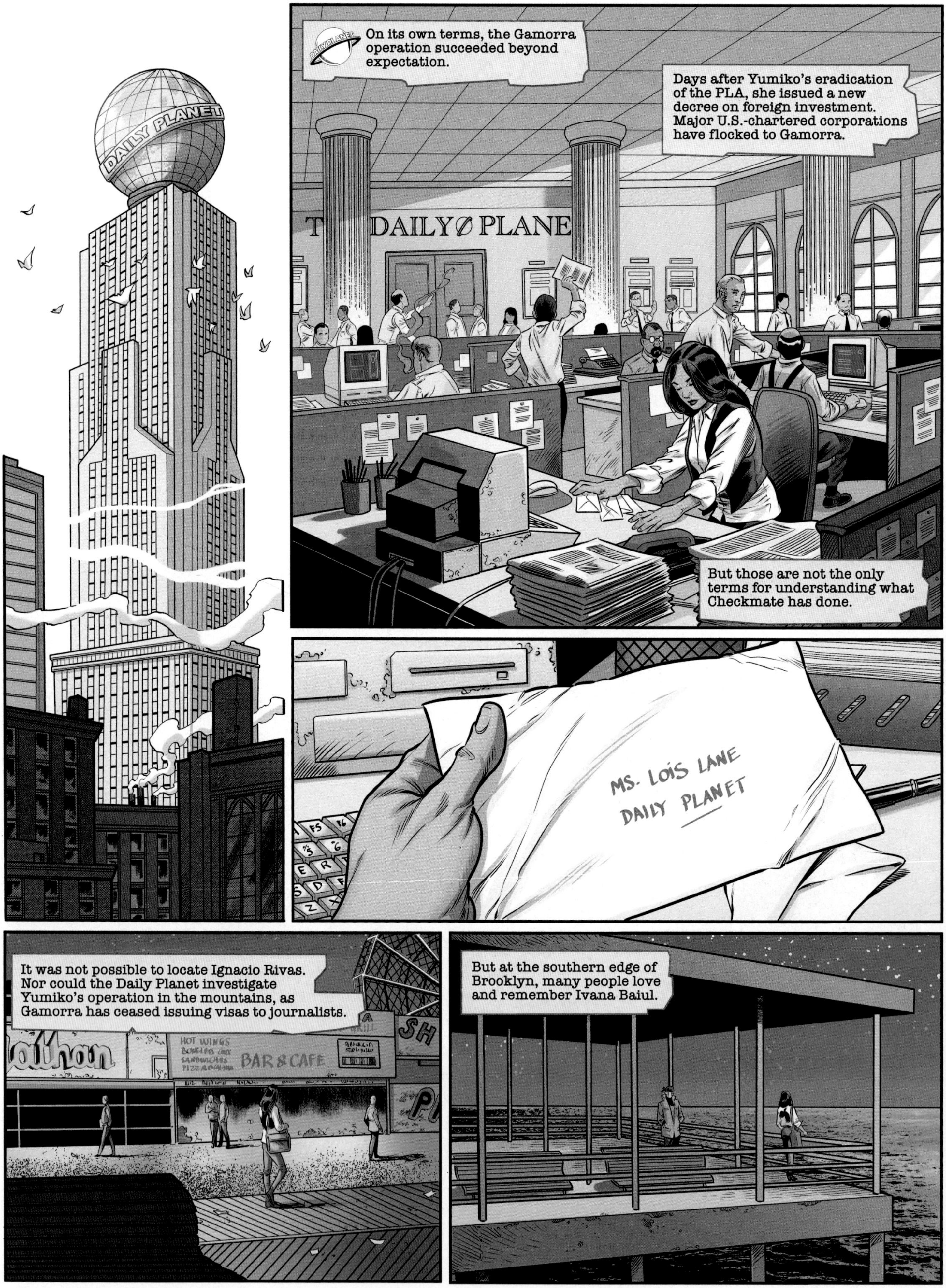
DAILY PLANET
On its own terms, the Gamorra operation succeeded beyond expectation.
Days after Yumiko's eradication of the PLA, she issued a new decree on foreign investment. Major U.S.-chartered corporations have flocked to Gamorra.
But those are not the only terms for understanding what Checkmate has done.
MS. LOIS LANE
DAILY PLANET
It was not possible to locate Ignacio Rivas. Nor could the Daily Planet investigate Yumiko's operation in the mountains, as Gamorra has ceased issuing visas to journalists.
HOT WINGS
BAR & CAFE
But at the southern edge of Brooklyn, many people love and remember Ivana Baiul.

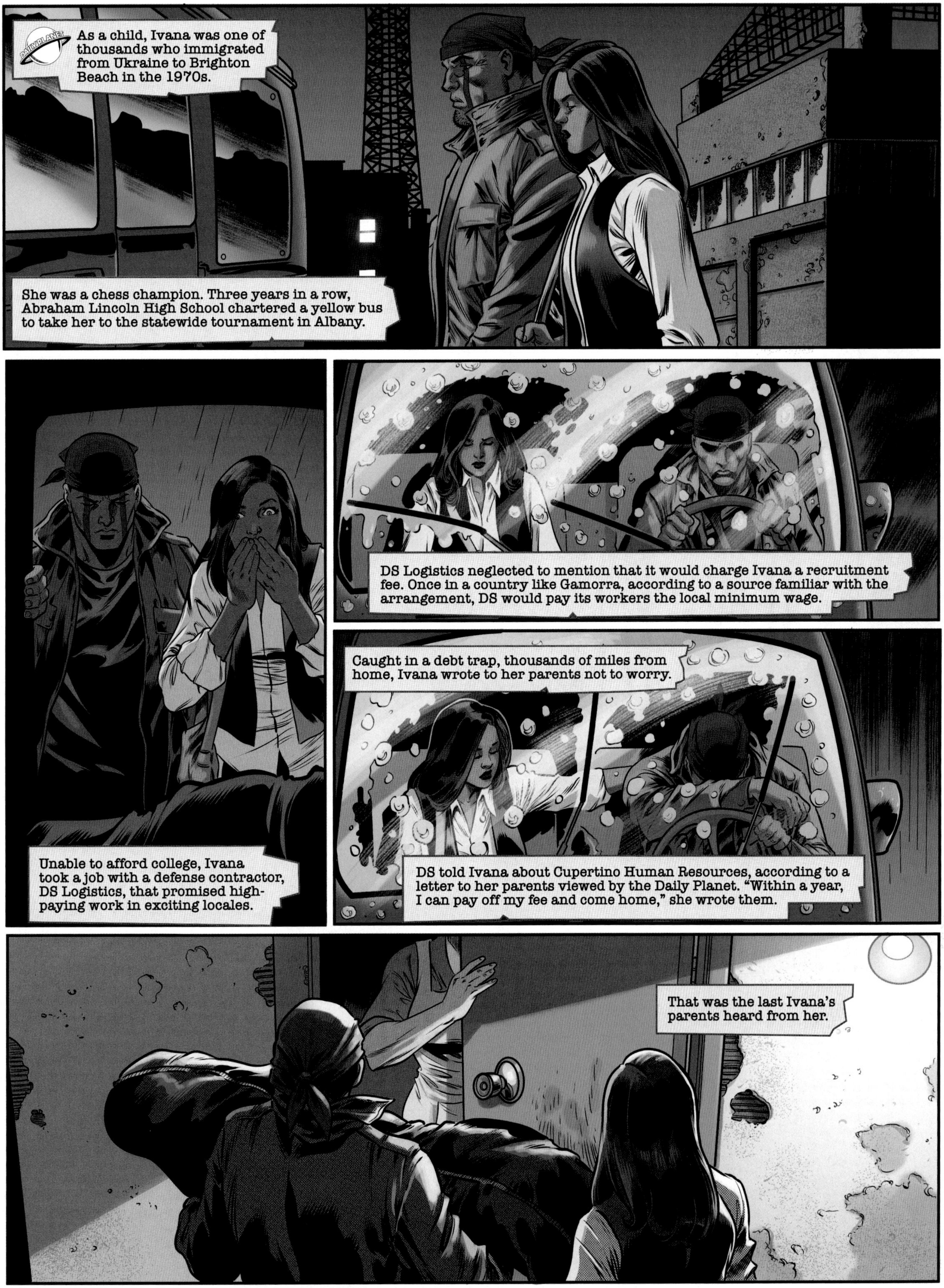
DAILY PLANET
As a child, Ivana was one of thousands who immigrated from Ukraine to Brighton Beach in the 1970s.
She was a chess champion. Three years in a row, Abraham Lincoln High School chartered a yellow bus to take her to the statewide tournament in Albany.
Unable to afford college, Ivana took a job with a defense contractor, DS Logistics, that promised high-paying work in exciting locales.
DS Logistics neglected to mention that it would charge Ivana a recruitment fee. Once in a country like Gamorra, according to a source familiar with the arrangement, DS would pay its workers the local minimum wage.
Caught in a debt trap, thousands of miles from home, Ivana wrote to her parents not to worry.
DS told Ivana about Cupertino Human Resources, according to a letter to her parents viewed by the Daily Planet. "Within a year, I can pay off my fee and come home," she wrote them.
That was the last Ivana's parents heard from her.

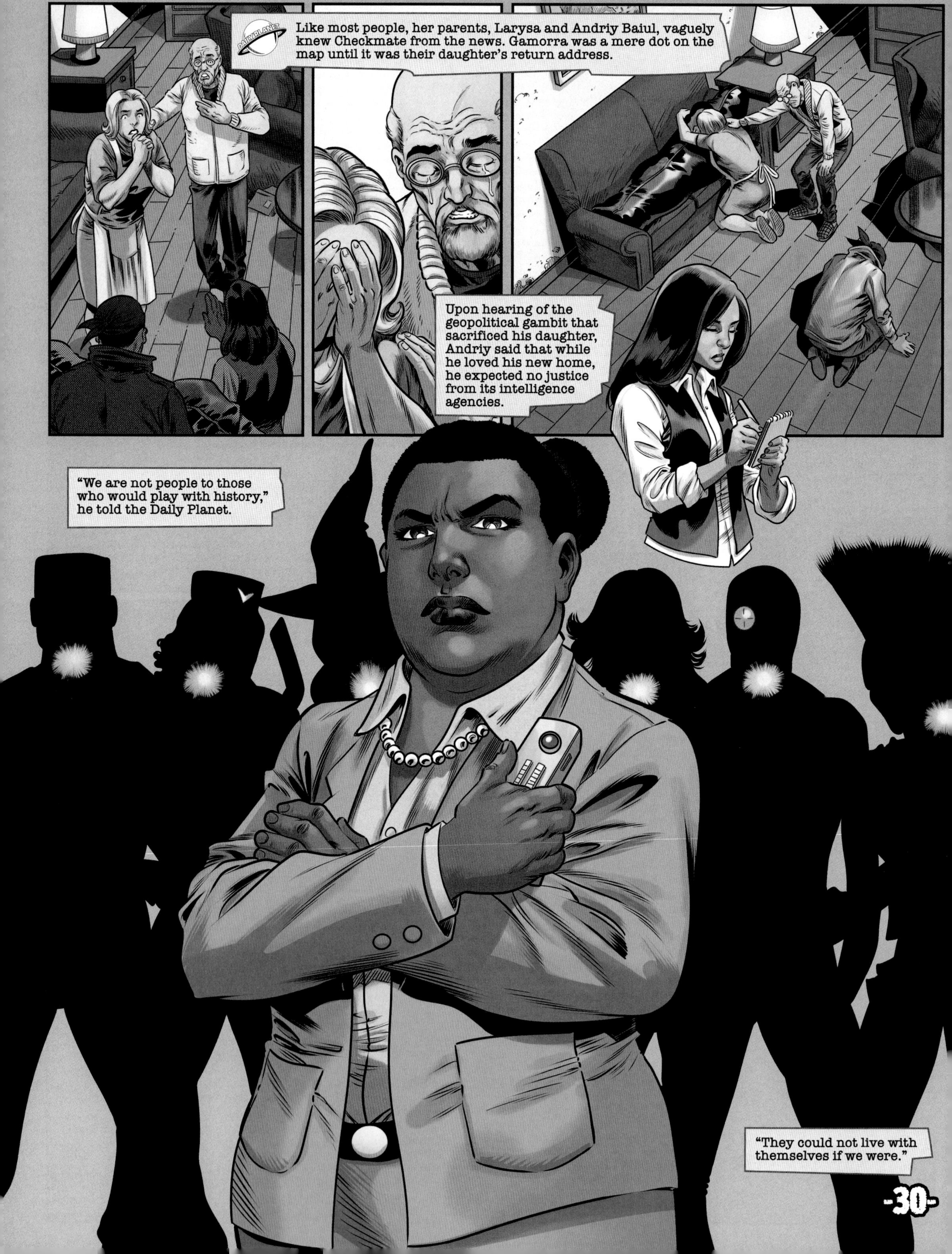
DAILY PLANET
Like most people, her parents, Larysa and Andriy Baiul, vaguely knew Checkmate from the news. Gamorra was a mere dot on the map until it was their daughter's return address.
Upon hearing of the geopolitical gambit that sacrificed his daughter, Andriy said that while he loved his new home, he expected no justice from its intelligence agencies.
"We are not people to those who would play with history," he told the Daily Planet.
"They could not live with themselves if we were."

VARIANT COVER GALLERY

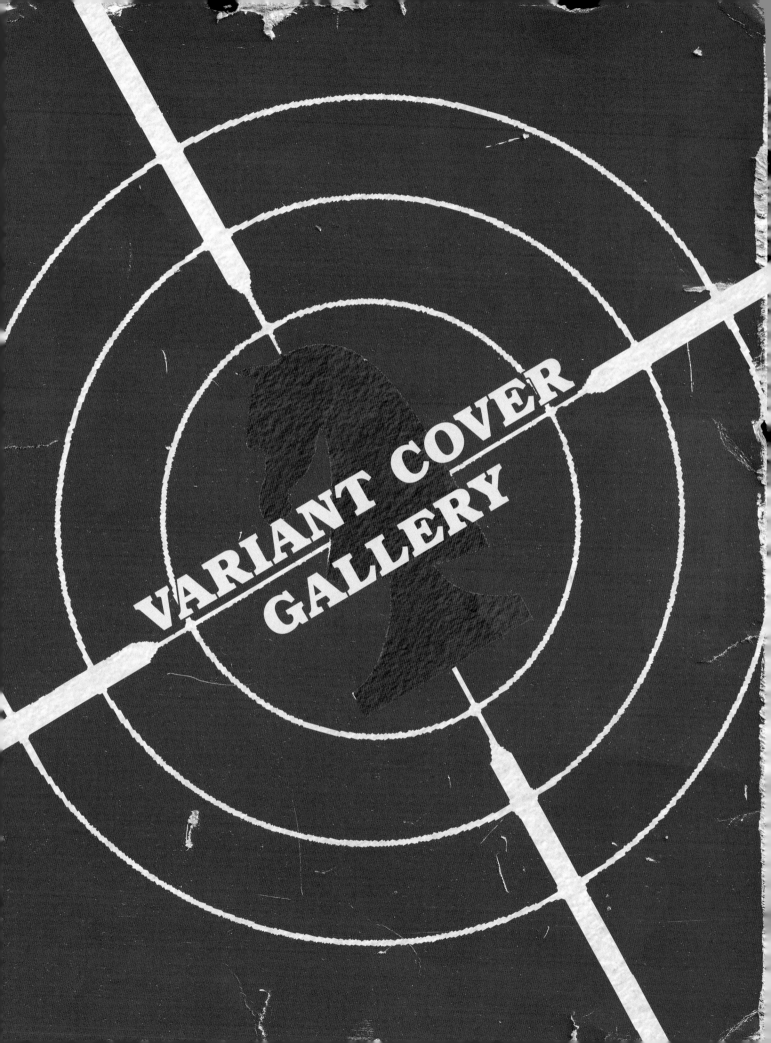

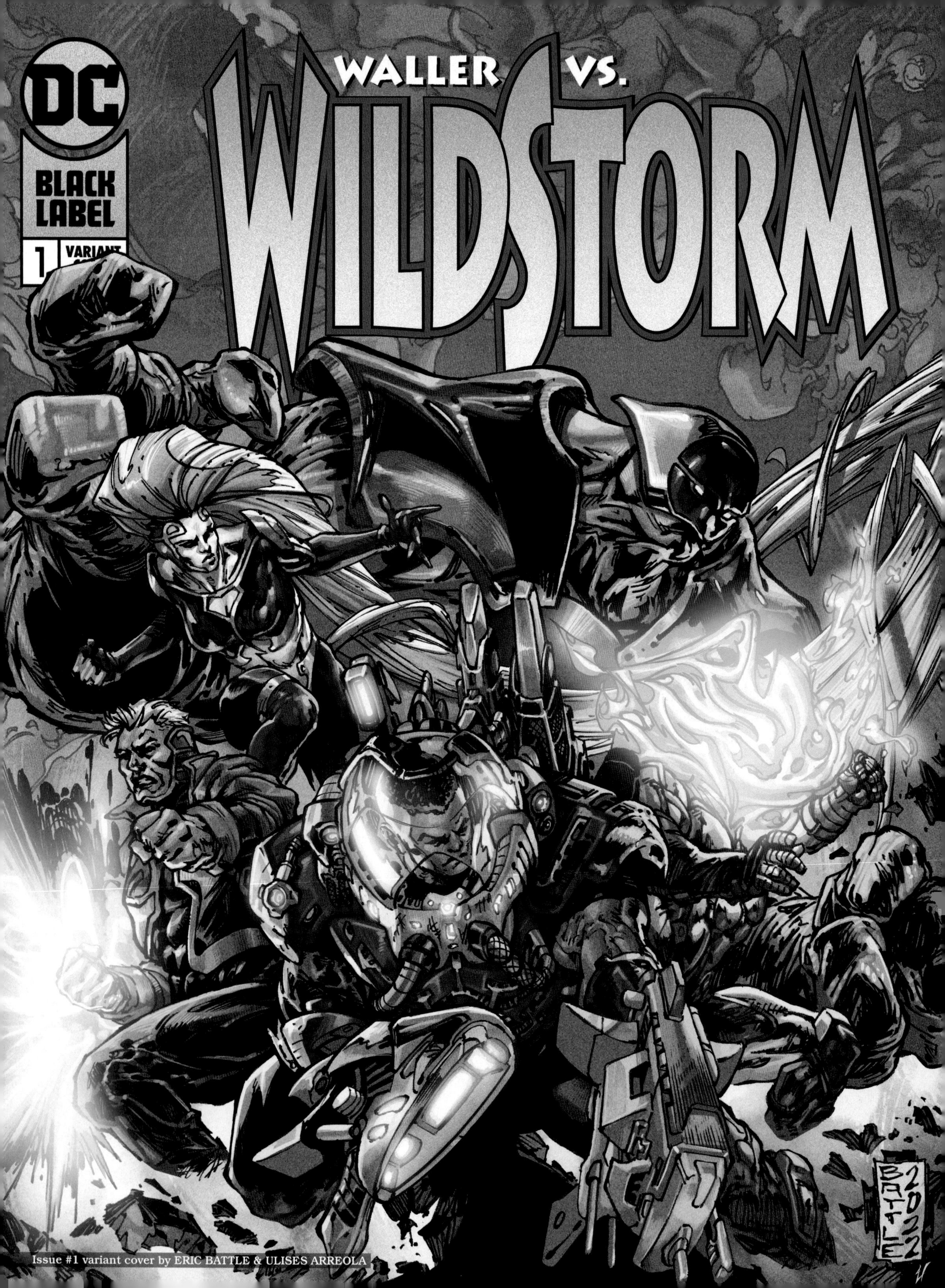
DC
BLACK LABEL
1
VARIANT
WALLER VS.
WILDSTORM
BATTLE 2022

Issue #1 variant cover by ERIC BATTLE & ULISES ARREOLA

Issue #1 1:25 variant cover by MIKE PERKINS

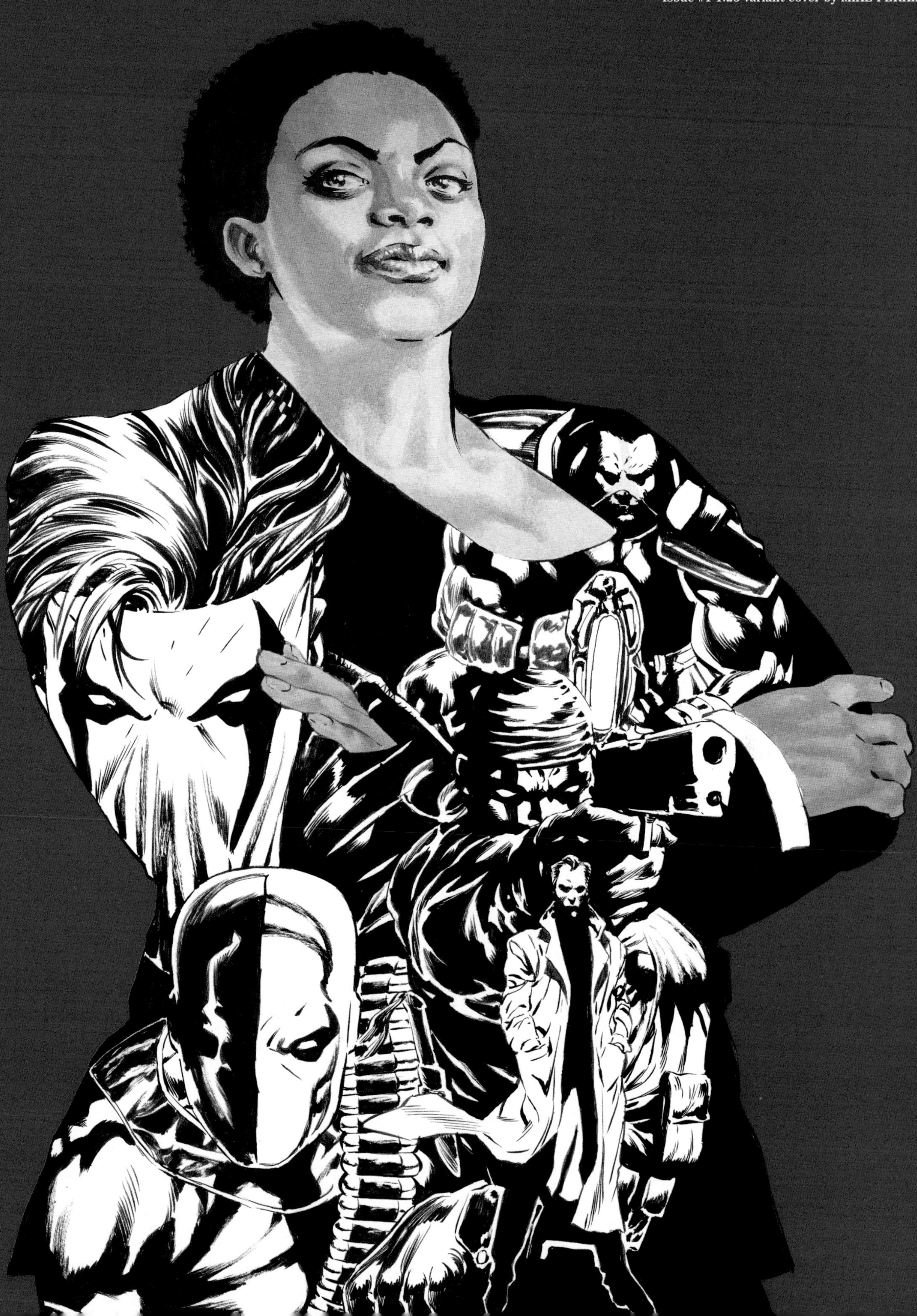

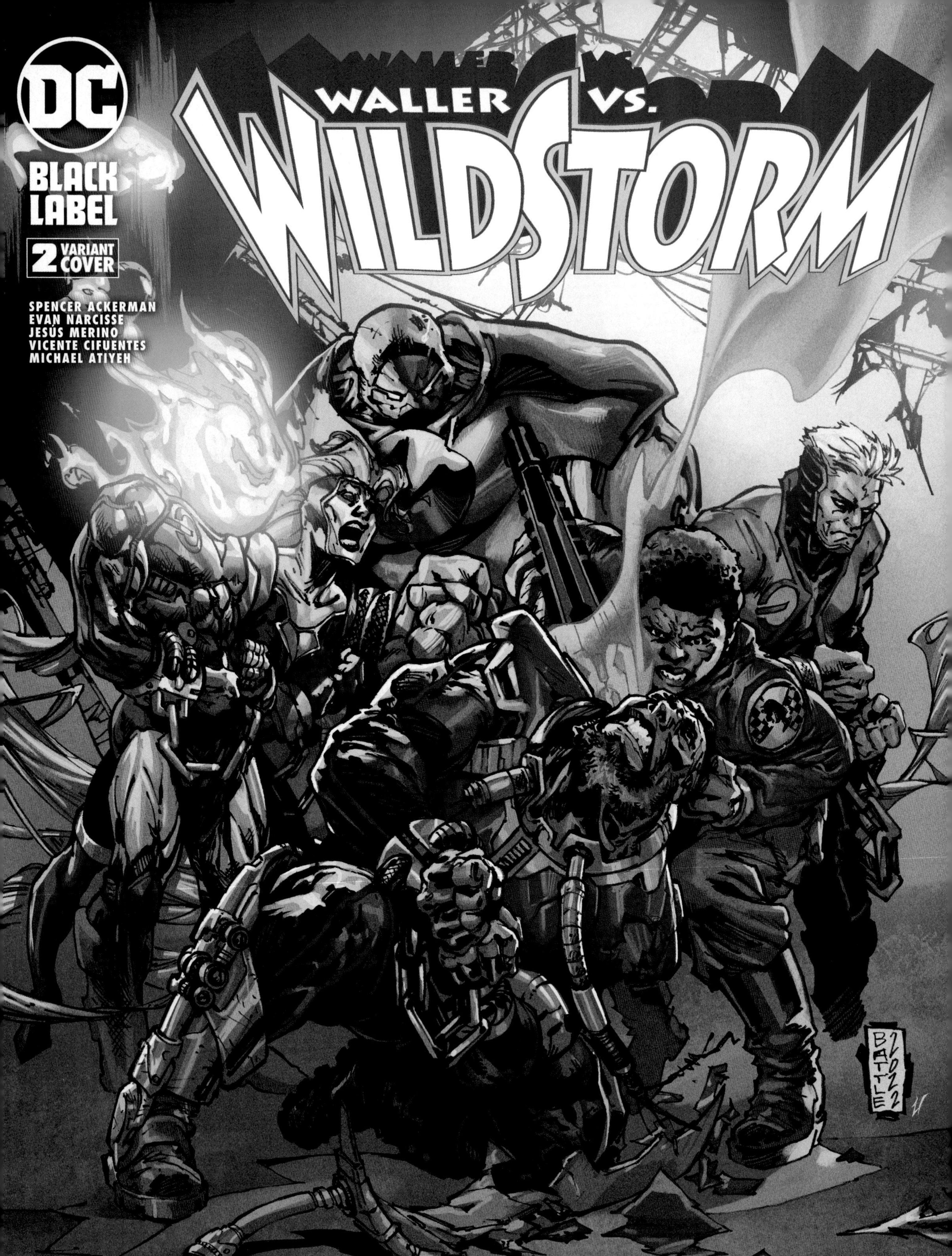
DC
BLACK LABEL
WALLER VS. WILDSTORM
2 VARIANT COVER
SPENCER ACKERMAN
EVAN NARCISSE
JESÚS MERINO
VICENTE CIFUENTES
MICHAEL ATIYEH
BATTLE 2022

Issue #2 variant cover by ERIC BATTLE & ULISES ARREOLA

Issue #2 1:25 variant cover by TOM RANEY with MICHAEL ATIYEH

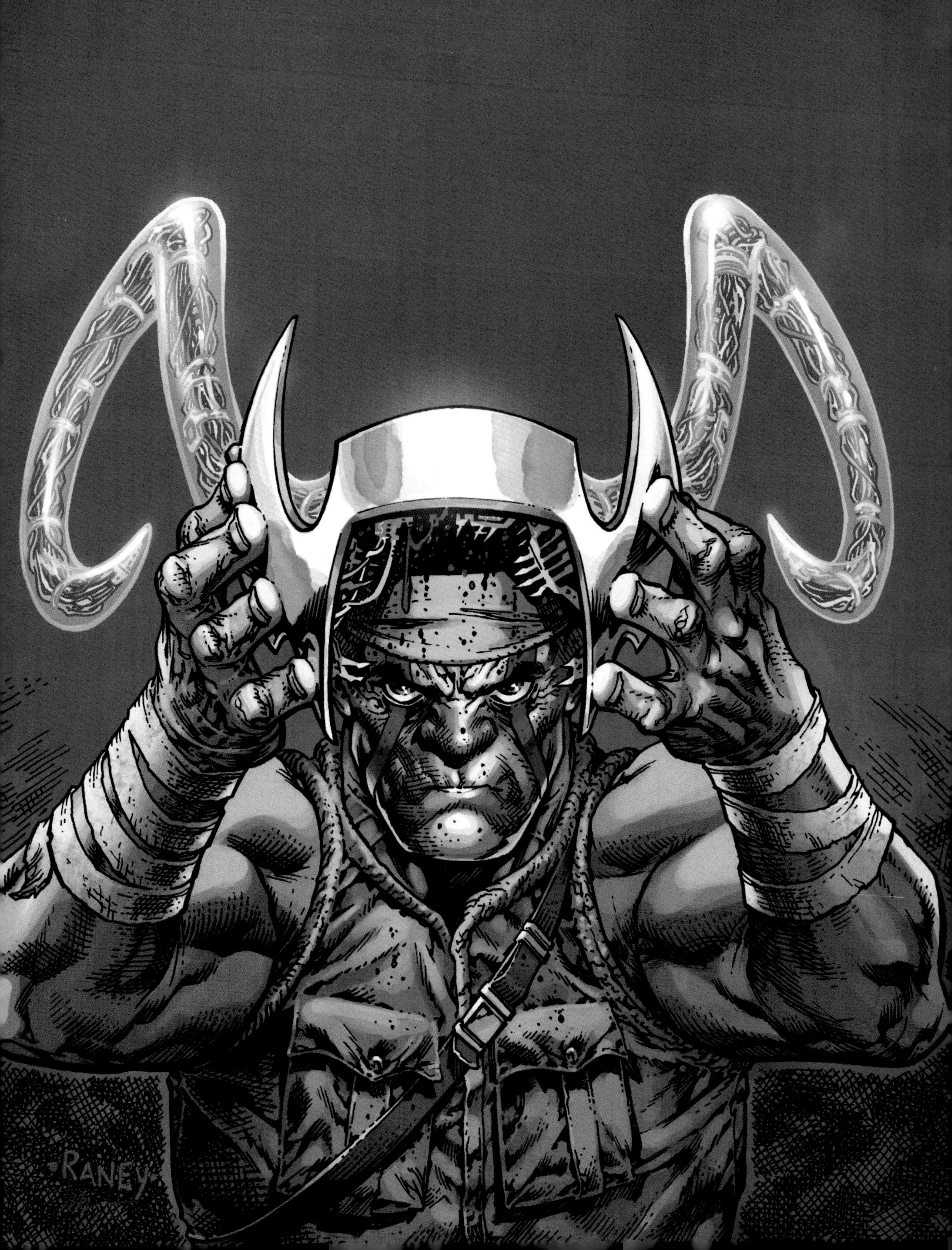

Issue #3 variant cover by ERIC BATTLE & ULISES ARREOLA

Issue #3 1:25 variant cover by AARON CAMPBELL

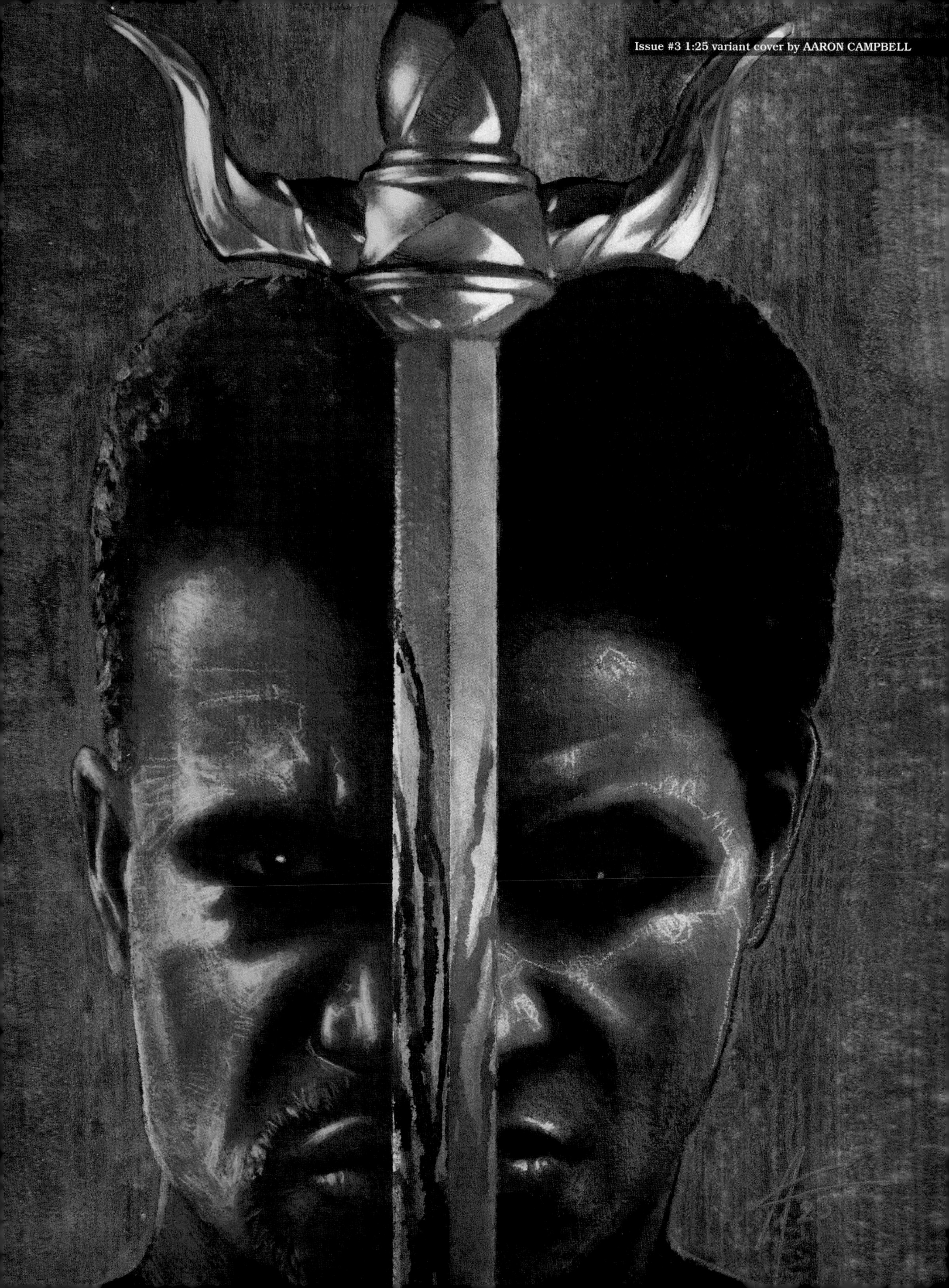

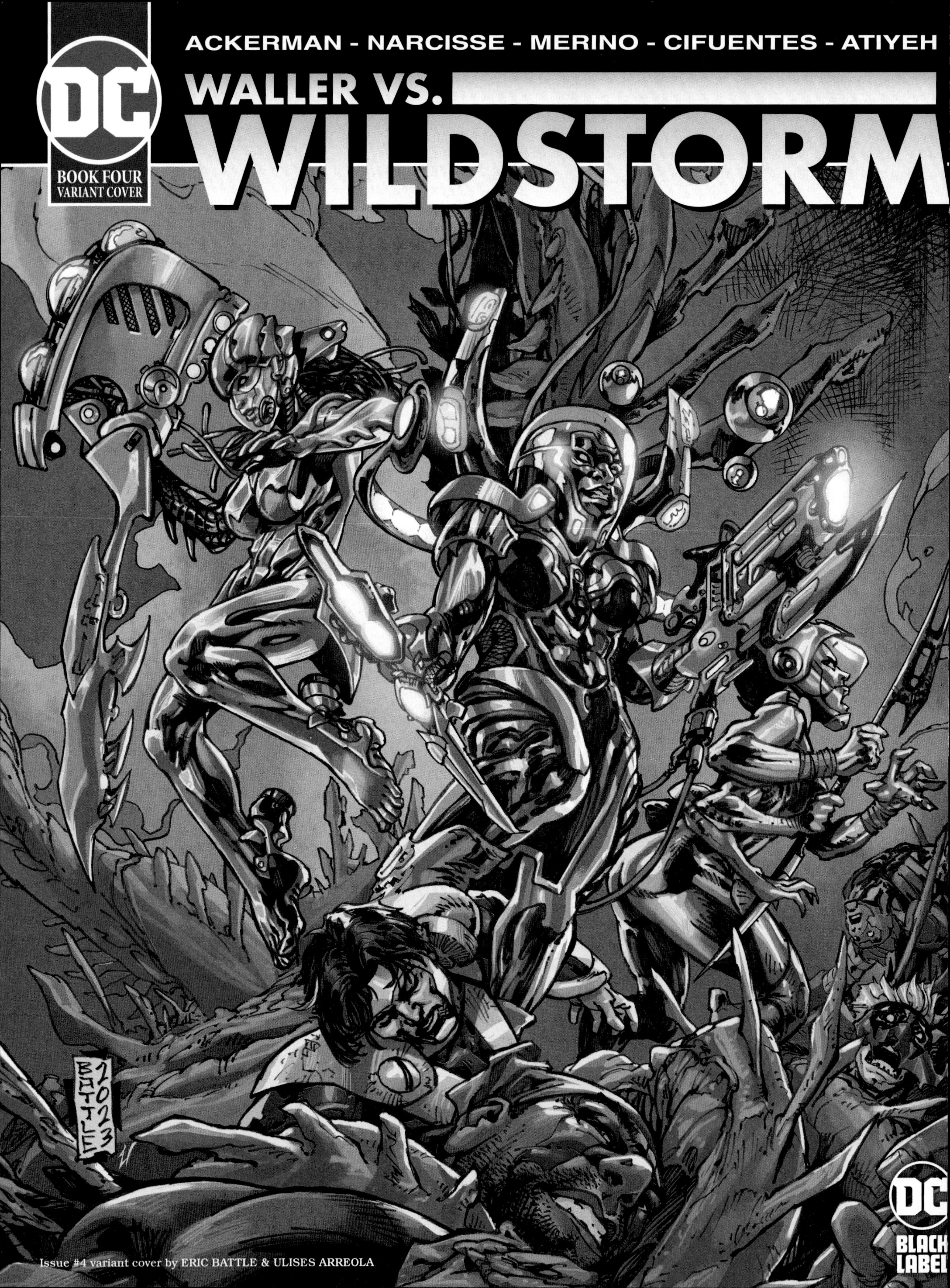
DC
BOOK FOUR
VARIANT COVER
ACKERMAN - NARCISSE - MERINO - CIFUENTES - ATIYEH
WALLER VS.
WILDSTORM
BATTLE 12023
DC
BLACK LABEL

Issue #4 variant cover by ERIC BATTLE & ULISES ARREOLA

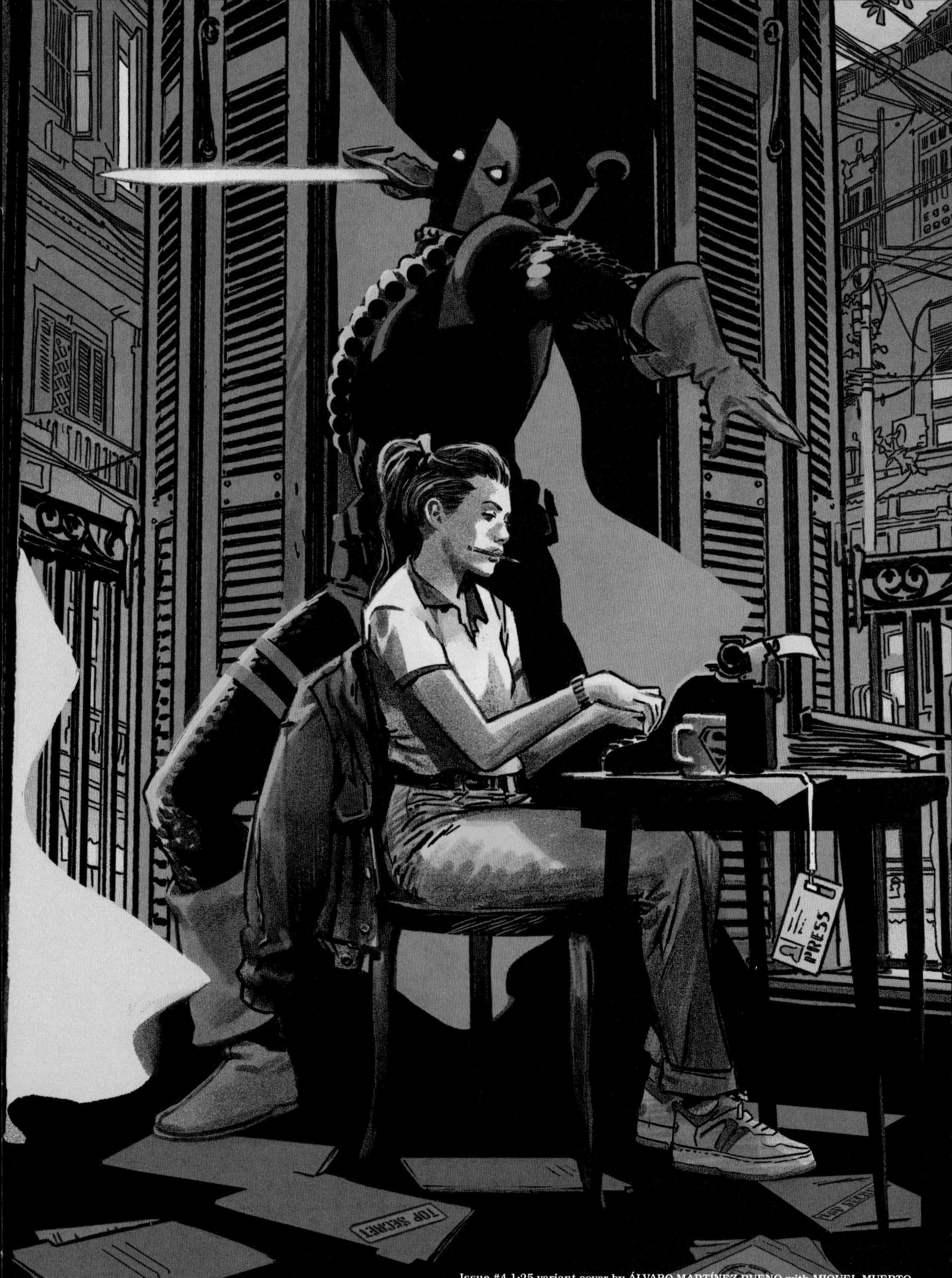
PRESS
TOP SECRET
TOP SECRET

Issue #4 1:25 variant cover by ÁLVARO MARTÍNEZ BUENO with MIQUEL MUERTO

AFTERWORD by SPENCER ACKERMAN

So who was right?

Was Amanda right? Was Jackson right? Was Lois right?

Or maybe: What were they right *about*? Was Amanda right that America will intensify the horrors its most vulnerable already suffer if it sees its geopolitical power decline? Was Jackson right that Amanda's efforts to forestall decline would push Checkmate into the moral abyss? Was Lois right that Checkmate was always going to produce an Amanda Waller?

Or do the various things they each get *wrong*—that they each *do*—stop us from considering *any* of them right?

Everyone on the immensely talented *Waller vs. WildStorm* team has their own perspective. I sure have mine.

But along with my friend Evan Narcisse, I wanted to construct a story that destabilized *everyone's* perspective at various points. Just not in a cheap way where the book ends up saying nothing. Or worse, shrugging its shoulders at atrocities.

That sort of discomfort is part and parcel of my day job as a national-security reporter and columnist. For over 20 years, my work has taken me to places like Iraq, Afghanistan, Guantanamo Bay, the Pentagon, and CIA headquarters. I've documented crimes of the state—crimes that emerge from the standard operations of the state. I've also personally witnessed heroism performed by people inside the machinery of those operations.

I've sure been where Lois is in issue #1: across the table from sources who tell you you're full of shit after you

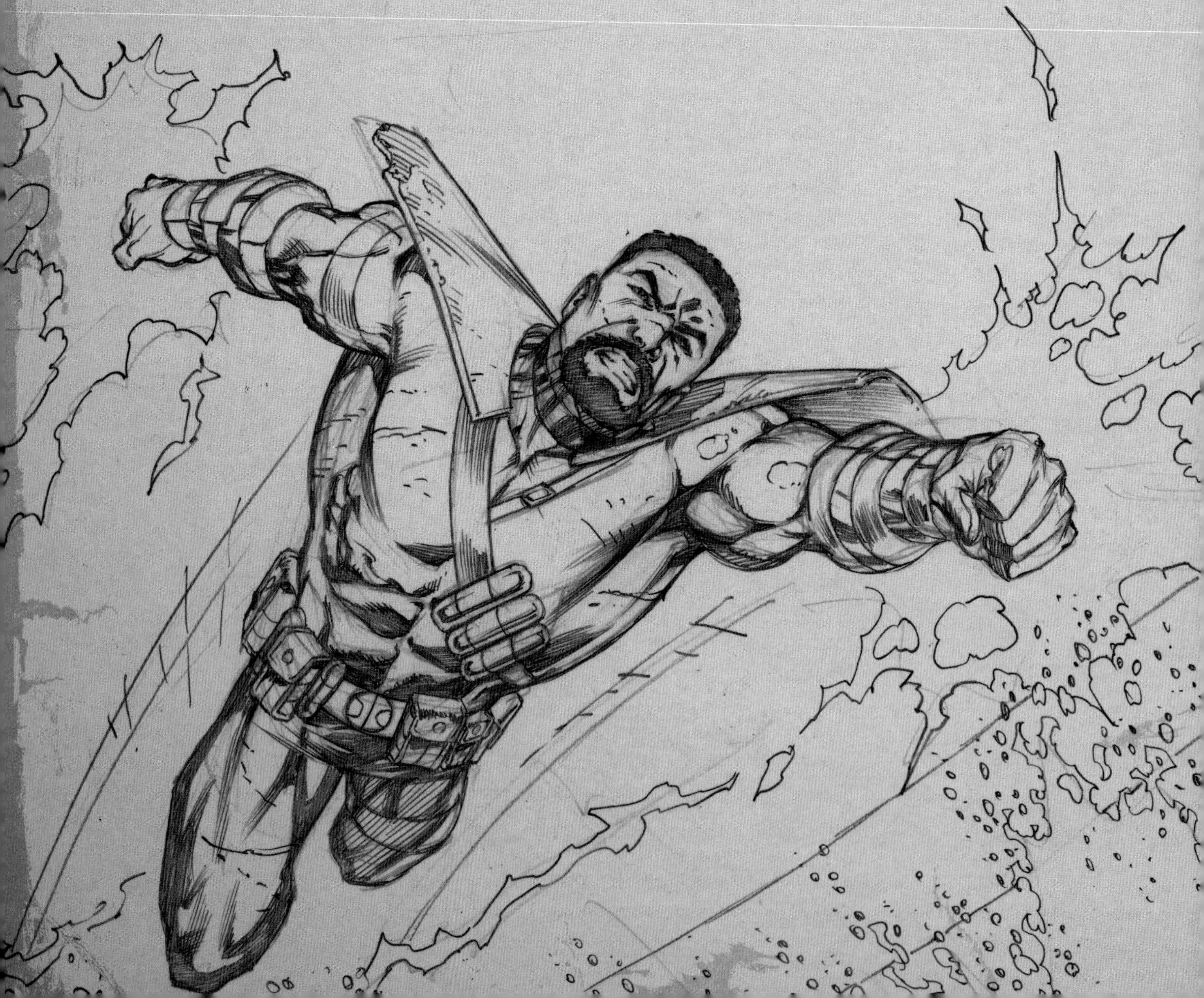

push back on them. And just because *they're* full of shit concerning *other* things doesn't make them wrong about *that*. Truth isn't a scalpel. It's a grenade.

Because I'm a comics lifer—I learned to read with superhero comics and never kicked the habit—sometimes when I've gone to a war zone, or dug through a trove of secret government documents, I've wondered: *How would this work in a superhero universe?* I've covered intelligence chiefs while a voice in my head whispered: *Amanda Waller.* I've watched factional struggles unfold inside security agencies and thought: *Wow, WildStorm got a lot right.*

But none of that meant I knew how to write comics. I'm grateful to have gotten a crash course from some of the best. Namely Evan, who's shared his scripts with me over the years and showed me what true craftsmanship in comics writing looks like. And Jesús Merino, whom I cannot believe my luck at working with my first time out. Vicente Cifuentes, Michael Atiyeh, Dave Sharpe, and Eric Battle demonstrated how comics pros turn an ugly idea into a beautiful page. They taught me that comics, like journalism, is a team sport. And we couldn't have had a better captain than Chris Conroy.

So: When all is said and done—when we factor in people's results, not just their motivations—who do *you* think was right?

SPENCER ACKERMAN
October 2023

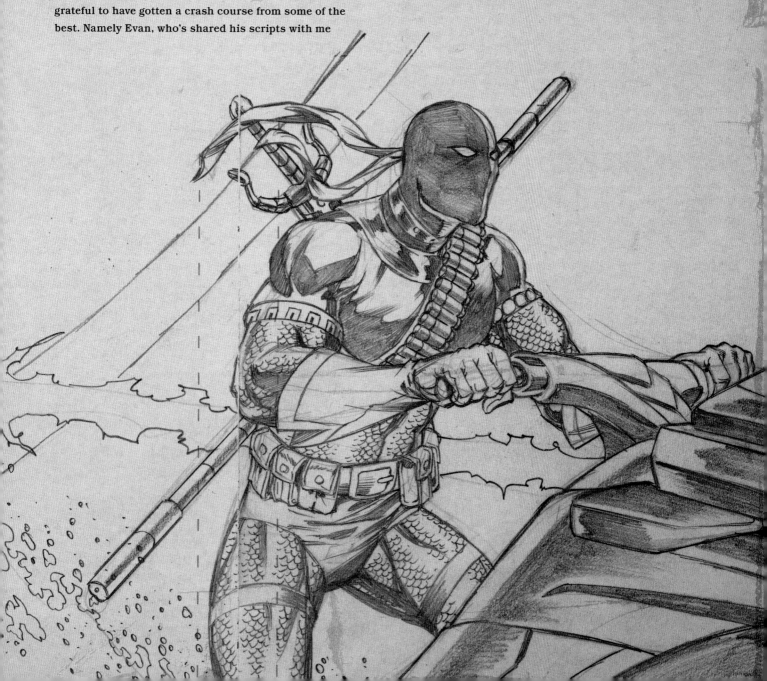

SPENCER ACKERMAN

Spencer Ackerman, a Pulitzer Prize and National Magazine Award-winning reporter, is a columnist for *The Nation* magazine and the author of *Reign of Terror: How The 9/11 Era Destabilized America and Produced Trump*, which won a 2022 American Book Award.

EVAN NARCISSE

Evan Narcisse is the senior writer at Brass Lion Entertainment. He's worked as a screenwriter, producer, and narrative design consultant in video games, comic books, film, and TV, often focusing on the intersection of Blackness and pop culture. As a journalist and critic, he wrote for the *Atlantic*, *Time* magazine, *Kotaku*, and the *New York Times*, in addition to teaching game journalism at New York University and appearances as an expert guest on CNN and NPR. He's also the author of the *Rise of the Black Panther* graphic novel, Marvel's *Black Panther: Wakanda Atlas*, and *The New Day: Power of Positivity*. As a narrative design consultant, he's worked on *Marvel's Spider-Man: Miles Morales*, *Redfall*, *Marvel's Avengers*, *Gotham Knights*, and the award-winning *Dot's Home*. A native New Yorker, he now lives in Austin, Texas.

JESÚS MERINO

Jesus Merino is an illustrator who first got his start in fanzines before receiving wider recognition through the Spanish publisher Planeta-DeAgostini in works such as *Aníbal Gris*, *Checkmate*, and *Triada Vértice*. Since 1998 he has worked primarily as an inker for Marvel Comics and DC Comics on such well-known series as *Fantastic Four*, *Avengers Forever*, *Green Lantern*, and *Superman*. From 2008 to 2010, he illustrated *Justice Society of America* before taking on art duties on the New 52 relaunch of *Superman* scripted by George Pérez. Aside from his work on *Superman*, Merino has also had stints on titles such as *Team 7*, *Futures End*, *The Flash*, *Aquaman*, *Justice League*, *Astro City* (with writer Kurt Busiek), *Hellblazer*, *Detective Comics*, *Wonder Woman*, *Teen Titans*, *Supergirl*, *Dark Nights*, and *Infinite Frontier* among many others. His most recent project is *The Joker Presents: A Puzzlebook*.

MICHAEL ATIYEH

Michael Atiyeh is a 30-year veteran comic book colorist based in Northern California. He has worked on an extensive list of characters and titles, including *Green Lantern*, *Flash*, and *Supergirl*. Believing a single style does not fit every artist, he enjoys altering his color style to fit each project he works on.